I, WANDERING JEW

I, Wandering Jew

A FIVE-CENTURY HISTORY
OF OUR MODERN CONDITION

YAIR MINTZKER

PRINCETON UNIVERSITY PRESS

PRINCETON AND OXFORD

Book epigraph from "On Death, without Exaggeration," from *View With A Grain Of Sand* by Wisława Szymborska. English translation copyright © 1995 by HarperCollins Publishers. Used by permission of HarperCollins Publishers and Faber and Faber Ltd. Epigraph to chapter 5 from *In the Margins: On the Pleasures of Reading and Writing* by Elena Ferrante. English translation by Ann Goldstein. New York: Europa Editions, 2022, p. 80.

Published by Princeton University Press
41 William Street, Princeton, New Jersey 08540
99 Banbury Road, Oxford OX2 6JX

press.princeton.edu

GPSR Authorized Representative: Easy Access System Europe - Mustamäe tee 50, 10621 Tallinn, Estonia, gpsr.requests@easproject.com

All Rights Reserved

ISBN 9780691272702
ISBN (e-book) 9780691272726

Library of Congress Control Number: 2025938391

British Library Cataloging-in-Publication Data is available

Editorial: Priya Nelson and Emma Wagh
Production Editorial: Sara Lerner
Jacket Design: Katie Osborne
Production: Erin Suydam
Publicity: Alyssa Sanford and Kathryn Stevens
Copyeditor: Jennifer Harris

Jacket Credit: *The Wandering Jew*, 19th century (Epinal print), photography © Leonard de Selva / Bridgeman Images. Desert landscape by TanyaJoy / iStock. Jacket text: *The Wandering Jew; or, The Shoemaker of Jerusalem* (1750), HEH 289746, The Huntington Library, San Marino, California. Mendele Moykher-Sforim, *Di Klyatshe, oder Tsa'ar Ba'alei Chayim: A Mayse* (n.p., n.d.), 6. Arnold Greve, *Memoria Pauli Ab Eitzen, Doctoris Theologi Et Superintendentis Hamburgensis Instaurata* (Hamburg: Bohnius, 1744), 279.

This book has been composed in Arno

Printed in the United States of America

10 9 8 7 6 5 4 3 2 1

MIX
Paper | Supporting
responsible forestry
FSC
www.fsc.org   FSC® C008955

For Itai, with love

There's no life that couldn't be immortal if only for a moment.

—WISŁAWA SZYMBORSKA,
"ON DEATH, WITHOUT EXAGGERATION"

CONTENTS

NOTE ON TRANSLATION AND TRANSLITERATION

Unless noted otherwise, all translations in this book are mine. In transliterating words in Hebrew and Yiddish in the body of the text, I followed a simplified version of the Library of Congress guidelines, omitting diacritical signs, leaving a more exact method to the footnotes and bibliography. Hebrew and Yiddish words widely used follow the common spelling in American English (for example, yeshiva), and place names in Eastern Europe are transliterated according to the historical context. Throughout, I strove for simplicity and readability rather than exhaustive (and exhausting) exactitude.

TO THE READER

The book you are holding in your hands was born several years ago when, to my astonishment, I ran into a ghost. It was an otherwise unremarkable evening in central New Jersey: the kids were already in bed, their mother was downstairs, working on one of her projects, and Zoe, our little poodle, was standing just outside my study, scratching at the door. Earlier that day I had bought a new computer, and my plan for the evening was to create a backup of my old computer, transfer it to the new one, then hopefully go back to a short lecture I had been preparing about the sixteenth-century German alchemist Johann Georg Faust.

As it happens, I had developed a rather idiosyncratic backup method for my files over the years. Whenever I purchased a new computer, I would make a complete backup of the old one, then transfer it intact onto a separate folder on the new machine. I liked to think of the new backup folder as a crawl space or dusty attic: a place to store half-discarded objects that I might, perhaps, revisit one day. But here's the rub: because I was in the habit of buying a new computer once every few years, and because every old machine already had a folder with a backup of an even older one on its hard drive, my backup folders grew over time into a series of Russian dolls, one ensconced within another. The outermost doll was my current computer, the innermost one a backup of the earliest computer I had ever owned.

I opened the door to let the dog in, sat back down, and decided to explore the old backup folders. The reason? Plain old procrastination. What I found there, in any case, gave me pause. St. Augustine once remarked that the most important journeys in life are not through the physical world but through what's lying within us.[1] And so it was also in this case. For a few hours, I lost myself in backups-within-backups and worlds-within-worlds. At one point on my journey, I stopped to read emails, presumed lost, from a dear friend who had died by suicide. ("Why don't you write more often, you son-of-a-bitch?" began one of his messages.) Deeper still, I discovered a letter from the muse of my youth, long estranged, addressing me as her "dark-eyed poet." I felt engulfed by phantoms, wraith-persons, ghosts. The past sometimes does come back to haunt us.

It was a few hours into my mnemonic-digital journey that an even eerier feeling washed over me. Seemingly unrelated experiences and documents from different periods of my life formed strange patterns or connections in my mind: the contents of an enigmatic seventeenth-century pamphlet I had at one point scrutinized showed unmistakable similarities to a story I had just overheard about a mysterious man wandering in Israel in the early 1950s; an image of a great fire in Frankfurt in 1711 was relevant to my memories of traveling by train in Europe as a young man; and what to do about my favorite Yiddish story, published in Vilnius in 1873, that describes a talking horse? How was it that it, too, seemed so relevant to the other stories?

Following that evening in my study, I spent the better part of seven years excavating these and related fragmentary tales, slowly fleshing out their many meanings and interconnections. Having written down my findings, I now present them to you in the form of a book that bears the name of the ghostly figure that haunts them all: I, Wandering Jew.

I, WANDERING JEW

Introduction

TO A GENERAL audience, the term "wandering Jew" seems innocuous enough. In modern-day America, one encounters it in a variety of mostly random places. The term refers to a popular houseplant, but also to a movie production company in California and a deserted silver mine in Arizona. It appears in self-descriptions on social media by Jews who happen to move to a new city or switch jobs, and in various musical compositions ranging from the Christian folk song "Three Wandering Jews" to the opening lines of one of Paul Simon's most beautiful songs.[1]

Before it was bulldozed by the enormous weight of American culture, the Wandering Jew had a more precise and much darker meaning. For centuries, it referred to a legendary Jewish figure who allegedly betrayed Jesus Christ on his way to the Crucifixion and was consequently cursed by him to wander the earth until the end of time. Today these details are for the most part known only in literary circles, but before World War II, the legend of the Wandering Jew was extremely popular across Europe, if known by different names. Some called this figure the Wandering Jew, while others invoked the Eternal Jew, and yet others referred to Ahasverus or Ahasver.

The main source for the legend of the Wandering Jew is one of the most enigmatic pamphlets in European history. Published in German in 1602, the pamphlet is short and physically unremarkable. It nevertheless relates a most astonishing tale. According to the pamphlet, in the winter of 1542, a young German student by the name of Paul von Eitzen had traveled to visit his parents in the city of Hamburg. While in church the following Sunday, Eitzen saw an unusually tall man with long hair falling over his shoulders standing barefoot by the chancel and attentively listening to the sermon. Though it was winter, the stranger donned only "pants stretching to his feet, an outer garment reaching to his knees, and over that a coat down to his feet."[2] The calluses on his bare feet were so thick that "one could measure them with the thickness of two fingers across."[3] As he listened to the homily, the man didn't move, but when the priest mentioned the name of Jesus Christ, he "bowed, beat on his breast, and sighed deeply."[4] To Eitzen, the man seemed to be about fifty years old.

The 1602 pamphlet reports that in the days following Paul von Eitzen's encounter with this man, Eitzen approached him to inquire about his identity and asked him to clarify what business had brought him to Hamburg. The man replied in the Saxon dialect of the German language that his name was Ahasverus and that he had been born a Jew in Jerusalem in the time of Christ. He used to be a shoemaker and had a wife and child. Believing that Jesus was a heretic and a seducer of the Jews, Ahasverus joined the crowd at Pilate's palace and demanded that the murderer Barabbas be released and Jesus crucified. Afterward, he hurried back home and stood by his shop with his small child in his arms. When the procession to Calvary passed by Ahasverus's shop, Jesus stopped for a moment, and bearing the heavy cross on his back, leaned on a wall seeking respite.

But Ahasverus cursed him and egged him on. Jesus then turned to Ahasverus, looked at him sternly, and spoke with passion: "I will stand here and rest, but you must go!"[5]

Ever since that day (so reads the pamphlet), Ahasverus had remained alive. He left his wife and child behind and, after witnessing the Crucifixion, wandered all over the world. When he revisited Jerusalem centuries later, the city stood desolate and his wife and child were long gone. He consequently continued his peregrinations in the Orient and elsewhere, a fact he allegedly proved to his interlocutor in Hamburg in 1542 by answering the latter's learned questions about circumstances concerning the Crucifixion, the history of the Orient, and the lives, sufferings, and deaths of the Apostles. During his stay in Hamburg, the stranger was never seen laughing, and when people offered him money, he immediately gave it over to the poor. His fate, he said, was to continue his wanderings until the Second Coming. The pamphlet also reports that Ahasverus speaks many languages other than German, and that whenever anyone takes the Lord's name in vain, he reproaches that person with great force.

———

As was common in Baroque Germany, the short pamphlet describing the figure that came to be known as the Wandering or Eternal Jew has a very long title. It begins with the words "A short description and tale of a Jew named Ahasverus, who was present in person at the Crucifixion of Christ . . . and a few years ago came to Hamburg."[6] For the sake of brevity, scholars usually refer to it as the "Short Description" or *Kurtze Beschreibung* in German (pronounced KOOR-tsay besh-RYE-boong), a practice we too shall adopt in this book. (See figure 1.)

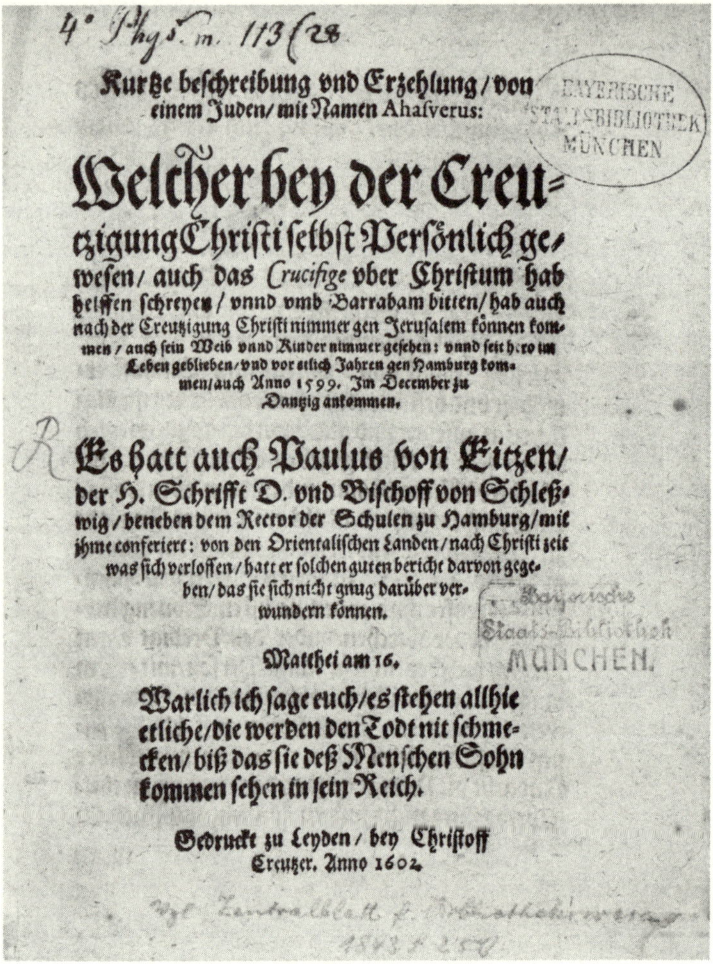

Kurtze beschreibung vnd Erzehlung / von
einem Juden / mit Namen Ahasverus:

Welcher bey der Creu=

tzigung Christi selbst Persönlich ge=
wesen / auch das Crucifige vber Christum hab
helffen schreyen / vnnd vmb Barrabam bitten / hab auch
nach der Creutzigung Christi nimmer gen Jerusalem können kommen / auch sein Weib vnnd Kinder nimmer gesehen: vnnd seit h. ro im
Leben geblieben / vnd vor etlich Jahren gen Hamburg kommen / auch Anno 1599. Im December zu
Dantzig ankommen.

Es hatt auch Paulus von Eitzen /
der H. Schrifft D. vnd Bischoff von Schleßwig / beneben dem Rector der Schulen zu Hamburg / mit
ihme conferiret: von den Orientalischen Landen / nach Christi zeit
was sich verloffen / hatt er solchen guten bericht darvon gegeben / das sie sich nicht gnug darüber ver-
wundern können.

Matthei am 16.

Warlich ich sage euch / es stehen allhie
etliche / die werden den Todt nit schmecken / biß das sie deß Menschen Sohn
kommen sehen in sein Reich.

Gedruckt zu Leyden / bey Christoff
Creutzer. Anno 1602.

FIGURE 1. Title page of the earliest known edition of the Kurtze
Beschreibung as identified by Leonhard Neubaur (1893).
Source: BSB, Rar. 825.

More than four centuries after the publication of the Kurtze Beschreibung, scholars still don't know much about it. Despite a great deal of speculation, the pamphlet's author, publisher, and place of publication remain unknown, and the significance of certain details in the story, including the setting in 1542 Hamburg, or the decision to call the man "Ahasverus" (the name of the Persian king in the Book of Esther), have never been clarified.[7] What is unquestionably clear, however, is that almost as soon as the pamphlet was published, the story about the wandering Ahasverus spread like wildfire across Northern Europe. The pamphlet came out in at least eleven more German editions by the end of 1602, and more than thirty additional ones by the end of the century. Translations into other languages, including French, Dutch, English, Polish, Swedish, and even Icelandic, also ensued.[8]

But there is more. Already in the seventeenth century, Ahasverus began to feature in proverbs and folk art, and from there, this figure wandered into ballads, poems, novellas, and novels, including by such luminaries as Alexandre Dumas, Johann Wolfgang von Goethe, Pushkin, Byron, Shelley, Dickens, and Nathaniel Hawthorne, to name but a few. (See figure 2.)

Moreover, reports of purported sightings of Ahasverus proliferated after 1602. (See figure 3.) Presumptive eyewitnesses placed him in dozens of cities across Europe and beyond, including Danzig, Madrid, Brussels, London, Paris, and even upstate New York.[9] By the late nineteenth century, Ahasverus was such a popular figure in some contexts that one could find him mentioned in political essays, parliamentary speeches, and antisemitic newspapers, but also in descriptions of ordinary people's dreams and in medical reports about very real wanderers who seemed to have lost both their way and their mind.[10] The following description came from the great

The WANDERING JEW;

OR,

The Shoe-maker of *Jerusalem*, who lived when our Saviour Christ was crucified, and appointed to live until his coming again.

To the Tune of, *The Ladies Fall.*

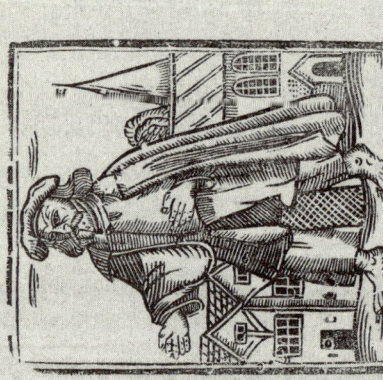

WHEN as in fair *Jerusalem*,
Our Saviour Christ did live,
And for the Sins of all the World,
His own dear Life did give.

The wicked *Jews* with Scoffs and Scorns,
Did daily him molest,
That never till he left this Life,
Our Saviour could have Rest.

Repent now therefore, O *England*!
Repent, whilst y have Space,
And do not like this wicked Jew,
Despise God's proffer'd Grace.

When they crowned his Head with Thorns,
And scourg'd him with Disgrace;
In scornful sort they led him forth,
Unto his dying Place.

Where Thousands, Thousands in the Streets,
Did see him pass along,
Yet such unhappy ones was there,
That did play his Wrong.

Both Old and Young revil'd him,
As in the Streets he went,
And nothing found but churlish Taunts,
By every one's Content.

His own dear Cross he bore himself,
A Burthen far too great,
Which made him in the Street to faint,
With Blood and heavy Sweat.

Being weary thus, he fought to Rest,
To ease his burthen'd Soul
Upon a Stone, this wicked Wretch,
Did churlishly controul.

And said, *Away! thou King of th' Jews,*
Thou shalt not rest thee here;
Pass to thy Execution Place,
Thou feest how drawing near.

And thereupon he thrust him thence,
At which our Saviour said,
I sure will stand and rest, said, walk,
Thy Steps shall ne'er be staid.

With that this cursed Shoe-maker,
For offering Christ this wrong,
Left Wife and Children, House, and all,
And went from thence along.

Where after he had seen the Blood
Of Jesu Christ thus shed,
And to the Cross his Body nail'd,
Away with Speed he fled.

Without returning back again,
Unto his Dwelling-place;
And wandering up and down the World,
A Run-a-gate most bale.

No resting could he find at all,
No Ease, or Heart's Content;
No House, no Home, no Dwelling place,
But far from Home he went.

From Town to Town in foreign Lands,
With his grieved Conscience,
Repenting for the heinous Guilt,
Of his past great Offence.

Thus after some few Ages pass,
In wandering up and down,
He much again defired to fee,
Jerusalem's Renown.

But finding it all quite defiroy'd,
He went from thence with Wo,
Our Saviour's Words which he had fpoke,
To verifie and how.

I'll reft, said he, *but thou shalt walk,*
So doth this wandring Jew,
From Place to Place, but cannot stay,
For feeking Counfel new.

Declaring fill the Power of him,
Where e'er he comes or goes;
And of all Things done in the East,
Since Christ his Death he shows.

The World he hath encompafs'd round,
And feen thofe Nations strange,
That hearing of the Name of Christ,
Their Idol Gods do change.

To whom he had told wond'rous Things,
Of Times fore paft and gone,

And to the Princes of this World,
He makes a grievous Moan.

Defiring fill to be diffolv'd,
And yield his mortal Breath:
But if the Lord has thus decreed,
How fhall he yet fee Death.

For neither Looks he old or young
But as in thofe fad Times,
When Christ did fuffer on the Crofs,
For mortal Sinner's Crimes.

He pafs'd many a foreign Land,
Arabia, Africa,
Grecia, Syria, and *Great Thrace,*
And through all *Hungaria.*

Where *Paul* and *Peter* preached Chrift,
Thofe blefs'd Apoftles dear;
Where he had told our Saviour's Words,
In Countries far and near.

And lately in *Bohemia,*
With many a *German* Town;
And now in *Flanders,* as 'tis thought,
He wandereth up and down.

Where learned Men with him confer,
Of thofe his lingering Days,
And wondering much to hear him tell,
His Journies and his Ways.

If People give this Jew an Alms,
The moft that he will take,
Is not above a Groat a Time,
Which he for Jefus's Sake

Will freely give unto the Poor,
And therefore makes no fpare;
Affirming fill that Jefu Chrift,
Of him hath daily Care.

He ne'er was feen to laugh or fmile,
But weep and make great moan;
Lamenting fill his Mifcries,
And Days fore paft and gone.

If he hear any one blafphemne,
Or take God's Name in vain,
He tells them that they crucify
Their Mafter Chrift again.

If thou hadst feen grim Death, fays he,
As thofe mine Eyes have done;
Ten thoufand, thoufand Times would you,
His Torments think upon.

And fuffer for his Sake all Pains,
All Torments, and all Woes;
This is the Life, and thefe his Words,
Where e'er he comes or goes.

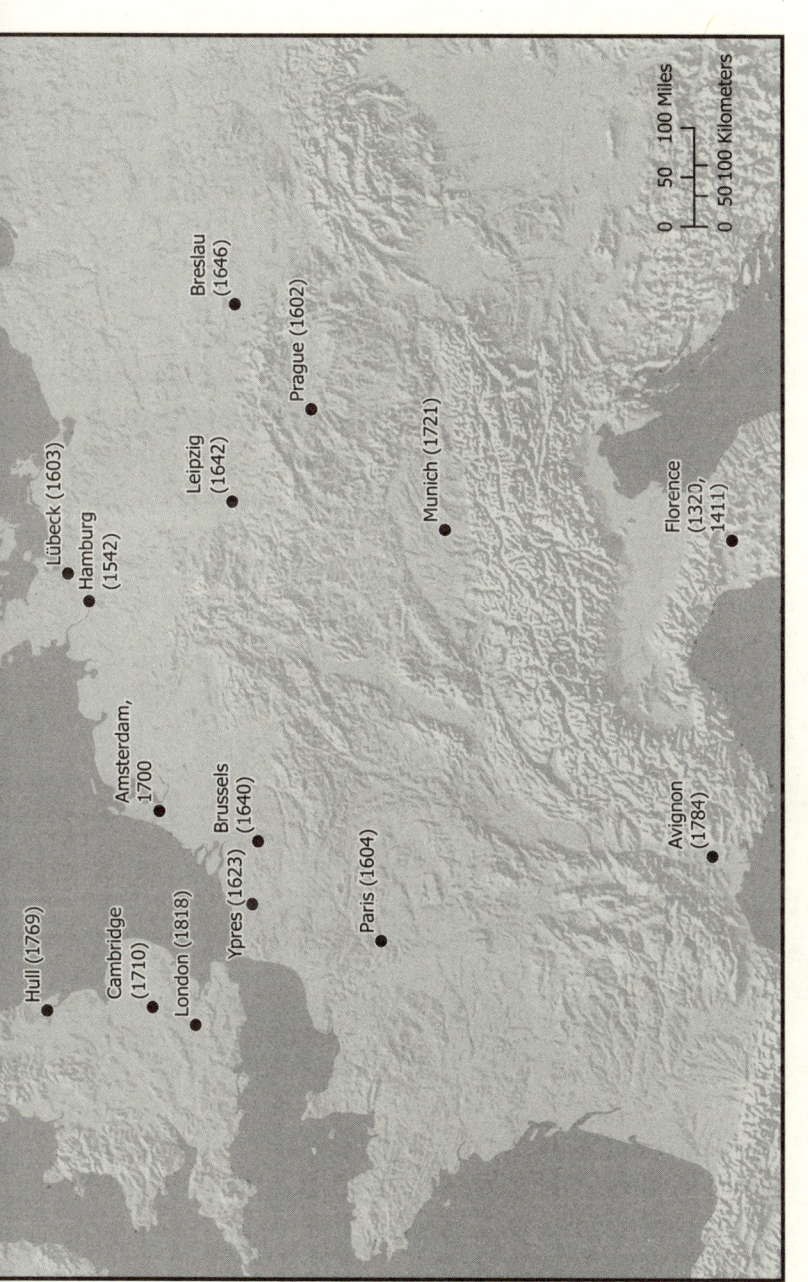

FIGURE 3. Spotting the Wandering Jew in early modern Europe. Source: Martin Gilbert, *The Routledge Atlas of Jewish History* (London and New York: Routledge, 2010), 65.

nineteenth-century Hungarian statesman and writer Jozsef
Eotvos:

> Who doesn't know the mythical Ahasverus, the Eternal Jew,
> who by turning away from Our Savior as He was carrying the
> Cross and by refusing to give Him a glass of water, was con-
> demned to walk the earth among men, cursed and unable to
> die, alone, like the dry leaves of a by-gone spring, carried
> away by the currents of the times without a place on which
> to lay his tired head. Everybody knows the legend; one would
> be hard pressed to find a place, especially among the north
> European peoples, where it hasn't played an important role
> in local folklore. I know no sadder story, nothing that touches
> my soul more deeply, because this legend is the truth!
>
> The Wandering Jew is not a figment of our imagination.
> He lives and suffers among us. Go to the market place and
> there you shall find him, standing among the multitude in
> the midst of the hustle and bustle, spreading his wretched
> wares on a table or on the ground, offering to sell them with
> his shouts, almost begging; go to the great plateau, and you
> shall find him there, too, treading through the sand with a
> heavy load on his back, accompanied by the distant voices of
> a boisterous inn. Go anywhere, from one end of the home-
> land to the other, and you shall find him.[11]

As this description makes clear, the legend of Ahasverus pre-
sents a remarkable mixture of history and myth, truth and
fantasy.

———

Eotvos's description of Ahasverus is not particularly antisemitic, and the same is true of common contemporary uses of
the expression "wandering Jew." But ever since the publication

of the Kurtze Beschreibung in 1602, the figure of the wandering Ahasverus has also played a prominent role in the history of antisemitism. In the original 1602 pamphlet, the description of the Christ-denying Jewish cobbler contained anti-Jewish stereotypes that persisted for centuries, reaching a climax in an infamous Nazi propaganda exhibition titled *The Eternal Jew* and the eponymous and extremely vile film, directed by Fritz Hippler, in 1940.[12]

Opened in Munich's Deutsches Museum on November 8, 1937, the exhibition *The Eternal Jew* (Gr. *Der ewige Jude*) was named for one of Ahasverus's common appellations in German, and indeed it contained many implicit references to his legend, even without mentioning Ahasverus by name. (See figures 4 and 5.) The exhibition consisted of a series of rooms with displays of the alleged "curse" of Jewish existence in Europe, with one room featuring grotesque "Jewish" body parts (nose, lips, mouth), another showing photographs of famous Jews in politics and the arts, and a third displaying out-of-context excerpts from Jewish sources, allegedly demonstrating that Jews do not consider non-Jews to be fellow humans. Martin Luther, the great German reformer, also featured prominently in the exhibition in the form of some of his most disgusting anti-Jewish quotes. Behind the exhibition's inflammatory rhetoric stood the claim that coexistence between so called "Aryans" and Jews was impossible. According to Nazi ideology, the Jewish race had always been a foreign element in European society. This is why the Jews were universally hated and doomed to repeated expulsions.

The exhibition *The Eternal Jew* and the movie it inspired had of course little to do with historical reality. Jews are no less European than Christians, and Nazi racial theory had no basis in scientific fact. But in another sense, the exhibition and the movie rang true. In the 1930s, Nazi authorities forced Jews to

GROSSE POLITISCHE SCHAU IM BIBLIOTHEKSBAU DES DEUTSCHEN MUSEUMS
ZU MÜNCHEN · AB 8. NOVEMBER 1937 · TÄGLICH GEÖFFNET VON 10·21 UHR

FIGURE 4. Postmarked postcard of the exhibition *The Eternal Jew* (Munich, 1937). Source: United States Holocaust Memorial Museum Collection, Gift of the Katz Family, Accession Number: 2016.184.272.

FIGURE 5. A case featuring "typical Jewish external features" at the exhibition *The Eternal Jew*, Munich, Germany, November 1937. © SZ Photo / Bridgeman Images.

emigrate from Germany, and when the Wehrmacht invaded Poland in September 1939, it dispossessed Jews, driving them into ghettos (or worse). Thus, though the exhibition and film *The Eternal Jew* weren't true originally, they served as a kind of transcript for a future reality: they *became* reality when millions of homeless, desperate Jews turned into wandering Jews. This is a fundamental point that will inform this book at every turn. We often think of history as preceding fictional accounts, providing writers such as Homer, Shakespeare, or Tolstoy with material to shape into literary (fictional) accounts. But sometimes causation points in the opposite direction: literary descriptions often shape (rather than merely represent) reality. Some such depictions provide positive life models, as when Alexander the Great fashioned his own biography after the legendary hero Achilles or when Napoleon Bonaparte thought of his entire life as a kind of novel. ("Quel roman pourtant que ma vie!" he exclaimed to an interlocutor toward the end of his life.[13]) In other cases, fabrications affect people negatively: many an early modern woman lost her life because of fanciful fabrications about witches, and the prevarications contained in the Protocols of the Elders of Zion had disastrous effects on Jewish life in the twentieth century. The reader should expect to see the figure of the Wandering Jew serving in these two functions repeatedly in the pages of this book.

———

Because of its importance to European culture, Ahasverus's immense popularity after 1602 has led scholars to spill much ink trying to document and explain it.[14] Most have relied on one or two methods, often in combination. The first was to highlight the universal aspect of his tale. The legend of the Wandering Jew, we are told, is but a local example of a universal trope: human beings commit acts of injustice against one another or the gods, often wandering from place to place as a consequence.[15] True enough: folk narratives where the gods punish individual sinners by obligating them to long wanderings are indeed common. They exist in Greek mythology (Odysseus), in the Hebrew Bible and the Qur'an (Adam, Cain), in Nordic and Germanic mythologies (the Wild Hunter), and even in modern folktales (the Flying Dutchman, the Ancient Mariner). Clearly, Ahasverus isn't as unique as one might think at first. His figure seems to be a particular iteration of a general literary motif or anthropological archetype of a divinely punished exile. Alexandre Dumas captured this sentiment when he noted in his book on the Wandering Jew that "[i]t is not the history of a single person which we are telling, but the history of humanity."[16]

There is much to be said in favor of this understanding of Ahasverus's story. It explains, at least in part, why writers with no knowledge of early modern Germany or Jewish history have been attracted to the figure of the Wandering Jew: they saw in Ahasverus also a reflection of themselves and their particular life circumstances. But this approach also comes at a price.[17]

Consider, for example, the Kurtze Beschreibung and its enigmatic historical context. The original Ahasverus might have
been a local example of a larger, even universal, trope. But why
was the pamphlet about him published in 1602 and not earlier
or later? Who wrote and published it, where, for what particular
purpose, and with what specific audience in mind? The main
drawback of treating stories like that of Ahasverus as an expression of a universal symbolic grammar is that it deprives them of
their historical specificity. If we are to better understand Ahasverus's gravitational pull in the modern world, we must supplant
the anthropological mode of analysis with at least a modicum
of history.

A second way of coming to terms with Ahasverus's story is
by analyzing artistic representations. Especially in the second
half of the twentieth century, important works of scholarship
have enumerated and examined such representations in
European literature, music, and the visual arts.[18] The results of
these investigations have often been illuminating, as the case of
the Kurtze Beschreibung once again convincingly shows. As
several scholars have demonstrated, wandering figures associated with Christ's Passion appeared centuries before the 1602
pamphlet, notably in thirteenth-century chronicles such as the
work of the English monk Matthew Paris. Like the description
in the later Kurtze Beschreibung, these early accounts relate
how Jesus, on the eve of his Crucifixion, cursed a person before
telling him, "I go now, but you will await me till I come back."[19]
Across sources, the names vary. Some call this figure Cartaphilus,
other sources mention Butadeus, and a third group invokes the
Apostle John, about whom Jesus reportedly said, "If I will that
he tarry till I come, what is that to thee?" (John 21:22–23). No
matter: the similarities between these stories and the 1602 pamphlet are so striking that they cannot possibly be coincidental.

The author of the Kurtze Beschreibung most certainly did not cut the figure of Ahasverus out of whole cloth.

What is true for the 1602 pamphlet applies just as well to other representations of the Wandering Jew in history. Literary scholars, folklorists, and art historians have contributed immensely to our understanding of the legend of the Wandering Jew by shedding light on what artists and writers borrowed from one another in describing him and how they added new details to his tale. This is often wonderfully well done, and the following pages draw extensively on this scholarship. But just as with the anthropological approach to the story of the Wandering Jew, a heavy focus on artistic representations of Ahasverus tends to concentrate on the general and philosophical, rather than the particular, as no lesser authority than Aristotle once pointed out.[20] Consider again the example of the 1602 pamphlet. The existence of earlier accounts of a wandering figure cursed by Jesus is enlightening, but it still doesn't explain who resurrected the story in 1602, where this happened, or why. Moreover, the story the Kurtze Beschreibung told is full of historical allusions. According to the 1602 pamphlet, in 1542 Ahasverus appeared in Hamburg—a real city in northern Germany—where he met Paul von Eitzen and introduced himself as the Jew Ahasverus. Why this specificity of description? Why the meeting with Paul von Eitzen of all people, why in 1542, why in Hamburg, and why the name "Ahasverus" and not Cartaphilus, Butadeus, or John? We have already noted this same mixture of fiction and history in the exhibition *The Eternal Jew* in Nazi Germany and in Eotvos's writings. My point is that, while the legend of Ahasverus has important anthropological and artistic dimensions, the story cannot be reduced to them and them alone. Ahasverus also has a history, and historical work begins not where the text is most general, but on the

contrary, where it is so specific that at first "it makes no sense"
(Robert Darnton).[21]

———

The following pages discuss several crucial incidents in Ahasverus's historical–fictional life. They consist of five chapters that
proceed, for reasons that will become clear later, in reverse
chronological order, starting in the twentieth century, and then
moving deeper into the past. One can read them as stand-alone
pieces, each describing an isolated moment when Ahasverus's
anthropological and literary aspects intermingled with very real
historical circumstances. Taken together, however, the chapters
also constitute a whole that is greater than the individual parts.
As such, it constitutes a general, if also necessarily fragmentary,
biography of the ghostly figure of the Wandering Jew.

The book's first chapter, "The Apparition (1952)," tells the
story of a recent sighting of Ahasverus. It takes place in the early
1950s in the young State of Israel, where dozens of reliable eyewitnesses over the course of some three years came across a
man who fit the description of the Kurtze Beschreibung to a T.
Because the historical moment this chapter describes is still
recent, the events it discusses illumine what a serious historical
approach to Ahasverus's legend can help us see. Reports of
sightings of Ahasverus should not be dismissed out of hand.
However strange it sounds, they can represent an important
aspect of historical reality.

Chapter 2, "When Ahasverus Turned Jewish (1873)," travels
further back in time to the Russian empire of the late nineteenth century. The folklore specialist Galit Hasan-Rokem has
already suggested that Jews might have helped in shaping the
legend of the Wandering Jew over the centuries.[22] Under what

exact historical circumstances, however, could a tale based on anti-Jewish stereotypes be accepted, and eventually even celebrated, by Jews? What psychological and cultural mechanisms could possibly bring about such a transformation? The chapter sheds light on these important historical questions by reconstructing the life story of the man who tried to come to terms with this phenomenon for the first time.

Chapter 3, "A True Story That Never Happened (1711)," descends deeper into the well of the past. Its topic is the great fire that devastated the Jewish ghetto in Frankfurt am Main in 1711 and the image of Ahasverus that emerged from its ashes. Already in the early modern period, some scholars noted the strange mixture of history and fabrication in the story of the Wandering Jew. In the wake of the Frankfurt fire, one local scholar sat down to explain it. The result was the most influential historical–theological explanation for how Ahasverus's story could be simultaneously false and real.

The book's fourth chapter, "The Case of Ahasverus in Hamburg (1602)," reaches the origin point of Ahasverus's modern story—the enigmatic circumstances surrounding the creation of the Kurtze Beschreibung. Although the pamphlet lacks the name of an author, publisher, or place of publication, a detective-like investigation of its shape and content tells us a great deal about the intention behind it, and whether it was based, however loosely, on a historical encounter between a German student and a mysterious Jew. Insights from the previous three chapters combine here to conjure a powerful picture of the original "Ahasverus moment." From its inception, there were universal and literary but also historical dimensions to the story of Ahasverus, the Wandering Jew.

Having completed a journey that spans some three continents and more than 400 years, the book's fifth and final chapter, "I, Ahasverus (2025)," asks what is true and fictional about Ahasverus's story today. Do people still intimately identify with Ahasverus and perhaps even spot him in real life? If so, who are they, where do they live, and what exactly do they see in Ahasverus? What seemed all along like a dispassionate historical account of a premodern legendary figure assumes a very personal turn here. Imagine, once again, this book's opening scene: a middle-aged scholar sets up a new computer in his Princeton study. Suddenly, a ghost from his past appears on the screen.

1

The Apparition (1952)

The Wandering Jew is not a figment of our imagination.
He lives and suffers among us.

—JÓZSEF EÖTVÖS[1]

THE PLACE is Haifa Bay, Israel, the time the early 1950s. (See figure 6.) Under a blue Mediterranean sky, a vessel is seen heading out of harbor. The ship is snow white except for its funnel, which is adorned with seven golden Stars of David between two vertical blue lines, and the mast just behind it, which is painted black to mask the soot created by the smoke from the funnel. On closer inspection, some of the passengers appear: on the upper and main decks, sitting, walking, or leaning against the railings. Many more, no doubt, are in the ship's hull, hidden from view. On the stern, the vessel's name is painted in both Hebrew and English: *Artsa*.[2]

The ship's presence in this time and place is germane to our story, which occurs in the decade following World War II. The destruction of many thousands of ships in the global conflict

s. s. "ARTSA"   א.ק. "ארצה"

FIGURE 6. SS *Artsa*. Source: ZIM Archive.

that ended in 1945 created an acute shortage of maritime vessels. This deficit affected almost all countries to some extent, but had special meaning for the young State of Israel. Until the Reparations Agreement between Israel and West Germany came into effect in 1953, Israel's merchant marine (known as ZIM) made do with only a handful of small, rusty steam-powered liners. Like the ancient Ship of Theseus, these vessels seemed to contain not a single original part. Beneath their coats of whitewash, they were little more than floating heaps of maritime wreckage, "worthy, in reality," one passenger remembered later, "only of immediate scrapping in one of the ship cemeteries of the Far East."[3]

Our ship is one of these early ZIM vessels. While her name in 1952 is *Artsa*, she had been known by three other names in the past. Built in Bremen in 1930, she initially served as a banana boat named *Panther*, running between Cameroon and Hamburg. In 1938, during the rapid expansion of the German Navy ("Plan Z"), the *Panther*, alongside several German merchant vessels, was turned into a submarine tender, and for the next seven years, she was known as the *Lech*.[4] First stationed in Kiel, the *Lech* set sail to Memel in East Prussia, then to Gotenhafen (Gdynia), and from there to Danzig (Gdansk) and Pillau (Baltiysk). How the ship survived the war is not altogether clear, but in March 1945, American troops captured her intact in Travemünde, near Lübeck.

Even in 1945, the vessel's odyssey wasn't quite over. The US Navy took possession of the *Lech* only to sell her to an Italian company in 1948. ZIM purchased her a year later. From then on, the ship was known as *Artsa* (roughly, "Israel-bound") and transported Israeli tourists to Europe and Jewish immigrants to their new homes in Palestine. Thus did the former banana boat turn into a transport for humans, and the quondam Nazi submarine tender set sail under the Israeli flag.

———

Eliezer Khodorov, *Artsa*'s captain in October 1952, was a legendary figure in the early years of the Israeli merchant marine.[5] He seemed proud to serve on *Artsa*, at least according to what he told the official ZIM journal at the time. "This is ZIM's flagship, literally," he told the journal, "and a ship to be proud of she is at that."[6] Contemporary postcards depicted the ship in similar vivid colors, and at least some of her passengers painted her retrospectively also in a positive light. In 1953, for instance, a passenger composed a poem dedicated to the ship. It concluded with the lines: "A toast to the people who sail this good ship, / Whose spirit will always be nice to recall! // A toast, all you friends, lift the cup to the lip! / To the Artsa! The captain and crew! To us all!"[7]

Other passengers had different recollections of this floating assemblage of scrap-iron and maritime garbage. There was petty crime on board—theft, smuggling, and the occasional kerfuffle—and at one point, a waitress who couldn't take the harsh conditions any longer jumped ship in Marseille.[8] The poet Esther Raab complained in the 1950s about conditions on board, which "explain the low price of the tickets!" and Shoshana Arbeli-Almozlino, the future Israeli minister, remembered *Artsa* as "small and old."[9] A later captain went even further in describing the ship: *Artsa* was not only old, cramped, and filthy. Bluntly put, *Artsa* was "a little piece of shit."[10]

———

David Giladi—the father of the author Shulamit Lapid and grandfather of Israeli politician Yair Lapid—was working as a journalist for the newspaper *Ma'ariv* when he boarded the *Artsa* on October 3, 1952. He was traveling back to Israel from London and changed ships in Marseille.[11] During his journey, Giladi made brief visits to two transit camps set up by the Jewish Agency in Marseille and Naples. There were so many "wandering Jews across Europe," he wrote.[12] *Ma'ariv*'s readers needed to hear their stories.

It was the festival of Sukkot then, when Jews around the world commemorate the Exodus from Egypt and the Israelites' wanderings in the desert for forty years. The sea was calm, *Artsa* was packed with passengers, and Giladi saw many a familiar face on board. On the main deck were the cabins of Yisrael Weiss, head of the Jewish Agency's office in Brussels (who, like Giladi, belonged to the religiously observant

Zionist movement, Hapo'el Hamizrahi [the Mizrahi Worker]);
Yaakov Azulai, a district court judge in Haifa; and a wealthy
American Jew by the name of Simmel (first name unknown).
For these passengers, the journey was almost luxurious: *Artsa*'s main deck boasted a lounge, bar, and pleasant dining
hall, and in the evenings, Captain Khodorov presided over
social events. During the captain's dinner, for instance, the
lights in the dining hall were turned off and seven waiters
stepped out of the kitchen, each holding a cake *en flambé* in
his hands.[13]

Down in the ship's hull, the situation was different. After ZIM
purchased the *Artsa*, it reconfigured it to carry 550 passengers
instead of the intended 350. The reconfiguration affected mainly
the lower decks, where hundreds of Jewish immigrants, mostly
from the Maghreb, were bound for the young State of Israel.
One immigrant remembered the place as "awfully overcrowded
and filthy," while another recalled how, when a few of them
tried to use one of the upper decks, "a crew member told [us]
to return immediately downstairs."[14] During his own voyage on
Artsa, Giladi visited the hull (his own cabin was located on the
main deck), and shared what he saw there with *Ma'ariv* readers.
The men, women, and children in the lower decks spent their
days in their own quarters, eating inferior food in a separate
dining hall.[15]

None of this was out of the ordinary, strictly speaking, in the
early days of the State of Israel, and so it was nothing, figuratively and literally, for Giladi to write home about. That Giladi's
journey on the *Artsa* did not pass into oblivion was due to a
remarkable figure he met during the voyage. The mysterious
man seemed to be both middle aged and ageless, and although
he evidently had a present, he lacked any identifiable past.
There is much speculation about his true identity, some

theories more plausible than others. Who he really was we will probably never find out.[16]

———

Rumors about this man had already reached Israel a couple of years earlier. Elie Wiesel (not yet famous) was working as a Paris correspondent for the Israeli daily newspaper *Yediot Ahronot* at the time. Alongside a host of other Jews living in Paris after liberation—including, significantly, Emmanuel Levinas[17]—Wiesel had met the mystery man right after the war and studied under him on and off for several years. In an article Wiesel published in Hebrew in September 1950, titled "A Madman or a Genius?," he describes the first impression made by this unusual man:

> They call him Sharoni. Just like that. Without a first name. Only in religious circles they also add: Rabbi. And at the university: Professor Sharoni. A most extraordinary individual. A mixture of kabbalist, comedian, and anarchist. A genius who at first makes the impression of a Parisian clochard. A short, ungainly body, long hands, big head, expressionless. His clothes, torn and old to the point of ridicule, are pitiable. Shoes which aren't really shoes, ripped trousers, and a small, clownish hat.[18]

Wiesel then describes the riddle of the man:

> No one knows his real name. And, in general, he is shrouded in mystery. Whence did he come? Where and when was he born? Where does he live? What does he live *on*? One cannot tell. And one shouldn't ask. The slightest hint at these questions and he would grow mad. They say about him that

he's very wealthy and that, once he dies, we shall find a hidden treasure. People tell stories about extraordinary sums of money his students pay him. . . . Most of these fables are probably true.[19]

Wiesel, a great man but perhaps not a particularly rigorous thinker, does not explain how a story can be both true and a fable, nor why the only two options to characterize Sharoni are a genius or a madman. From this point on, however, Wiesel takes Sharoni's wealth as a given and calls the man's strange behavior "a game." "What does he do with his money? And, especially, why this pathetic game? Why dress as a pauper, a beggar, a schnorrer?—I cannot tell. I said: a strange man. Strange but also a genius."[20]

Next in Wiesel's account comes the gaping contradiction between Sharoni's poor external appearance and the extraordinary richness of his mind. This part is worth quoting at some length:

I have never met a man who knew so much. A veritable fountainhead. A living encyclopedia. There is nothing in this world he doesn't know. He knows by rote the entire Talmud and its legends, the Zohar, Maimonides, Ibn Ezra, and much more. He is in full command of all the humanities, philosophy from Thales and Socrates to Kant and Henri Bergson. (They once asked him to lecture in front of Bergson's students.) Also extraordinary knowledge in mathematics, physics, and biology. He can explain Einstein's relativity theory or the mystery of the hydrogen bomb. In short: a miracle man. Truly omniscient.

Of course, he also reads many languages. Indeed, he speaks and writes fluently in 30 tongues. Lately, he taught himself Hungarian in two weeks. In France, a whole body of legends revolves around him. People who knew him 20 years ago testify that he hasn't changed at all. It's as if time itself has no control over him. If you were to hear him, you'd forget everything: the world, time itself. . . .

He loves riddles. He likes to evoke hidden problems, to attack, to destroy rock-solid truths. Hence the ridicule and belittlement in his speech, hence too the cynicism and irony in his entire being. He pokes fun, derisively, at everything: living people, the world.[21]

Taken together, Wiesel's writings leave no room for doubt that Sharoni's more common name in France was Monsieur Chouchani.[22] "A 'wandering Jew,' he was the man who made me who I am," Wiesel writes. "Whatever I know now I owe to him."[23]

———

For the rest of his life, Wiesel would return to the topic of his old enigmatic teacher, each time rehearsing the same basic description but often adding a few new facts. This was the case with a short story Wiesel wrote in 1966, titled "The Wandering Jew." According to Wiesel, it was the best description he ever wrote of Chouchani.[24]

The story begins with the two men's first encounter at a synagogue in Paris. One day after liberation, Wiesel enters the synagogue and sees a mysterious figure surrounded by many admirers. When he approaches the group, the man turns to him and strikes up a conversation. This eventually leads to a lasting, significant bond between them.

In his story, Wiesel remembers the first impression made by Chouchani as profound and unpleasant. He describes the man's voice as discordant and his demeanor as overpowering and odious.

> He closed his eyes and went into an explication [of a biblical passage] which utterly dazzled me. I was already his, I entrusted him with my will, my reason. He spoke and I could only admire the extent of his knowledge, the richness of his thought. His words wiped out distances: there was no longer beginning or end, only the voice, harsh and disagreeable, of a man explaining to the Creator the mysteries and inadequacies of his creation.[25]

The clear magical–realist elements in this excerpt were also present in Wiesel's 1950 description where he described Sharoni/Chouchani as a person over whom "time itself has no control." In 1966, he repeats the same description: "The years had no hold over his body or mind. He was ageless. He remained the same, defying the imagination, provoking time itself."[26] In his 1966 story, Wiesel reiterates his observation two more times: "Death stands in awe of his temper," and even more directly: "he denied time."[27]

Writing in 1950, Wiesel claimed that Sharoni's relationship with God was fraught. Sixteen years later, Wiesel repeated the same claim. Reporting that some in the Parisian synagogue considered Chouchani a particularly righteous person, Wiesel noted that there were also some who wondered whether he was an observant Jew at all. One member of the congregation even suspected that "he's in the service of Satan; it's Satan who protects him and assures him his victories."[28] In his 1966 short story, Wiesel buttresses this semi-demonic depiction of Chouchani with a series of thinly camouflaged literary allusions taken from Johann Wolfgang von Goethe's *Faust*. Early in Goethe's play, the devil reveals himself to Faust for the first time. Having sneaked into Faust's study in the form of a poodle, he morphs into an itinerant savant, refuses to reveal his name, claims that he is "the spirit of perpetual negation," questions Creation, and declares, in two of the most celebrated lines in world literature, that he is "*ein Teil von jener Kraft / Die stets das Böse will, und stets das Gute schaft*" ("Part of that power which would / Do evil constantly and constantly does good").[29]

Despite its title, Wiesel's 1966 piece "The Wandering Jew" owes more to *Faust* than to the classical tropes associated with Ahasverus, the Wandering Jew. The dark master Wiesel describes is an ageless figure, and his itinerant's outward appearance hides a remarkable inner life. Crucially, Wiesel's Chouchani is also a man who urges his hearers to negate the Creation. Indeed, Chouchani dazzles Wiesel (read: Faust) with his profound knowledge so that the latter "entrusts him with [his] reason," and although he is undeniably odious, Chouchani's influence on Wiesel is somehow mostly benign. "It was him I had been seeking since the end of the war," Wiesel writes, "he alone would be in a position to take the place [of my dead teachers] and show me what road to follow."[30]

The deployment of Faustian tropes in Wiesel's "The Wandering Jew" should make us wary when we read Wiesel's description of Chouchani. If we are to trust his account as a whole, or even just a little, we need to find an independent source to verify what it describes. At least at first glance, this evidence is exactly what we find in David Giladi's reporting on the 1952 trip on *Artsa*.

Two years after the publication of Wiesel's *Yediot Ahronot* article and seven years after Chouchani's sudden appearance in the synagogue in Paris, Giladi saw him on *Artsa*—"a 'preacher' in one of the synagogues of Paris," he calls him in his *Ma'ariv* article published a few days later.[31] "Many important passengers were on the ship," Giladi recounts, "including professors and judges, consuls, and rabbinical emissaries. But the most popular personality on board was a Jew named Ben Shoushan, who was always able to find an audience for his lessons." Ben Shoushan, whose name in Hebrew means "the one from Shoushan" (the capital of King Ahasverus from the Bible) claimed to have traveled to Haifa from Morocco. He consequently should have stayed in the ship's packed hull during the trip, alongside other new immigrants from North Africa. But because *Artsa*'s voyage took place over the festival of Sukkot, Ben Shoushan took advantage of a loophole in the strict upstairs–downstairs logic of *Artsa* and stayed in the sukkah on the upper deck during the day. At night, too, he remained there, curled up on a bench.

What comes next in Giladi's description is a section whose style is just as telling as its content. More than Wiesel, Giladi moved easily between different registers of the Hebrew language, evoking biblical imagery, rabbinic pearls of wisdom, and references to modern Hebrew literature in a single article while also touching on everything from ancient religion to modern-day Israeli politics. Giladi's literary palette was undeniably rich: his description of Ben Shoushan was consequently a matter of deliberate design.

"He neglected his outward appearance and was dressed in rags," Giladi writes of Ben Shoushan, "but appearances cannot be more misleading in his case":

> He is a true student of the sages, the likes of which one doesn't meet every day: an expert swimmer in the sea of Talmud, in midrashim, the interpreters of the Talmud, as

well as science in general. There is not a single question he cannot interpret in 150 different ways and not a single saying he doesn't know by heart and can trace back to its source.... His knowledge is like a fountainhead, his exegeses astonish their hearers, and his speech a wondrous combination of many different tongues.[32]

According to Giladi, Ben Shoushan was a sensation on the ship. He had worshippers of all ages who wondered about the riddle surrounding the man: "Where did he come from? Why haven't we heard his name before? Why is he not counted among the great sages of our generation?"[33]

As in the case of Wiesel's 1950 article, Giladi mentions Ben Shoushan's money issues—he reports how several passengers offered Ben Shoushan money only to be rejected out of hand. Like Wiesel in his early article, Giladi finds the figure of Ben Shoushan not only strange but also temporally enigmatic. He writes that one could find Ben Shoushan "preaching in the morning, noon, and in the evening, all through the six days of the voyage," and that in Ben Shoushan, he witnessed in the flesh, "an old way of life resurrected, as when students literally sat at their master's feet, listening to the lesson." Indeed, how extraordinary it was to "have seen Mr. Azulai and Mr. Weiss withdrawing each to a different corner, reciting noiselessly to themselves what they had just heard, lest the lesson be forgotten, like two young pupils studying with an ancient rabbi."[34]

Giladi does not seem to have read Wiesel's article ("Why haven't we heard his name before?" he asks), and yet he repeats Wiesel's description almost verbatim. Thus, in both men's accounts, the mystery man's external shell seems barren, but his inner life contains an unmistakable spark, and though he speaks in the flesh to some very real people, there is no information about Ben Shoushan's past. A further, uncanny similarity between the two authors' descriptions is that both claim that Sharoni/Ben Shoushan/Chouchani preaches continuously from dawn to dusk, and yet neither is able to reproduce the content of the sermons in anything but general terms. Wiesel and Giladi tell rather than show: Ben Shoushan talks and Ben Shoushan preaches, he explains and he scolds—but *what* or *what about* both authors fail to tell us. The hero of their respective portrayals both incessantly speechifies and comes close to being speechless; he has a remarkable presence but only an indistinct, muffled voice.

———

Artsa arrived in Haifa on Thursday, October 9, 1952. No doubt disembarking first from the ship were the paying passengers (Giladi, Azulai, Weiss), who then sailed through passport and customs control. The new immigrants' path was different. Before they could be admitted into the country, they had to undergo medical examination, be registered by the authorities, and receive blankets and food.

Because they were separated at the port of entry, Giladi never had a chance to describe what happened to Ben Shoushan once *Artsa* reached Haifa. We do, however, have reports from passengers about what usually transpired at the port. Ralph Klein, the future coach of the basketball team of Maccabi Tel Aviv, made aliyah on *Artsa* a few months before Ben Shoushan. Together with his mother and sister (his father had been murdered in Auschwitz), the Hungarian Klein was on his way to a new life in Israel, which he soon realized "looks much better from afar than from up close."[35] Living in the dirty hull of the

Artsa wasn't easy either, but it was at the harbor that reality began to sink in. "Insufferable noise and loud yelling . . . welcomed us at the harbor," he reminisced. "The native Israelis treated us like inferior creatures and with rudeness I still find hard to describe. They aggressively sprayed us with DDT guns and told us to stand in a long line for an oil lamp and a blanket."[36]

Also shedding light on what happened once Chouchani reached Haifa is the registry of new immigrants from the day of his arrival. On close examination, this seemingly unremarkable document contains a few interesting facts. The registry (*pinkas olim*), ordered alphabetically by family name, records each new immigrant's personal information as well as an alien registration number (*te'udat oleh*), and national health system number (*mispar kupat holim*). Often, it also includes the immigrant's intended final destination in Israel. The registry paints a picture of *Artsa*'s passengers as a motley bunch: the 216 immigrants on board hailed from fifteen countries and spanned a range of ages. The majority came from North Africa, following the trend in Haifa at the time.[37]

We know from the work of French journalist Salomon Malka that Chouchani/Ben Shoushan used a forged Moroccan birth certificate on his journey to Israel.[38] The certificate, issued in August 1952 by the Jewish community in Casablanca, listed Ben Shoushan's parents as Joseph and Ferha, the year of his birth as 1904, and his name as Mordechai. (The choice of this first name must have been at least partially a joke: Mordechai ben Shoushan is an unmistakable reference to Mordechai of the Book of Esther who, just like Ahasverus, lived in Shoushan.) The same information is recorded in the registry of new immigrants dated October 9, 1952, with his national health system number and a remark that Ben Shoushan traveled alone. Because of the assembly-line nature of procedures at the port, health system numbers were issued sequentially, one passenger at a time. Thus, unbeknownst to the immigration officer on duty that day, he or she recorded the hierarchical (racial) nature of the immigrant's entry into Israel. In exactly the same way that the process was described in popular Israeli culture both then and later, immigrants from Western countries entered Israel first, while those from elsewhere, especially the Maghreb, waited at the end of the line.[39] The only exception to this rule was Ben Shoushan. Despite his Moroccan birth certificate, Ben Shoushan was practically at the head of the immigration line (number seven out of 216), with the next holder of Moroccan identity papers very far behind.[40]

But there is more. Until the founding of the State of Israel in 1948, the ethnic composition of the Jewish community in Palestine was fairly homogenous—Eastern and Central European, fairly educated, and fairly young. But by 1952, with the waxing tide of immigrants from non-European countries, Israel's Jewish population had more than doubled in absolute numbers while undergoing a radical shift in its ethnic composition. A year before Ben Shoushan arrived in Israel, the Israeli government, spurred by harsh economic conditions in the country and not a small dose of European (Jewish) racism, restricted immigration from North Africa to only healthy youths or families with a breadwinner no older than thirty-five (later raised to forty years).[41] Judged by these standards, Ben Shoushan should never have been allowed to enter Israel: he claimed to be a forty-eight-year-old Jew from Morocco and he traveled alone. Indeed, no other immigrant on *Artsa* or, for that matter, on any other ship arriving in Israel that month, showed similar characteristics.[42] Certainly, Ben Shoushan received special treatment of some kind.

———

From the harbor, Ben Shoushan went to Sha'ar Ha'aliyah, a former British military installation serving as a transit camp for new immigrants. The camp, comprising long rows of tents and a few administrative buildings, was located a few miles west of the harbor on the Mediterranean coast. Typically, new immigrants stayed there while their cases were sorted out.[43]

By the time Ben Shoushan set foot in Sha'ar Ha'aliyah, the place had approximately 2,000 inhabitants. By late 1952, the massive first immigration wave to the State of Israel had subsided, in part because the country's dire financial straits deterred potential newcomers, in part because of the government restrictions mentioned earlier. Nevertheless, in late 1952, the transit camp still brimmed with carnivalesque characters. Natan Alterman, Israel's foremost poet in the 1950s, visited Sha'ar Ha'aliyah less than a year before Ben Shoushan arrived, and described it on a radio show with that unmistakable Zionist pathos so characteristic of the time:

> The transit camp of Sha'ar Ha'aliyah. Tents and huts and sheds stretch on either side, cut in the middle by a paved road, almost like a street. Here is an immense and most colorful assembly of people that is constantly mixing and growing: Persia and its ways, Iraq in tatters and purple hats, Romania, Poland. . . . A Sambation [legendary river] of exiles, tatters of anguish and insult and poverty and wretchedness, illnesses and pains of an enormous miracle. . . . Immigrants from 67 countries have passed through this camp, and the

torrent is still rising. Here is a river that doesn't go to the sea but flows from it as rivers are prophesied to do at the arrival of the Messiah. [Sha'ar Ha'aliyah is] the name of the greatest and most meaningful station of all the stations in the Jewish historical journey so far.[44]

Feeding Alterman's hyperbolic prose was a paradox of 1950s Zionism: the idea that the Jewish state was to be the place for the final ingathering of the exiles of Israel and therefore the fulfillment of an ancient biblical prophecy (*kibbuts galuyot*) while also serving as the birthplace of a revolutionary New Man in the Nietzschean tradition. (Only in 1950s Israel were there Nietzscheans who believed in the Bible.) What all this meant in practice was a curious process of gathering, welding, morphing, and renaming—not unlike the story of *Artsa*, in fact. In the many transit camps throughout the country, the government took the "human material" of immigrants (a contemporary term), threw it into the proverbial "melting pot," and hoped that a New Jew would emerge in the process. Indeed, these were the exact metaphors the Israeli press used in describing Sha'ar Ha'aliyah in the early 1950s, though there were quite a few variations on the theme. One visitor wrote that the camp most resembled an assembly line in a factory, "a giant machine into which the new immigrant enters on one end as a nameless person, and having undergone medical examination and after being registered . . . leaves from the other end a citizen, with a certification of immigration in hand and a little bit of [government] money in his pocket."[45]

It almost goes without saying that immigrants often experienced the place rather differently. Conditions in the camp were harsh, cultural misunderstandings abounded, and the government formed a special police force to handle protests and outbursts of violence inside the camp.[46] In fact, Sha'ar Ha'aliyah was soon surrounded with barbed wire. In that respect, it was not unlike a refugee or a European displaced-persons camp.

———

Following a short sojourn in Sha'ar Ha'aliyah and for the next three years, Ben Shoushan lived in Israel. Written sources about his stay are not easy to find. This is not a coincidence but a pattern: in Israel, Ben Shoushan abstained from talking about his past, never had a permanent address, and consistently refused to publish anything in print.[47] With his students never recording his lessons (perhaps per his instruction), the usual materials of an intellectual biography are all but absent in his case.[48]

Viewing his presence from another angle, however, Ben Shoushan does seem to have left telltale tracks in Israel. To see them, the trick is not to look in unsubstantiated rumors about his "true identity," but to trace Ben Shoushan's peregrinations on a cultural map of early-1950s Israel. (See figure 7.)

It is best to start with the parts of the map where Ben Shoushan's traces are conspicuously absent. For instance, despite his alleged mastery of many scientific disciplines, there is no indication that Ben Shoushan ever subjected himself to the scrutiny of scholars at the Hebrew University in Jerusalem, Israel's main university at the time. The same person who, according to Wiesel, was called "Professor Sharoni" in France and lectured in Paris in front of Bergson's students, showed in Israel no sign of academic élan. Mutatis mutandis, the same is also true for the world of religious Zionist yeshivot, of which Yeshivat Merkaz Harav in Jerusalem, or perhaps Yeshivat Kerem B'Yavneh, might have been Ben Shoushan's clearest choices.[49] This expert swimmer in the sea of Talmud chose to practice his

FIGURE 7. Ben Shoushan's whereabouts in Israel of the 1950s.

strokes in a different ocean. According to the evidence we have, his Israeli life was not centered on a yeshiva.

But the most conspicuous element in the map Ben Shoushan never drew sat right in the center. Though he was known and admired by many during his sojourn in Israel, Ben Shoushan never entered mainstream culture. Between 1952 and 1956, the regular press (with the exception of Giladi's article) did not mention his name, and the cultural tone-setters of the time seemed not to notice his existence. This phenomenon is both understandable and suggestive. It is understandable because Israeli culture in the 1950s was proudly secular, and it empha-sized youth, collectivity, self-sacrifice, and a sense of indige-nousness to the land. As a rule, its heroes were those who fought, and all too often fell, in the struggle for Jewish independence. Young and "dripping of Hebrew dew," these youthful figures were "the silver platter on which the Jewish State was given," in the famous words of the poet Alterman.[50]

Diasporic Jews like Ben Shoushan represented the antithesis of this youthful, homegrown ideal. Early Zionist leaders like Leon Pinsker or Theodore Herzl had already viewed Ahasverus with contempt, and the same sentiment was still very much present in Israel of the early 1950s.[51] "We keep our distance from everything that's foreign," declare the protagonists of the most important novel of the period, S. Yizhar's *Days of Ziklag*, and "we flee, as if from a fire, everything that's [religiously] Jew-ish."[52] Yizhar's characters use the term "Wandering Jew" only once in the 1,100-page novel and then only in a disparaging sense. "If you speak in this way," one says to another, "you won't become a farmer. What will you become? I think nothing at all. A Wandering Jew, at best."[53]

Ben Shoushan's absence from 1950s Israeli culture was no accident, then. From a mainstream Zionist perspective, this middle-aged, lonely, eccentric, diasporic Jew could have been useful only in exile or perhaps while making his way to the Promised Land—indeed, this is exactly how both Wiesel and Giladi described him in their respective newspaper articles in the early 1950s. Once Ben Shoushan was inside Israel, however, such an exilic luftmensch was not supposed to become a celebrity. This makes it all the more remarkable that in one particular social milieu, Ben Shoushan did attract attention, almost at once.[54]

———

For five weeks after his arrival, we lose track of Ben Shoushan in Sha'ar Ha'aliyah. But then, in mid-November 1952, he resurfaces, first in Kibbutz Sa'ad, just across the border from Egypt-occupied Gaza, and then in Kibbutz Be'erot Yitzhak, not far from Tel Aviv. Both kibbutzim belonged to the Religious Kibbutz Movement, an affiliate of the religious-Zionist Hapo'el Hamizrahi. The attentive reader will recall that David Giladi and at least one of Ben Shoushan's admirers on *Artsa*, Yisrael Weiss, shared the same political affiliation.[55]

Be'erot Yitzhak, where Ben Shoushan spent a few months in late 1952 and early 1953, bore an uncanny resemblance to *Artsa*. Just like the battered ZIM liner, the religious kibbutz was a place of both miracles and traumas, an ever-moving terrestrial vessel made of recycled objects, names, and pasts. The nucleus of the kibbutz consisted of German and Czech Jews who originally called their group Ramat Hashomron and lived in northern Palestine. A few years later and under the name Be'erot Yitzhak, they settled in a spot east of Gaza where, during the 1948 war, they came under a series of Egyptian attacks. The worst of these attacks, in July 1948, left seventeen of the defenders dead and many more wounded. The Egyptian army eventually withdrew, but the remaining kibbutz members decided not to return to the same location. This was the third time in fifteen years that the kibbutz had to change sites.[56]

As it turned out, even in 1948, the wanderings weren't over. First came a short stay in the deserted German colony of Wilhelma, and then the permanent location, near the Arab village of Al-Abbasiyya, depopulated by Jewish forces in 1948 and now rechristened as Yehud. This constant process of movement and renaming was typical of Zionism. It meant to conjure a lost biblical landscape while superseding (or erasing) the recent past. It was then, amid Jewish and non-Jewish violence, exile, and rechristening, that Ben Shoushan appeared at the gates of Be'erot Yitzhak.

Zvi (Walther) Bachrach was a member of the kibbutz in late 1952. Years later, he recalled how Ben Shoushan burst into his life. "He appeared one day at my doorstep, completely unannounced, and told me to give him room and board and that 'I will teach you whatever you'd like.'"[57] Bachrach remembered Ben Shoushan as a harsh man, almost unbearable.

> He neglected his external appearance, like a beggar. We thought he was an eccentric and couldn't just turn him away. So we gave him a little wooden hut in the kibbutz, and after a while said to ourselves: "Let's see what he has to say." He then gave us such a lecture on the Talmud. . . . We were utterly dazzled. We let him stay after that.[58]

In the following months, some became enthusiastic admirers of Ben Shoushan while others did not. This was not a matter of coincidence, as the story of Bachrach makes clear. Just like Wiesel, Bachrach was a Holocaust survivor. During World War II, the Germans murdered his parents, and his own

infernal ordeal had taken him through Ravensbrück, There-
sienstadt, Auschwitz, a slave labor camp, and finally a death
march. Upon liberation, Bachrach made aliyah (Wiesel did the
same, but left Israel), and—again like Wiesel—he eventually
dedicated his life to studying and teaching the Holocaust (in
his case, as a history professor). "From experience to research,"
Bachrach later called the journey of his life: from *havaya* to
mehkar.[59]

The similarities between Wiesel's and Bachrach's stories go
even deeper. Following separate interactions with Ben
Shoushan, both men came to share almost identical ideas
about man's relationship with God. Wiesel's "wounded faith"
is well known; following his personal ordeal, he refused to believe in God, but after meeting Chouchani in Paris, he changed
his mind, deciding to refuse to stop believing. Significantly,
Bachrach's intellectual trajectory developed along similar
lines.[60]

We know from his writings that Bachrach had a fairly standard religious education before World War II. But following the
Holocaust, and even after he made aliyah and joined a religious
kibbutz, Bachrach's relationship with God was quite strained.
He was in awe of God's wondrous creation, "the beautiful things
in man and nature . . . but I was also angry, and still am, at
him."[61] In a moving letter to his children in 1985, Bachrach explained, "I often feel that my whole life is one big fall,"[62] and on
a different occasion he wrote:

> My religiosity is a constant struggle. . . . I believe in God and
> pray to him but always within <u>strict limits</u>. I cannot forgive
> him that he let my parents be murdered, that he sent me to a
> concentration camp, that he made my life so difficult. I dare
> even say that I have a love–hate relationship with him.[63]

Throughout his adult life, Bachrach's faith, just like Wiesel's, remained in a state of belief *and* rebellion. The two concepts were closely related because to rebel against something is by definition also to believe in its existence. "The rebellious Jew who ponders the Holocaust faces a paradox," Bachrach explained. "The real religious crisis is not in forsaking God but in the conscious decision to believe in him out of unrest and rebelliousness."[64] There were powerful echoes of Wiesel here or, perhaps more accurately, of an ur-voice that both men had heard soon after the Holocaust. Indeed, in one of his academic articles, Bachrach quoted Wiesel on the revolt against God: "The rebellion must be constant. . . . One has to live one's rebellion, lest we shall slide into apathy. Each and every one of us has to say: 'Lord of the World, we both know that it is now time for prayer. . . . But I refuse, you hear me? I refuse!' "[65]

From today's perspective, Bachrach's paradoxical combination of belief and rebelliousness seems at odds with his religious-Zionist commitments. Today, religious Zionism is self-confident, overwhelmingly right wing (with a few notable exceptions), and politically powerful. The situation in the early 1950s was different. The movement's leader, Moshe Shapira, held dovish political views, and an important faction within the movement shared Bachrach's complicated relationship with God. Mainstream Zionists had no such theological compunctions because they were mostly atheists, and Orthodox (anti-Zionist) Jews often came up with some kind of "comforting [theological] truth about the Holocaust," as historian Eliezer Schweid once put it, which made the problem disappear.[66] (Bachrach later called such facile solutions to the theological problem of the Holocaust "appalling."[67]) Many religious Zionists were caught between Scylla and Charybdis: they shared with

Orthodox anti-Zionists a belief in the existence of a benign providence, but alongside secular Zionists, they refused to search for any faith-affirming meaning in the Nazi genocide. Where, after all, was God? "How can I stay quiet in the face of the memory of my father, my mother, my sister, and my brothers??," wrote Shalom Karniel, a religious-Zionist author, in his diary in 1945, for instance. "Can one still pray to God when one also wonders whether there is justice and law in the universe? . . . How could [the Holocaust] have happened in a world whose Creator is supposed to be good and benevolent?"[68]

Throughout his life, and indeed long after religious Zionism took a sharp political turn to the right, Bachrach persisted in his decision to navigate between his Jewish faith, on the one hand, and an imperfect Creator on the other. He believed in God ("within strict limits") while stubbornly seeking historical (nontheological) answers to what happened to him during the war. Summing up his academic career in the early 2000s, Bachrach recalled how in his research, he was driven by the attempt to understand "Why my family was targeted? What motivated the perpetrators, what did they hope to achieve?"[69] As it turned out, history, like theology, provided few definitive answers. Shortly before his death, Bachrach was asked by the French–Israeli filmmaker Michael Grynszpan whether he could now, after so many years of study, understand the causes of his personal tragedy. In a far cry from the know-it-all triumphalism of post-1967 religious Zionism, Bachrach's reply was an unambiguous "No." "I still cannot fathom it," he told Grynszpan. "I do not understand the Holocaust even though the Holocaust is my profession. I do not understand it at all."[70]

Apart from Bachrach's recollections, we also possess con-
temporary sources about Ben Shoushan's stay in Sa'ad and
Be'erot Yitzhak. According to the Kibbutz Sa'ad newsletter, Ben
Shoushan first arrived at the kibbutz exactly five weeks after
Artsa dropped anchor in Haifa.[71] The newsletter reports that
Ben Shoushan didn't just show up in the western Negev out of
the blue, but that he had been sent by the Center for Jewish
Culture in Israel's Ministry of Education. This is an important
detail. In the early 1950s, Avraham Chen, a well-connected
religious-Zionist rabbi who had previously served as a rabbinical emissary in France, headed the center. Hence, in all likelihood, the Chouchani/Ben Shoushan connection at Sa'ad and
Be'erot Yitzhak, and perhaps also on *Artsa*.[72]

The Sa'ad newsletter describes Ben Shoushan's presence in
the kibbutz in some detail:

> The Center for Jewish Culture [in the Ministry of Education]
> sent us Dr. Ben Shoushan. He was to give us lectures during
> the Shabbat on which the Torah portion Hayei Sarah [life of
> Sarah] is read. We found it curious that one person would be
> willing to lecture and teach seven times over the course of a
> single day . . . but anyone who was fortunate enough to
> attend the lectures stopped wondering. Never before have
> we met a man like him. His knowledge encompasses all
> the realms of culture, and he surveys in his mind's eye the
> whole wide world. . . . That Saturday was consequently only
> the opening salvo, and in the following three days, he taught
> many classes, covering Ecclesiastes, Proverbs, Habakkuk,
> then the Eight Chapters of Maimonides, and ending with
> philosophy. Kibbutz members rushed to his lectures from
> work, and even those who do not usually attend such events
> came to hear him—and enjoyed the experience.[73]

Despite the range of topics he covered, Ben Shoushan seems to have followed a logical progression in his lectures. Reconstructing it today is bound to be speculative—the reader is invited to disagree—but the exercise is revealing nonetheless. Ben Shoushan's course of lectures started with biblical works that are famous for questioning the meaning and goodness of God's Creation. This is the crux of the powerful opening verses in Ecclesiastes ("Utter futility! All is futile!" Ecclesiastes 1:1), and that is the case too with Habakkuk. The discussion of the latter at Sa'ad must have struck a chord with kibbutz members. Like their counterparts at Be'erot Yitzhak, many kibbutzniks at Sa'ad were personally affected by the Holocaust and the heavy losses of Israel's War of Independence; also like them, they were observant Jews. Hence, the unmistakable force of the first verses of Habakkuk: "How long, O LORD, shall I cry out, and You not listen, shall I shout to You 'Violence!' and You not save?" (Habakkuk 1:2).

After these early lectures, Ben Shoushan continued with Maimonides's Eight Chapters, in which the celebrated medieval Jewish philosopher discusses ethics, man's place in the world, and his philosophical method. The latter, Maimonides famously explains in the introduction, follows a plan by which one sheds light on the Mishnah by "gather(ing) from the discourse of the sages in the Midrash, the Talmud, and other compositions of theirs, as well as from the discourse of both ancient and modern philosophers, and from the compositions of many men."[74] Finally, and as if following in Maimonides's footsteps, Ben Shoushan touches on philosophical questions that may or may not have shed new light on the relationship between man and God.

The kibbutz newsletter then expands on Ben Shoushan's lectures while repeating what seems to be the same logical progression we have just observed—a circuitous movement from the words of the Torah to general philosophy and back.

What we heard from him, though it was clearly just an ap-
petizer, gives us a sense of his way of learning and thinking.
As far as the Bible is concerned, he places special emphasis
on exactitude in language and style, and—in terms of content—on the fact that the key to understanding all things is
faithfulness to the Bible's internal logic. When it comes to
other cultural realms, he proceeds by way of exact defini-
tions, a careful distinction between what is essential and
what is not, and logical deduction.[75]

The short text concludes with what seems like a rare direct
quote from one of Ben Shoushan's lectures, a statement whose
deep and theologically rebellious overtones might have been lost
on most if not all of the kibbutzniks. "Above all else," the newsletter states, "he believes that wonder is the beginning of all study—
and the beginning of all wonder is study."[76] These seemingly
harmless words are a clear reference to Greek philosophy (that
wonder is the beginning of all philosophy can be found in Plato's
Theaetetus and Aristotle's *Metaphysics*) and an inversion of a celebrated early verse in Proverbs—one of the biblical books, we
remember, that Ben Shoushan discussed in his lectures. There, it
is stated that it is not wonder, but "The fear of the LORD [that] is
the beginning of knowledge" (Proverbs 1:7). This point is subtle
but suggestive: in front of a group of religious Zionists who had
experienced a great deal of trauma, Ben Shoushan replaced acquired knowledge (*da'at*) with the process of exploration or study
(*mehkar*), and used "wonder" as a substitute for "fear of the Lord."

———

The news about Ben Shoushan we have from the following year
and a half comes from several sources. According to a

December 1952 report, Ben Shoushan had just finished a week-long stay at Sa'ad, and decided to split his time from then on between Sa'ad and Be'erot Yitzhak.[77] According to this source, Ben Shoushan's condition for this arrangement was that he would be allowed to give regular lessons at both kibbutzim, and that students would commit to regularly attending them.

For about a year, Ben Shoushan remained committed to this arrangement. In early January 1953, for example, he was ill but insisted on giving several lectures at Sa'ad.[78] Topics included a brief discussion of the Talmud, followed by a much longer discussion of the biblical book of Malachi, which Ben Shoushan continued teaching the following month.[79] It might not be coincidental that Malachi, just like Ecclesiastes and Habakkuk, which Ben Shoushan had discussed earlier, also opens with doubts about God's benevolence: " 'I have shown you love,' said the LORD. But you ask, 'How have you shown us love?' " (Malachi 1:2).

Ben Shoushan's material life in the two kibbutzim is also fairly well documented. The kibbutzniks at Sa'ad assigned him a private room, and at Be'erot Yitzhak he received—just as Bachrach recalled—a hut with the rare luxury of a private bathroom, as well as regular payments to cover his personal expenses.[80] Then money became an issue. At one point, Ben Shoushan insists that the kibbutz pay for his reading glasses and electric razor, and receives money but fails to show up to class.[81] Other reports cast doubt on Bachrach's retrospective description of Ben Shoushan. Fifty years later, the aging Israeli historian recalled how Ben Shoushan had appeared at Be'erot Yitzhak completely unannounced. The historical record shows otherwise: Ben Shoushan was sent to Be'erot Yitzhak by the Center for Jewish Culture in the Ministry of Education, and the decision to give him a hut wasn't made in the moment but well in advance.[82]

What is true about Ben Shoushan's sudden appearances at Be'erot Yitzhak applies also to how he eventually disappeared. Eyewitnesses later recalled that at one point, Ben Shoushan simply vanished into thin air, like a new Elijah. Contemporary records offer a more mundane explanation. After several months at Sa'ad and Be'erot Yitzhak, both kibbutzim asked Ben Shoushan to leave. At a meeting of Be'erot Yitzhak's executive in July 1954, participants complained that "[Ben Shoushan] has not been teaching or lecturing here for quite some time, and since to the best of our knowledge he has no intention of resuming his classes, we have decided to ask him to leave."[83]

In April 1953, while Ben Shoushan was still dividing his time between Sa'ad and Be'erot Yitzhak, the Center for Jewish Culture sent him to Haifa to lecture on the Jewish High Holidays to a group of young members of Hapo'el Hamizrahi.[84] Over time, such lectures became Ben Shoushan's main source of income. (Whether he also gave private lessons we simply do not know; such lessons would leave no trace in official records.) Public lectures were usually two-hour affairs during which Ben Shoushan spoke in front of large audiences of members of Hapo'el Hamizrahi. For each lecture, the center paid him a small sum.[85]

A first series of lectures is documented in Haifa, starting in September 1953, and a second took place in Petah Tikva in January 1954.[86] Later, Ben Shoushan moved his activities to the biblical seminary of Hapo'el Hamizrahi in Tel Aviv.[87] We do not have the written texts of the lectures, but we do know the titles of these presentations and that they were always intended for members of Hapo'el Hamizrahi. Occasionally, Ben Shoushan

spoke on general topics, but more often than not, his favorite subject was Maimonides. In February 1954, Ben Shoushan
spoke in Haifa on "The Significance of Maimonides in Light of
Jewish History," and not long afterward, he gave a lecture in Tel
Aviv titled, "The Torah Speaks in the Language of Men, According to Maimonides."[88] The impression one gets is that facing a
post-Holocaust, post-1948, religious-Zionist audience, Ben
Shoushan repeatedly explored the gap between rationality
and faith: this was the case with Ecclesiastics, Habakkuk, and
Malachi at Sa'ad; this was true with "The Torah Speaks in the
Language of Men"; and this, perhaps most symbolically, was
the case in an early 1955 lecture in Haifa, where Ben Shoushan
discussed Maimonides's masterpiece, the appropriately titled *A
Guide for the Perplexed*.

————

We are slowly nearing the end of Ben Shoushan's Israel story,
which is fittingly also its starting point. Those who met Ben
Shoushan wondered about his past. Who was he? Where did
he come from? What was his life like before and during the
war? The time Ben Shoushan spent in Israel helps to shed
light on such questions even if it does not solve them once
and for all.

    According to common conjecture, Ben Shoushan was born
Hillel Perelman in Latvia in the 1890s and spent time studying
under Rabbi Abraham Isaac Kook in Mandatory Palestine.[89]
Perelman immigrated to the United States and then returned to
Europe, where he likely spent the war, finally moving to Israel
in 1952. From the perspective of a professional historian, this hypothesis, based on conjecture and lacking definitive proofs for
its claims, is hardly compelling. Moreover, if the man's original

name was Perelman, then what? What is the difference that would make a difference in this case?

More important than assigning the name "Perelman" to Ben Shoushan is realizing what identifying him as a follower of Rabbi Kook achieves in present-day Israel. Rabbi Abraham Isaac Kook (1865–1935) was the Chief Rabbi of Mandatory Palestine, but his messianic, mystical theology became significant for religious Zionism especially after the Six-Day War. Before 1967, Kook's legacy was important, but many religious Zionists also kept their distance from him and his followers, preferring a more moderate political and theological stance. To insist on a connection between Ben Shoushan and Rabbi Kook thus carries political intent and forces Ben Shoushan into a specific mold. According to the sources we possess, Ben Shoushan's worldview, at least in the early 1950s, involved a defiant, Ahasverus-like stance vis-à-vis God and the man he created in his own image. This is a far cry from the way Rabbi Kook–inspired religious Zionists view the world.

A second hypothesis regarding Ben Shoushan's true identity is also quite telling. Many early Zionists Hebraized their names as a symbolic rejection of diasporic life. Wiesel surmised that Ben Shoushan's story must have been similar. He assumed his original name to have been Rosenbaum-Shoshani, because "rose" in Hebrew is *shoshan*, and Shoshani to Israeli ears is almost indistinguishable from Chouchani or Ben Shoushan.

The source of Wiesel's identification of Ben Shoushan with a Rosenbaum-Shoshani is unknown, but the story is suggestive. In the 1920s, there was indeed a Rabbi Shoshani in Palestine who had changed his name from Rosenbaum. His full name was Yehezkel Shoshani-Rosenbaum, he was born in Poland in 1895, and as a young man studied under Reb Haim Brisker before making aliyah. In the early 1920s, Shoshani-Rosenbaum settled in Haifa, where he soon joined—you've guessed it—the movement of Hapo'el Hamizrahi. During his stay in Palestine, Shoshani-Rosenbaum preached, taught, and traveled extensively.[90] For a while, he even served as an elected member of the governing body of Hapo'el Hamizrahi.

Let there be no mistake about it: Ben Shoushan and Rosenbaum-Shoshani were not—and could never have been—one and the same person. Rosenbaum-Shoshani returned to Poland in 1929 and was eventually murdered in Treblinka. After the war, his son, a refugee in Sweden, announced his name on a popular radio show that helped Israelis locate relatives they had lost contact with during the war. Perhaps this is how the two biographies became entangled: the parallel life stories of two rabbis with similar sounding names, who lived in Palestine for a period, traveled extensively, and were affiliated with Hapo'el Hamizrahi.

Alas, Rosenbaum-Shoshani's son's hope that his father could have survived Treblinka was a cruel, impossible fantasy. Of the 900,000 Jews the Germans shipped to the death camp in the early 1940s, fewer than 100 survived. Conflating the postwar Ben Shoushan with the prewar Rosenbaum-Shoshani, and even more so, hoping that the latter somehow survived the war, are psychologically revealing errors of judgment. They may not tell us much about Ben Shoushan's background, but they shed important light on his apparition in 1950s Israel. Ben Shoushan was an actual person, with real parents, and an all too real Holocaust-related trauma. But he was also, and not least, a projection of literary motifs and post-Holocaust cultural fantasies. This is, and must be, an important aspect of any attempt to reconstruct his personal, and undoubtedly tragic, history.

And yet Ben Shoushan's figure was not only tragic or a mere projection of other people's phobias or fantasies. Far from it.

Indeed, Ben Shoushan's Israeli story contains many farcical elements, combining mockery, parody, and extremely dark irony. This is so, first of all, because the whole Zionist project had always been so unlikely, self-contradictory, and full of pathos that it constantly hovered on the verge of the absurd. ("In Basle I founded the Jewish state," Theodore Herzl wrote in his diary following the first Zionist congress of 1897, "were I to say it out loud, *the response would be a general laughter.*"[91]) Ben Shoushan's Israeli story was consequently bound to have its many ironies, gaps between what ought to have been and what actually was. This, we saw, was the case of *Artsa*, at once an exemplary, proud vessel and "a little piece of shit," and the reality for new immigrants to the country, who soon realized that Israel looked great but "especially from afar." Irony has always been a part of Israel's self-perception, a "country of every possible contradiction, and every possible paradox" (Saul Friedländer).[92] As such, it was also an important aspect of the Israeli story of Ben Shoushan.

A different comic element that colored the Israeli act in Ben Shoushan's biography had to do with the man's actions. Wiesel highlighted this side of Ben Shoushan's personality when he wrote in 1950 that Ben Shoushan was "[a] mixture of kabbalist, *comedian*, and anarchist."[93] Other eyewitnesses concurred. A woman who had run into Ben Shoushan at an engagement party in 1953 Jerusalem recalled years later how, as she walked into the room, she saw Ben Shoushan standing on a chair, parodying a Jewish sermon.[94] Ben Shoushan seems to have basked in such moments: he loved serving mockery to the merriment of the crowd.

Which leads us to one last element of mockery in Ben Shoushan's story that is both very important and outright

sacrilegious. Many reports claim that Ben Shoushan used de-
structive irony to poke fun not only at other people but also at
God. As we saw, this attitude resonated with Wiesel and Bachrach, among others, after the war. The poet Alterman, in four
of his most famous lines, explains why a post-Holocaust God
must also be an object of bitter mockery: "When our children
sobbed in the gallows' shadow / We didn't witness the world's
wrath / For you have chosen us of all other peoples / Loved
us and taken pleasure in us."[95] To be chosen for *that*, to be in
this utterly absurd way "loved" by God, was a cruel joke, a most
bitter gag. Not only the Israeli stage, therefore, and not only the
peculiarities of the main protagonist turn Ben Shoushan's Israeli story into a scene from a parody or a farce. A fundamental
element in this whole fantastic story—a fundamental element
in modern Jewish history as a whole—is also the scandalously
cynical, shameless, pathetic excuse of a God *who exists*, and who
treats his beloved people thus.[96]

———

The rest can be summarized briefly because the end of Ben
Shoushan's Jewish-Israeli story is the reverse image of how it
began. Over the course of 1955, Ben Shoushan's lectures petered
out until, by late 1955, they ceased completely. By early 1956, at
the latest, Ben Shoushan left Israel behind.[97]

No one depicted his departure. There was no Giladi this
time, no *Artsa*, no Bachrach, and no Be'erot Yitzhak. As he was
making his exit, the Israelis of the 1950s paid no attention to Ben
Shoushan.

Years went by and the land changed its face. The once small
State of Israel expanded, first just for a few months in 1956, and
then permanently in 1967. During the Six-Day War, East

Jerusalem, the West Bank, Gaza, the Sinai Peninsula, and the Golan Heights were conquered (or occupied, or liberated), and soon a tidal wave of Rabbi Kook–inspired religious-Zionist messianism swept the land. Many features of the place where Ben Shoushan had made his apparition were washed over in the process. What was hard to recognize to begin with, was all but completely unrecognizable now.[98]

It is against this backdrop that in October 1967, a journalist of the religious-Zionist newspaper *Hatsofe* gave Israelis one final sign of life from Ben Shoushan. He saw him in Montevideo, Uruguay, "a beautiful, quiet, and peaceful country . . . where the Jewish community is rather small, about 40,000 souls in all, and sharply divided among itself like any other Jewish community in the world."[99] The picture the journalist sketched will by now be familiar to the reader. Ben Shoushan was a "strange and extraordinary Jew, a genius the likes of which one probably cannot find throughout the Jewish world."[100] He had survived all the horrors of the Holocaust in Europe "and wandered over many years, constantly drifting and metamorphosing." Then he spent some time in the young State of Israel, where the Center for Jewish Culture at the Ministry of Education paid his expenses, including financing his lecture circuit "through the length and breadth of the land." Soon he left, however, and kept wandering, "until he found some peace and quiet—if a Jew like him can ever find such things—in this distant corner of the globe."[101]

Two months later, Ben Shoushan died in Uruguay, where he was then buried. And yes, in case you were wondering, reliable eyewitnesses were at hand.[102]

What remained from Ben Shoushan was not an organized, written body of theology but an unexplained name and a theatrical performance that we now know were closely intertwined. Like all of us, Ben Shoushan was a creation of those around him, but like all of us, he was also his own man. His curious behavior and decision to call himself "the one from Shoushan" (that is, Ahasverus) were choices Ben Shoushan himself made, on his own terms, for his own reasons, and at a time he himself deemed to be right. Not only a madman or a genius, therefore, and not just a projection of other people's phobias and fantasies, Ben Shoushan appeared in 1950s Israel as a *gilgul* or transmigration, an ancient midrash come to life and a cruel, pathetic joke, too. Amid revolutionary change stood a man who proclaimed through his actions, his name, through his very figure: Here I am—I, Ahasverus—the ever-drifting, accursed, God-deriding living legend; I am the Wandering Jew.

2

When Ahasverus Turned
Jewish (1873)

THE GREAT Yiddish writer Sholem Aleichem recalled once what it felt like to read the novel *Di Kliyatshe* (Yiddish: "The Nag") for the first time. The year was 1873, the novel's hero a talking horse, and the author Sholem Yakev Abramovitch, a man better known to modern readers by his Yiddish pen name, Mendele Mokher Sfoyrim ("Mendele the Book Peddler"). Sholem Aleichem read the novel, as was his custom, in a circle of friends, and the group, finding the premise of the novel funny, began by poking fun at the author for composing it. Suddenly, they realized what the book was really about, and fell silent. *The Nag*'s topic, it turned out, was very serious indeed.[1]

The Russian censor seems to have had the same exact intuition about *The Nag*. After examining the manuscript for government approval, the censor invited Abramovitch to his office and informed him that the novel was under suspicion of being an antigovernmental treatise in disguise. Although Abramovitch professed as much all but explicitly in the book—("[m]y shape is that of a horse," the novel's heroine says at one point, "but in reality I'm something else altogether"[2])—in front of the censor, he pleaded ignorance. Full of false praise for the Russian official and with his characteristic Jewish self-abnegation, he told the censor that "it's an honor and a privilege to think that a great personality like yourself takes the time to interpret my work so creatively."[3] If we believe Abramovitch's account of the incident, the flattered censor left him in peace after that.

———

A few months after the encounter between Abramovitch and the censor, copies of *The Nag* were indeed printed. It was done at the Romm publishing house in Vilnius: a famous establishment located in Žmudski Street in Vilnius's old town. About halfway down the street was the owner's residence, and another few doors down, two low structures facing each other, in which books like *The Nag* were produced. Peering through windows, passersby on the street reported seeing heavy printing presses on the ground floor, and between them many a busy figure: lithographers, bookbinders, proofreaders, floor sweepers, carriers, and of course the typesetters, "their hands black from ink, their lungs full of metal dust."[4] "Here the presses work day and night," an eyewitness described the scene, "composing, printing, and distributing all the books of Israel."[5]

Despite its humble location in central Vilnius, in 1873 the Romm publishing house catered to a vast and rapidly changing Jewish readership. Hot off its presses rolled out simple prayer books and Hebrew Bibles, editions of the Mishnah and the Talmud, philosophy books and newspapers, some of the earliest plays and novels to appear in modern Hebrew and Yiddish literatures, and even some translations into Hebrew and Yiddish of foreign (non-Jewish) works. Book shipments left Vilnius by train, bound for wholesale merchants in Warsaw or Berdychiv,[6] while individual works were carried away also by book peddlers (Yiddish: *pakntregers*) who wandered from town to town on foot or in rackety carriages.[7]

In 1873, the owner of the publishing house on Žmudski Street was Devorah Romm.[8] In Jewish Vilnius, many called Romm "the princess" (Hebrew: *hagevirah*), but on the books she helped issue (including *The Nag*), she referred to herself as "the Widow Romm." David Romm, Devorah's late husband, died in the early 1860s, and since then his widow had taken care of the business side of the family enterprise. Devorah Romm left many day-to-day operations in the hands of Shmuel Shraga Feigensohn, a bibliograph and Hebrew author who, like many other characters in this book (Ben Shoushan among them), went by a pseudonym. In his case, it was "Shafan Hasofer"— "Shafan the Scribe."

The location, physical appearance, and management structure of the Romm publishing house in late nineteenth-century Vilnius reflected contemporary Jewish society at large: the wealthy elite often living somewhat separately from other social classes, while white-collar workers and manual laborers sharing space, at least in part. This spatial arrangement expressed the logic of late nineteenth-century European capitalism. Gone were the days of the early printing revolution, when different stages of book production were carried out in separate artisans' workshops; no longer was printing mainly a *craft*. The factory-like organization of labor in the Romm Press was based on a different production logic. By keeping all workers under a single roof, Devorah Romm and Shafan saved on unnecessary expenses while also keeping a watchful eye on manual workers and administrative staff.

The laborers in the Romm Press, for their part, were no passive objects of Devorah Romm, Shafan Hasofer, or the abstract

FIGURE 8. Creating a stereotype. Source: © Deutsche Fotothek /
Roger und Renate Rössing https://www.deutschefotothek.de/gallery
/freitext/df_roe-neg_0006484_033.

forces of late nineteenth-century capitalism. On the contrary,
they were readers and often authors themselves, and working
alongside one another, they forged a shared class consciousness, which in turn influenced the kind of works that the Romm
Press put out, including *The Nag*.[9] In the late 1860s, Devorah
and Shafan tried to introduce into their business the new technology of stereotype (rotary) printing, to which the workers
responded by going on strike. Instead of using flatbed presses
as before, stereotype printing was based on cylindrical metal
plates ("stereotypes"), which were more durable, simpler to
use, and easier to store for future editions than anything printers had used in the past. (See figure 8.) This development
threatened to make part of the typesetters' work superfluous—
hence the decision to strike. Shafan eventually cut a deal with
his disgruntled workers: in exchange for their acceptance of the

new technology, he gave them a pay raise and promised to expand the Romm Press's offerings to include new literary works in Hebrew and Yiddish.[10] While guaranteeing future work for the typesetters, the agreement also met better the changing literary tastes of the day.

The introduction of stereotype printing into the Romm Press's production process is entangled with the story of how the Wandering Jew, which was originally an anti-Jewish figure, became an identification model for Jews. Stereotype printing proved revolutionary not only in Vilnius but also throughout Europe. The cheaper printing process led to a dramatic increase in the number of titles published, which in turn made many books affordable that once proved too expensive for ordinary people to buy. All types of printed materials now circulated more widely, including encyclopedias, newspapers, textbooks, and enlightened treatises, but also many works that were deeply prejudicial against Jews. Print culture and Jew-baiting came together to create what historian William Hagen once called print-antisemitism; stereotypes begot stereotypes begot stereotypes.[11]

———

Part of the issue was how seriously many Jews regarded the printed word. For instance, one employee in the Romm publishing house in the 1860s and 1870s was the editor and translator Kalman Schulman.[12] Like many Eastern European Jews of his generation, Schulman was no stranger to the peripatetic life. Born to a Hasidic family in Belarus, Schulman traveled to Volozhin as a teenager to attend the flagship of all Lithuanian yeshivas and somehow found time there to expand his intellectual horizons by learning foreign languages, literature, and

general history on his own. He later moved to Vilnius, first finding work as a teacher and then with the Romms, and befriended
a long list of local Jewish intellectuals known for their
(relatively) liberal views. Among Schulman's close associates in
those years were Mordecai Aaron Günzburg, the first writer to
compose a biography in modern Hebrew, Abraham Dov Ber
Lebensohn (also known by his pen name, Adam Hakohen), the
pioneering Hebrew poet, and Micah Joseph, his son. To varying
degrees, these men were all associated with the publishing
house of the Romms.[13]

During his decades of editorial work at the Romm publishing
house, Kalman Schulman tirelessly worked to spread knowledge of European history and literature among his coreligionists. That was part of the project of the Jewish Enlightenment,
or Haskalah, to which Schulman, Günzburg, and the Lebensohns subscribed. The Maskilim (adherents of the Haskalah)
believed that Jews could retain their Jewish identity while inte-
grating more fully into general European society. Education
provided the means: reading and study were universal values
that Jews shared with, and that connected them to, other human
beings. The Romms paid Schulman, but not much, and for
decades he lived with his wife in a decrepit two-bedroom apartment in central Vilnius.[14] He dedicated his life to books. A visitor once described Schulman as a person whose life passes
slowly, like "the water of the Siloam [a small spring in
Jerusalem]—without any major events; his books were the
only events in his life."[15]

With the financial backing of the Jewish Enlightened Society
of St. Petersburg, where he had influential acquaintances,
Schulman managed to translate and publish dozens of works
by prominent European authors. These included, among many
others, a nine-volume oeuvre on world history originally

published by the German historian Georg Weber, a book on the history of St. Petersburg, and works on world, Russian, and ancient geography and ethnography.[16] Schulman did not neglect literature either: the most commercially successful project of his editorial career with the Romms was a translation into Hebrew of the novel *The Mysteries of Paris* (*Les Mystères de Paris*, 1842–1843) by the French writer Eugène Sue.[17]

Schulman's translation of *The Mysteries of Paris* unleashed a heated debate among Jewish intellectuals about the appropriateness of using Hebrew, traditionally referred to as the Holy Tongue, for writing or translating novels, and the appropriateness of Jews reading European novels at all. Reacting to Schulman's translation of Sue, the Hebrew writer Abraham Mapu criticized him for facilitating what he called "an intermarriage between Lady Hebrew and the Frenchman Eugène Sue"[18]— intermarriage, of course, is forbidden for observant Jews. Another critic echoed the same sentiment, writing that the European novel as such was a foreign element in Jewish culture, "an imported vine in the vineyard of our Holy Tongue."[19] Even the Lebensohns, close friends of Schulman's, doubted whether Jews should read novels. "From the time novels began to appear in all languages," Lebensohn Sr. wrote, "they became the main topic of discussion by day, and the main pleasure by night."[20] Reading non-Jewish novels was a waste of one's time. Indeed, reading them could sometime be outright dangerous.

———

Vilnius, home to the Romm publishing house, sat in the northernmost part of the Jewish Pale of Settlement in czarist Russia. (See figure 9.) As such, the books the Romms produced were supervised by Russian censorship rules. For much of the

FIGURE 9. Map of the Pale of Settlement in late nineteenth-century Russia.

nineteenth century, the Romms maintained good relations with the Russian authorities (many censors were former Jews), and at one point, they even enjoyed a near-monopoly over the printing of Hebrew books in Russia. This coincided with the early years of Czar Alexander II's reign (r. 1855–81), when the young monarch implemented (albeit reluctantly) a series of liberal reforms, including the relaxation of censorship.[21] The years immediately before 1873, however, saw a worsening of the political situation in the Russian empire and in Eastern Europe more generally. After a failed attempt on his life, Alexander II rolled back some of his political reforms, and physical attacks against Jews grew in number, with particularly nasty violence taking place in Odessa in 1871 and Rumania (outside the Russian empire) in 1871 and 1872. The protagonist in Peretz Smolenskin's great Hebrew novel, *Hato'e Bedarkhey Hahayim* ("The Wanderer in the Ways of Life," 1867–71) eventually dies in the Odessa pogrom of 1871, and in *The Nag* Abramovitch mentions the Rumanian attacks by name, describing "throngs of people running wild, descending like locusts upon houses, hurling stones at windows, breaking down doors, smashing and crushing everything in their path, attacking young and old with bestial ferocity."[22]

———

In the year that he published *The Nag* with the Romms in Vilnius, Abramovitch lived in Ukraine, far to the south. But he certainly wasn't a stranger to Vilnius and he had published with the Romm Press before. Born in a small town in modern-day Belarus, Abramovitch lost his father at a young age, while his mother, preoccupied with caring for Abramovitch's younger siblings, sent the thirteen-year-old to a yeshiva in Vilnius all by himself. (This was, almost verbatim, also the story of Kalman Schulman.) It is impossible to corroborate many details from Abramovitch's childhood before this move, because Abramovitch's papers are mostly gone, and in an autobiographical piece he wrote decades later, he says very little about his early years. Still, even in his old age, it was important for Abramovitch to describe how early and how well he had learned to read, and what reading meant to him throughout his life. "When I was six years old," Abramovitch reminisced, "I already knew how to read a book. [My father] had hired an excellent tutor . . . who spent up to twelve hours a day teaching me the Holy Scripture and its interpretations. After three years, I knew all twenty-four books [of the Hebrew Bible] by heart, and the Torah was as if a sinew of my very body."[23]

Later periods in Abramovitch's life, including during his stay in Vilnius as an adolescent, are better documented. In the early 1900s, Abramovitch's daughter lived with her husband in a suburb of Vilnius. Once, visiting her, Abramovitch brought his friend, the Jewish publisher Shlomo Srebrek, for a stroll around Vilnius's old town. "Slowly we ambled through the alleys,"[24] Srebrek describes their walk together: "The old man moving about with his head held up high and his breast protruding as was his custom, looking with keen eyes at every house and into every little backyard, stopping occasionally, lost in his thoughts."[25] Every corner brought back memories to the old man, to whom "every pole, every fence . . . without change, seemed exactly as it had been in his youth."[26]

At one point during their stroll through old Vilnius, Abramovitch and Srebrek stopped in front of a house at Rodnitzky Street where one of Abramovitch's relatives had hosted the boy years earlier as he was making his first steps in town. At the Jewish Street, next to the famous synagogue complex,

Abramovitch pointed out to Srebrek the building of the yeshiva, where "I studied sixty years ago with Rabbi Sander, head of the yeshiva, for a few months."[27] Abramovitch wanted to show Srebrek other important sights in the city: the synagogue of Rabbi Elijah ben Solomon Zalman, better known as the Vilna Gaon, and the booths and shops of the Jews in adjacent alleys and courtyards. The two men spent several hours ambling through the old town, and Srebrek reports how, in Abramovitch's company, the lines separating literature and life were often blurred. Walking through the city, he felt "as if I saw a whole book unfolding, page after page, and I read in it beautiful facts, events, histories, memories, and astonishing tales."[28] About halfway through their walk, the two men found themselves in front of the Romm Press building in central Vilnius. Abramovitch paused in front of it, lost in his thoughts. He "remember[ed] how, sixty years earlier, he had sneaked into the building in order to see how Hebrew books were being made." It was a meaningful moment for the celebrated author. Back in his youth, "he could never have dreamt that one day he would become one of the most important writers in the whole Jewish world."[29]

———

Notwithstanding his future celebrity status as the "grandfather of Yiddish literature"[30] (Sholem Aleichem), there were at first few signs that Abramovitch would one day become the extraordinary writer of *The Nag* and other pathbreaking literary works. His time at the yeshiva in Vilnius, for example, was typical for many young Jewish men. It was there that Abramovitch encountered not only the religious texts he was supposed to study, but also certain enlightened texts that circulated clandestinely among his fellow students. For Abramovitch, this clash resembled a military battle, waged between "the [rational] mind and old prejudices, so that there is no peace in [one's] bones because of all the many ruminations and doubts."[31]

The following years, though adventurous, were also not atypical for an Eastern European Jew of Abramovitch's generation. After his stay in Vilnius, Abramovitch went back to Belarus to his mother's house (she had remarried), and then decided to accompany his aunt on a journey south to Ukraine, where he spent time in Berdychiv and then Zhitomir, among other places. Still in his early twenties, Abramovitch got married, found a job as a schoolteacher, and began to publish essays in Maskilic journals. The essays showed little of the brilliance to come. "In the first years of his literary activity," explains an early critic of Abramovitch's work, he "was a typical Maskil: Maskil in his language, Maskil in his style, Maskil in his ambition, and Maskil in his system, that is in the way he tried to influence his readers."[32]

The Jewish Haskalah in Eastern Europe was a remarkably rich cultural movement that took on many shapes and forms and often meant different things to different people, or even different things to the same person over time. In principle, however, the Maskilim wished to create a new type of Jew who, in the words of historian Israel Bartal, "could be both 'a Jew' and 'a man.'"[33] The state of the Jews of Eastern Europe, according to the Maskilim, led them to focus on their own particular interests at the expense of what they shared in common with the rest of humanity. The Maskilim rejected what they perceived as the Jews' superstitions and ignorance and sought to cleanse the Hebrew language of what they considered foreign elements that had contaminated the biblical language over time.

At the beginning of his publishing career, the young Abramovitch adhered to these values.[34] Like Schulman and his friends the Lebensohns in Vilnius, he wrote his early essays in Maskilic Hebrew, often discussing pedagogical issues, and called for disseminating an appreciation of general works of science, literature, and the arts among Eastern European Jews. Abramovitch also practiced what he preached. His early publications are littered with references to central works of European literature (Cervantes, Goethe, Heine, Dostoevsky) and with the backing of a financial sponsor,[35] he translated into Hebrew an entire German encyclopedia on natural history. The book came out with the Romm publishing house.[36]

Though Devorah Romm was politically conservative, many Maskilim used her press to meet their own needs. The Maskil Abraham Mapu published the first modern novel in Hebrew with the Romms in 1852 (*Ahavat Tziyon*, "Love of Zion"); Shafan Hasofer was himself a Maskil and a writer; and so too were Schulman and many of the typesetters who worked on the first floor of the building on Žmudski Street. That in 1860 Abramovitch entrusted the publication of his earliest Maskilic collection of essays to the Romms is consequently hardly surprising. Crucially, as a typical Maskil, Abramovitch showed no interest in the figure of Ahasverus, at least in the beginning. The legend of the Wandering Jew was not a story that appealed to the Maskilim.

———

To be sure, Jewish Maskilim before Abramovitch had shown little or no proclivity for discussing Ahasverus. Most ignored his legend completely, even in discussions of wanderings and Jews (paradigmatic case: Smolenskin's *The Wanderer in the Ways of Life*), while writers who did talk about Ahasverus did so only to attack him, explicitly or implicitly.[37]

The novel *Spinoza* by the German–Jewish writer Berthold Auerbach, published in 1837, is the first known appearance of Ahasverus in a novel written by a Jew.[38] The book celebrates the life of the great early modern philosopher Benedict Spinoza, presenting him as the first modern, enlightened Jew. Spinoza, in Auerbach's telling, had fashioned himself according to rational principles, and this personal example earned him eternal life. "In everlasting unalterable harmony, as the legend says of the Gods . . . lived Benedict Spinoza," the novel declares in its last chapter. "What [Spinoza] had attained to by knowledge became to him blissful habit, and as he had once planned life in his thoughts, so his thoughts now gave him life."[39]

In a short epilogue to his Spinoza biography, Auerbach revisits an early moment in the famous philosopher's life, describing a fictional dream where the Wandering Jew appears to Spinoza, telling him how the source of his afflictions is a meeting he had, many centuries before, with "Jesus, son of Joseph and Mary of Nazareth, who called himself our Messiah." "I spurned him with my foot," Ahasverus explains to the somnolent Spinoza, to which Jesus replied by saying "come with me, thy foot which hath spurned me shall find no rest until the day when I return."[40] The symbolic key to this dreamy encounter in Auerbach's novel is not hard to find. Indeed, we have already encountered a version of it in Abramovitch's description of the battle he waged within himself between the rational mind, on the one hand, and old prejudices, on the other. "Thou art come to be a Savior to mankind," Ahasverus tells Spinoza, but "me too thou wilt save."[41] The scene ends, like the novel, with Ahasverus kissing Spinoza on the forehead and dying. Rational thinking (Spinoza) won the battle against old superstition (Ahasverus); the Dark Ages are dead and a new, rational dawn is breaking.

A year after the appearance of Auerbach's novel, Ahasverus became the subject of a heated argument between two German intellectuals, one non-Jewish, the other a Jew.[42] In August 1838, the editor and essayist Karl Gutzkow published two short anti-Jewish essays, drawing parallels between the fate of the Jews as a people and that of Ahasverus, the Wandering Jew.[43] Gutzkow was a liberal thinker and a passionate critic of the religious establishment in Germany. Although he rejected the Ahasverus legend as historically absurd, Gutzkow believed that it contained an important grain of truth. Just like the mythical Ahasverus who mocked a condemned man on the way to his execution, so too modern Jews showed for Gutzkow a remarkable lack of that "moral, noble, and beautiful human feeling of love."[44] "I do not condemn the Jews for not being Christian," Gutzkow insists in his essay, "but for the same reason that Plato, Socrates, Confucius, and Mohammad too would have condemned them,"[45] namely, an inability to believe in anything other than themselves. "Time itself may be renewed again and again, new peoples born, new heroes, new kingdoms—only Ahasverus stays as he is, a living corpse, a dead man walking."[46]

In late 1838, Gutzkow's essay elicited a strong response from Ludwig Philippson, the leading Maskil of his generation in German-speaking lands. "There have been at least thirty different literary treatments of Ahasver's legend in the past several decades," Philippson explains in his essay.[47] Indeed, more pieces were being published about Ahasverus every day. But did any of these writers stop to ponder whether the Jews wanted to be associated with the figure of the Wandering Jew? Jews, Philippson claims, have nothing against the legend of Ahasverus if by that one understands the story of a certain "wretched cobbler who mocked Jesus on his way to Calvary." Indeed, "we leave protestations against such a description to the guilds of the cobblers, if they'd like to do that."[48] One can't stay silent, however, when an important liberal intellectual like Gutzkow argues that Ahasverus is a true representation of the spirit of Judaism. Jews should not be idolized or paraded as symbols of virtue, Philippson writes. Indeed, "as God is my witness, we have in true fact many faults and weaknesses that are entirely our own."[49] But when Jews are demonized by seeing behind their actions nothing but material interests and claiming that they lack the very ability to love, "we have no other choice but to declare this a lie."[50] Philippson thus makes explicit what other Jewish Maskilim alluded to through silence (for example, Smolenskin) or literary means (Auerbach). Not only had Ahasverus never existed as a real person; he also made no sense as a symbol for Judaism. Ahasverus was but a mockery of what it meant to be modern and Jewish. Judaism was about love, rationality, optimism. It had nothing to do with the old stereotypical figure of the Wandering Jew.

———

If one looks hard enough, one can detect even in Abramovitch's early writings certain ideas which complicated and at times actually superseded the core group of Maskilic ideals. Included in Abramovitch's earliest collection of essays (published by the Romm Press in 1860), was a poem about an apparition of the ghost of an old man, complete with a short conversation with Satan, and in his first novel (*The Small Man*, 1865), one of Abramovitch's characters claims that "[t]oo much knowledge is often a great disadvantage. The world hates it. Beware of it like fire. . . . Educated people often walk in worn-out boots without soles."[51] Three years later, in his rendering of Ivan Turgenev's novel *Fathers and Sons* into Hebrew, Abramovitch returned to the same theme, warning that too much education too fast might be damaging to one's psyche: "Beware of the sons of Torah who turn into Maskilim overnight. A spirit contained in a small place, once unleashed, breaks forth with anger."[52]

What began as a small stream swelled into a flood over the course of the 1860s and 70s. Abramovitch was never an opponent of the Haskalah. But his attitude toward it became more nuanced, self-reflective, complex. From extolling the Hebrew language in the spirit of the Haskalah as "the only source for the education of the Jews,"[53] and "the language that turned the Jewish people, once exiled, into the People of the Book,"[54] Abramovitch, after 1865, moved to write primarily in Yiddish. From employing a satirical style that poked fun at the incredulity of common people, he turned more to realistic descriptions of, and pity for, the lives of ordinary Jews. (An early example: *Fishke the Lame*, 1868.) Now there were even curious echoes of the ugly anti-Jewish sentiments that Gutzkow promoted and Philippson so strongly decried. Abramovitch made comments about the ugliness of the Jewish body, and even claimed that many flesh-and-blood Jewish characters resembled ghostly apparitions more than living and breathing human beings.

Just as Abramovitch's views about the Hebrew language and common people expanded and shifted, so too did his descriptions of God and the latter's relationship with the world.[55] Long before Abramovitch, the Maskilim had used satire for poking fun at their enemies (thus, most importantly, Joseph Perl in a pathbreaking work against Hasidism in 1819, but also Isaac Baer Levinsohn, Isaac Erter, and many others).[56] Abramovitch, however, used satire also to poke fun at God. In the opening lines of his play *The Tax* (1869), Abramovitch praises God for creating mountains, oceans, and the animal kingdom. But then he also lauds him, sarcastically, for "choosing us Jews, out of all the people in the world, for conferring on us a tax, a money box, inspectors, communal leaders, attorneys, arbitrators, persons of high principles, intercessors, and great many idlers."[57] In the opening pages of *The Nag*, Abramovich uses a similar tone. He glorifies God for creating a marvelous universe but also "man, who is justly called *olam katan* [a microcosm], since man, if you look at him closely, combines in himself all species of creatures and creations." Such creatures include a hound, a cat, a monkey, a devil, a werewolf, a clown, a chicken, a Jew-hater, and "thousands of things no less amazing."[58]

In these and similar moments, Abramovitch echoes the writing of earlier Maskilim while also marking a decisive departure from some of the premises of the Haskalah, including its positive stance vis-à-vis the nature of humanity and the benevolence of God. In the 1860s and 1870s, Abramovitch was a wanderer, both in person and spirit. Traveling across Ukraine, he distanced himself from the optimism of the Haskalah. In a private letter, he compared himself to a traveler on a ship, sailing through "a stormy world-ocean, without a mast or an oar, and I don't see in front of me any haven."[59]

———

It was under these circumstances that Abramovitch invented Mendele the Book Peddler as the narrator of his stories. This invention struck a deep chord with readers: Mendele was so important that the boundary between life and literature collapsed, and they started referring to Abramovitch by that name. Just like the *pakntregers* who carried Devorah Romm's merchandise from Vilnius to every corner of Eastern Europe, so too was Mendele an itinerant seller of books. He traversed roads in his rackety carriage and sold religious books in Hebrew to shtetl Jews but also "prayer shawls, fringed undergarments, tassels, shofars, tefillin, amulets, mezuzas, and wolf teeth charms."[60] Because "most of the year I'm on the road," Mendele explains in one of Abramovitch's stories, "people know me in every city and town,"[61] and because he "knows all about printing books" he can listen to the stories of a Jew in one place, then have it printed and distributed "all around Poland."[62]

Mendele, the literary character, was a figure of many contradictions. He was an embodiment of what literary scholar Gershon Shaked called the typical Yiddish combination of laughter and tears, but also, and more important, a figment of the imagination that many an early reader perceived as painfully real. Mendele combined love for simple Jews with an ironic stance vis-à-vis their social existence, mixing empathy with incessant criticism of the spiritual conditions of his fellow Jews. Dan Miron, one of Abramovitch's most insightful modern readers, claims that through this figure, Abramovitch reflected on the intellectual tensions in his own life. "A traveler disguised," as Miron called him, Mendele stood for the quintessential Jewish wanderer, looking at the world as a member of the Jewish people while also looking at it (and himself), with a heavy dose of alienation and irony, from the outside.[63]

———

In 1873, Abramovitch published *The Nag* with Romm Press in Vilnius.[64] Like all books, *The Nag* has a double nature: it is a physical object and a nonmaterial story. As the first of the two, *The Nag* is made up of sheets of paper that Devorah Romm's workers imprinted with stereotypes, then cut, sewed together, bound, and distributed. On several occasions, the novel refers to its own materiality. In that respect, but not in that alone, *The Nag* is self-referential.

As a nonmaterial story, in the meantime, *The Nag* has an unstable structure, resembling that of a Russian nesting doll (matryoshka). It is comprised of three interrelated, nested stories. The novel's outermost frame story relates how Mendele the Book Peddler came across an unpublished manuscript by one Isrulik the Madman. The manuscript's title is "The Nag." Inside this first story is a full transcription of "The Nag," in which, apparently in a moment of sanity, Isrulik relates how he lost his mind after reading too many foreign books. Finally, nestled within the second frame story is a description of a series of hallucinations Isrulik had during his psychotic attacks. It is there that Abramovitch makes the connection between the Wandering Jew and the nag.

The three stories that make up the novel *The Nag* differ from one another in terms of style, themes, characters, and plot. What holds *The Nag* together as a novel are three literary devices: (1) the fictional character of Isrulik, who appears in all three stories; (2) an inward-moving progression from a description of Isrulik's place in society (external frame story), through his conscious thought (second frame story), to his deteriorating psychic life (the innermost matryoshka); and (3) a persistent preoccupation with the way life shapes literature, and literature shapes life.

The outermost frame story of *The Nag* alludes to the intimate ties between lived life and its many representations by way of a humorous dialogue. It opens with Mendele bemoaning the loss of the faithful horse that dragged his tottering carriage for many years. A friend of his then walks in and asks Mendele whether he'd like to buy a nag. "I'd buy one with pleasure," Mendele replies with a sign, "but where would I get the money?" The friend replies that Mendele shouldn't worry, because the nag is in his pocket. "What do you mean?" Mendele asks with astonishment. The friend then takes from under his coat a stack of papers and tells Mendele that it consists of a series of stories by one Isrulik the Madman, and that one of these stories bears the title, "The Nag."[65]

The basic device Abramovitch uses in this exchange is of course conflation: Mendele's acquaintance deliberately confuses the thing (a nag) with its representation (a story by Isrulik the Madman called "The Nag"). The tone in this passage is humorous. At this point in the novel, conflating life and literature seems harmless enough.

Inside the first frame story we find the second matryoshka: the very content of the manuscript "The Nag," written by Isrulik the Madman after his psychotic attacks. In the manuscript, Isrulik relates how he acquired his moniker. The plot proceeds as follows: Isrulik (nickname for Israel) is a fatherless Jewish boy who lives in one of the many shtetlach in the Pale of Settlement. When we first meet him, he lives with his doting mother Tzipa who urges him to find a bride and settle down. But Isrulik, refusing to listen, decides to leave home and study medicine at the university. Isrulik's decision sounds good in theory. In practice, however, there's a catch. To pass the university entrance exam, Isrulik must study not only the natural sciences, in which he excels, but also history and literature, which he feels are little more than incoherent jabber.[66] "Just think of it!," he explains:

I had to learn by heart, to know word for word, all sorts of inane fairy tales and resumés of famous battles, things having to do with how often people all over the world, from the creation of the universe down to our own time, had been spoiling for a fight, had mauled and killed one another and, on top of that, I had to remember in just what spots and on exactly what dates these disgraceful goings-on had taken place. This was the sum and total of what men called History![67]

"What the Russians call literature," Isrulik adds, is even worse. It consists of "countless fables of wondrous strong men, amazing drunkards and unheard-of cutthroats, tales of were-wolves, wood-demons, and witches, of Waters-of-Life and Waters-of-Death, of firebirds and golden apples."[68]

While preparing for his exam, all the histories and fables Is-rulik had consumed become mixed up in his head. They create a powerful allegory about the fate of the Jewish people that frays Isrulik's sense of self at the seams. The young man then suffers a nervous breakdown. The phantasmagorical visions Isrulik then sees make up the innermost matryoshka of *The Nag*.[69]

———

That reading European literature spurred Isrulik's mental break-down is an argument that Abramovich often puts in his charac-ters' mouths in *The Nag*. While studying for the exam, Isrulik realizes the negative effects that literature has on his psyche:

To me, at least, all these stories came with immeasurable dif-ficulty. My brain simply became clogged up from the con-stant grind, my strength and health were going, and little by little I was turning into a wooden dummy. . . . My head was as if filled with fumes of some narcotic drug, and something was tapping, hitting, whirling. . . . I was so upset that I had even contemplated suicide.[70]

Later in the novel, Isrulik's mother, Tzipa, sees things in a similar light. To a visitor at home, she relates that Isrulik's madness, "like it or not, was due to those secular books in which he had become so engrossed,"[71] and toward the novel's end, she looks at her demented son and exclaims:

> Oh, what a mess those books have made of your life, my son! . . . I wish you had listened to your mother and married early, as is usual not only with Jewish children but throughout the world. Both of us would have been spared all this misery. Oh, when I think of those weird tales of yours![72]

The second matryoshka of *The Nag* highlights how literature can undermine one's sense of self also by way of its plot structure. The background for this claim is that in the late eighteenth and early nineteenth centuries, one of the most important subgenres of the European novel was the *Bildungsroman* ("education-novel" or "coming-of-age story"). This was typically a romance of wanderings: of a young man who, afflicted by a personal loss at a tender age, travels through the world and experiences many hardships only to learn from his experience and mature in the process. Many Bildungsromans end with the protagonist's triumphal return to his birthplace. Johann Wolfgang von Goethe's *Wilhelm Meister's Apprenticeship Years* (1795–96) is considered the first and most important of all Bildungsromans, but examples in other national literatures also abound.[73]

In recounting how Isrulik lost his mind after leaving home and seeking education, Abramovitch takes some of the common themes of the European Bildungsroman and turns them upside down. Leaving home and expanding one's intellectual horizons through reading leads in Isrulik's case not to enlightenment but to insanity, and the traditional triumphal return of the son metamorphoses into the disgraceful homecoming of a meshuggener. *The Nag*'s second frame story thus criticizes modern assumptions about the supposedly straightforward relationship between reading and progress. Almost a hundred years before French philosopher Michel Foucault made his famous claim about the relationship between madness and enlightenment, Abramovitch already made it in *The Nag*, and in Yiddish at that. In the case of Jews, as he succinctly puts it, "[madness] is the natural fruit of enlightenment."[74]

———

The Nag's third matryoshka—the story within a story within a story—is a description of the visions Isrulik has after his mental breakdown. It is the novel's innermost core, structurally and thematically, and a stunning piece of world literature if ever there was one. Here, in the description of Israel's hallucinations, we finally encounter the creature that gives its name both to Isrulik's manuscript and to Abramovitch's entire novel. Here, too, the reader suddenly realizes that what he reads is a Jewish adaptation of the originally antisemitic figure of the Wandering Jew.

The story of *The Nag*'s third matryoshka begins with a description of Isrulik's collapse. Like the novel in which he is the hero, Isrulik has two natures: bodily and spiritual. In the process of going insane he completely loses the former. "It seemed to me that I was plunging into a bottomless, stagnant pool," Isrulik says, and "I had leaped out of my skin to become isolated from my body, and was not at all the Isrulik I had been,

but something ethereal, devoid of flesh, of organs."[75] Soon
enough Isrulik starts hearing voices:

> Shouts and the barking of a whole pack of hounds came
> floating to me. At first I wondered whether this commotion
> might not be the villagers hurrying pell-mell to drive the un-
> invited guests out of their grain fields. But the voices began
> to recede, and finally shifted altogether. My curiosity was
> aroused. I jumped up and started off in the direction of the
> voices, until at last I came out on a rolling meadow, where a
> horrible scene met my sight. Some urchins were harassing a
> nag, so gaunt that she was no more than a bag of skin and
> bones, throwing stones at her and setting a whole pack of
> dogs on her, curs of every conceivable and inconceivable
> breed. Some of the hounds—those who were more
> timorous—limited themselves only to barking and howling
> in every key—while others, more lively, were bent upon
> sinking their teeth into the nag and biting her wherever they
> could. It wasn't in my nature to stand by cold-bloodedly and
> watch this cruel sport with indifference . . . pity and humane-
> ness will not permit one to watch such tortures inflicted on
> a living thing.[76]

In his hallucinatory state, Isrulik sees how following the
dogs' attack on the nag, the urchins drive the haggard creature
into a mudhole. Later that day, he goes to see her there. "She was
lying on the mud," he reports, "weary to the point of death."[77]
Trying to encourage her in the language of horsemen, to his
astonishment, she answers him in the language of man. "My
shape is that of a horse," the nag says, "but in reality I'm something else altogether. If you but knew the things that have happened to me in this world, you would understand everything

for yourself and wouldn't be amazed."[78] Isrulik, still aghast, now looks at her intently:

> The two eyes staring at me were filled with suffering and weariness, and, at the same time, with prayer and infinite kindliness. One can come upon such eyes only in some impotent, disinherited, unjustly injured, grief-stricken man, who regards you in silence, while his looks alone attest to the inner torments he is enduring. Each such eloquent look calls and implores for mercy and rends your heart into tatters. I looked and looked. What sort of nag was this, where had it come from? Why, the face before me was a human face. Where did it come from?[79]

That Isrulik views the nag with compassion, recognizing the humanity behind her bestial façade, recalls an important cultural development in nineteenth-century Europe. In previous centuries, the main motivation for hatred of Jews was religious: the refusal of Jews to accept Jesus Christ as their Lord and Savior. With the advent of modern biological racism, however, hatred of Jews acquired a racial component. No longer was the main problem with Jews their belief system; from now on, Jewishness was also perceived as a biological fact. Abramovitch, and Isrulik, seem to be pointing to this development. In late nineteenth-century Russia, Jews were treated quite literally as less than human. This is one reason why Abramovitch decided to represent Judaism by way of a nag.

———

Shortly after the first encounter between Isrulik and the nag, the latter shares with Isrulik the contours of her life story. The humanity Isrulik had glimpsed in her eyes was not a figment of his imagination; before she metamorphosed into an equine, the nag had indeed been a person. The nag explains to Isrulik how this transformation happened by way of a parable that is worth quoting at some length:

At that time, by the way, there lived a certain prince, a king's son, a noble lad, not at all foolish—a fine fellow on all counts. In the days of his youth this king's son had wandered a great deal through the world trying to get to know people, and no matter where he went his fame preceded him. One Pharaoh, the sovereign of a domain celebrated for its gypsies and tricksters, became angry because our prince had outstayed his welcome. Immeasurably afraid lest the prince retaliate by deposing him, the Pharaoh called his magi and wizards together and told them: "*Ava nitkhakmo-lo,*" which meant: "Brothers, let's sneak up on this prince and fix him in our own way!" And the wonder-workers conjured up their spells and transformed the king's son into a work-horse which was forced to perform untold labors for them.

The poor nag hauled bricks and clay, carted whole mountains of materials, and built two cities—Pithom and Ramses. For many years the gypsies lorded over the poor beast and made its existence a misery, until at last the Lord God took mercy on it. And there came a certain great man of the Word who mocked at the gypsy breed and all their wizardry. He wrought still greater miracles with the help of God's Word. The Word was fulfilled and the nag became a prince again.

As long as that great man was among the living, and as long as his wondrous disciples lived on after him, so long did the prince have the likeness of a man, dwelling in wealth and respect in his domain. But afterward, when all the disciples had died, his enemies turned him back into a nag and in that shape drove him from one land to another, to this very day. The nickname of the Wandering Nag truly befits the unfortunate prince. Forever does the nag wander, traversing all the world. And whoever believes in God deems it his duty to ride this nag, and even he that has the fear of God in him will not deny himself the pleasure of a kick or a slap on its neck. Every passerby puts his load on it. The nag is eternally passing from one harness into another. It drags the cart, the unfortunate creature, it drags the cart loaded with brick and clay. It drags whole mountains along and has already built many, many towns out of clay and those bricks.[80]

Certainly, the parable about the nag is an allegory of the history of the Jewish people. The reference to the sojourn in Egypt, complete with the cities of Pithom and Ramses (Exodus 1:11), as well as the allusion to Moses ("a man of the Word"), makes the connection clear, as does the description of a long exile preceded by a time of prosperity in the Promised Land ("dwelling in wealth and respect in his domain"). But because of his precarious mental state, Isrulik needs some help making explicit what the reader already suspects: "tell me," Isrulik finally says to the nag, "I beg you—tell me, where is [the prince] now?" "That prince," the nag replies, "that miserable prince is now lying in the foul pit before you, in the image and likeness of a nag."[81]

———

Hidden in plain sight in this passage is a historically significant reference to the figure of the Wandering Jew. The epithet "Wandering Nag" is a clear reference to Ahasverus, one which Abramovitch would reuse three more times in the novel, in case the message wasn't already clear to readers.[82] Later references in the novel to the creature's many peregrinations in the world serve the same purpose, as do the many instances where Abramovitch endows the nag with the characteristics that had defined the wandering Ahasverus for centuries. Thus we read that the nag is unable to live but unable to die; that she is particularly reticent and pitiful looking; that "[f]orever does the nag wander, traversing all the world";[83] and that an ancient king-magician (read: Jesus) had cast a spell on her and was consequently the cause for all her misfortunes. Though at first Abramovitch claims that the nag's transformation had begun under Pharaoh, later he refers to her as a creature leading a peripatetic life only for "as long as the Exile [of the Jews]."[84]

Already in 1837, Auerbach mentioned Ahasverus in a piece of Jewish literature, albeit very briefly, at the very end of his book on Spinoza, and as a figure to be rejected—a thing of the past. Abramovitch's take on Ahasverus 36 years later is fundamentally different. Ahasverus-the-nag stands at the center of Abramovitch's novel, he is meant to arise in the reader pity and sympathy, and he is certainly still very much among the living. No less important is that in his novel Abramovitch sheds light on the psychological mechanism by which Jews begin to identify with the figure of the Wandering Jew in the late nineteenth century. Isrulik explains:

At a time when my head was, even without this, filled with amazing stories about wizards and sorcerers, at a time when, in addition to the fairy tales from the Thousand and One Nights and similar works which I devoured avidly in my childhood, I had just taken on a new cargo of fables. . . . At a time when my heart was like a seething cauldron, my blood at the boiling point, my fancy like a vehement flame, when my emotions had turned to gunpowder, igniting and exploding from the least fume, when my eyes were well-springs in

which every sufferer found scalding, salty tears—at that time
it befell me to hear the tale of the unfortunate prince.

Isrulik's point is this: his own psychic health was undermined by the constant barrage of histories and fables he consumed. It was then that the story of the wandering Ahasverus
seeped into his consciousness and turned into an allegory about
the fate of the Jewish people, made up, as all allegories are, from
fragments of various literary tales.[85] Earlier in the novel,
Abramovitch commented on the blurry lines between fictional
and reality-oriented representation by way of a joke (first matryoshka), and later he alluded to them through a series of statements by Isrulik and his mother (second matryoshka). Now
he's about to show it to his readers in a third way as well.

The Wandering Nag that Isrulik sees in his hallucinations is
made up in part of references to Ahasverus: the wanderings, the
sudden transformation by a magician, certainly also the epi-
taph. But as it turns out, the nag also has the characteristics of
other literary figures. It is hard to miss the fact that in creating
the nag, Abramovitch drew on Don Quixote's Rocinante, and
various readers of the novel have noted how the scene of the
dogs barking and biting the nag was lifted from Dostoevsky's
Crime and Punishment and the story of the prince who turned
into an animal borrowed from Heinrich Heine's poem *Princess
Sabbath*.[86] Earlier in *The Nag*, Abramovitch *told* us that many
different stories became entangled or mixed up in Isrulik's head.
In his characterization of the nag—a creature, we remember,
that Isrulik encounters in his demented state following an over-
dose of reading—Abramovitch *shows* this to us, too. The nag is
a living thing *and* a pastiche of well-known literary characters.

In the novel's second matryoshka, Isrulik's mother claimed
that her son's books, "in which he had become so engrossed,"[87]

had undermined his mental health. In the novel's innermost core, we see this process in action. Some critics doubted Abramovitch's originality precisely because of his many literary borrowings, while others minimized the depth of the psychological portrayal of his characters, particularly in his subsequent books.[88] These readers overlooked what are some of the most skillful sections of *The Nag*. Abramovitch's inclusions of broken pieces from European literature in his description of the nag is not a sign of his unoriginality but rather of his writerly virtuosity. He tells but also shows us how Israel's madness is a product of faulty reading practices. *The Nag* is about Jewish reading gone awry.

———

For those readers still unconvinced of the parallels between the nag, Ahasverus, and other famous literary figures, Abramovitch spells out these connections repeatedly. The nag is a living, breathing thing ("that miserable prince is now lying in the foul pit before you!"), but she is also a literary (textual) creation; the lines dividing fiction and life in her case are hazy. Thus, at one point in *The Nag*'s innermost matryoshka, Abramovitch has the wandering old horse comparing herself to historical chronicles which, the reader will remember, also contributed to Isrulik's mental collapse:

> Once, for instance, a certain drove of [my enemies], sent to war in the land of the Turks, knocked me down on their way, just like that. They kicked me and beat me till the blood came. And then, later on, how many times did they try to skin me alive, to draw the sinews out of me, to brand me and roast me over live coals? Upon my body you will find

depicted, in scars, legends of the world's cruelty, savagery, and stupidity. My chafed hide is all bruised; my back, all raw, is covered with swellings and blisters. There you have the written history of former generations. Look at my skin and read it![89]

In a later passage, Abramovitch goes further still. It is part of a scene where, now borrowing from Goethe's *Faust*, Isrulik rides on the back of Asmodeus (Mephistopheles) and observes the earth from above. This passage's extraordinary beauty is only one reason to quote it in length:

How long the flight lasted is something that I cannot tell definitely. All I know is that I flew for what seemed a long time until we arrived over a spreading abysmal valley, surrounded by mountains towering so high that their summits were capped with clouds. Shivers run down my spine even now when I recall the dreary waste and horror of that yawning bottomland. There was hardly a trace of grass or even scrubwood. All one could make out were some scattered thorny growths and piles of stones strewn all over, among which snakes, vipers, and lizards slithered and darted. The cacophony created by the wild beasts and birds of prey in their dens and nests—a diversity of mournful and depressing sounds—was earsplitting. A stench of sulfur and devil's dung assailed one's nostrils. Here and there clouds of smoke spurted out of the ground, dispersing like fog through the vale. And this was the region chosen by the demons for their abode!

A gorge between the rocks led to a yawning cavern, the interior of which was so terrifying as to baffle all description. A river of black ink ran through it, and its banks were covered with forests of quill-pens teeming with bizarre creatures that were a cross between ape and man. In the distance, I caught sight of them watering the poor nag and then dunking her several times in the inky river until she came out jet black.

"That's my office," Asmodeus informed me. "The stream and the forests you see I intend for your brethren. They will furnish writing materials as long as there's an inkwell and a penknife left. Behold! There are the conduits leading from the river of ink unto the remotest editorial rooms and the private offices of certain men. . . . Not only is the supply of ink and quills inexhaustible, but the writers as well are past all counting, like unto the sands of the sea."[90]

The nag is all too real. Isrulik sees, caresses, and even converses with her. But she is also a creature "dunked in ink," crafted in editorial rooms, spread by the hand of journalists and poets. We return full circle to an earlier scene in this chapter and the description of the printing house on Vilnius's Žmudski Street—the printing house, we remember, where *The Nag* was printed (*sic*!) for the first time. Unlike in his earlier, more naïve-Maskilic stage, in 1873 Abramovitch views ink and printing presses as no longer necessarily good. Instead, they describe and contribute to an ugly reality. They claim to spread reason and enlightenment but often spread maddening negative stereotypes about Jews, "lies, slanders, statements with no basis in fact meant to breed hatred and envy and many other such ugly things calculated to arouse enmity."[91] Such stereotypes then seep into the consciousness of the acculturating Jew—shuffling it and undermining it from within.

This same underlying message runs like a red thread throughout Abramovitch's astonishing novel. Its point of origin is in the first frame story, when Mendele and his interlocutor joked about conflating description (the manuscript titled "The Nag") with reality (a flesh-and-blood equine creature), and it continued in the second matryoshka when Tzipa, Isrulik's mother, described how her demented son couldn't separate representation from reality and consequently lost his mind. Here, in the innermost part of the novel, this insight finds its most poetic formulation. The sufferings of the Wandering Nag (read: the Jewish people) are all too real—"how many times did they try to skin me alive, to draw the sinews out of me, to brand me and roast me over live coals?"—but this reality has also been shaped by literary devices. "My chafed hide is all bruised . . . there you have the written history of former generations. Look at my skin and read it!"[92]

––––––

The novel imprinted on the Romm Press's stereotypes in 1873 was deliberately multifaceted. Its author states in the introduction that "each man will understand it in his own way" and "in keeping with his own common sense."[93] Still, it was also important for Abramovitch to emphasize that despite other possible readings, he saw in it an allegory about the Jewish people, a "reflection," as he puts it, "of all our little Jewish souls."[94]

If the main plotline of *The Nag* is about how Isrulik turned mad, and if Isrulik's case stands *pars pro toto* for the story of Eastern European Jewry in general, what then is the exact connection between Jewishness and insanity here? In what way are all modern, acculturated Jews mad? In one common reading of *The Nag*, Isrulik had been prone to mental illness all along. He turned mad because of his very nature. As historian Sander Gilman reminds us, over the centuries many have made the same claim about the Jewish people as a whole. Quoting Heinrich Heine, Gilman describes how especially in the nineteenth century, Jewishness was often seen as a mental sickness. "No help can be looked for [it] from steam-baths, shower-baths, or all the implements of surgery"; it is "that thousand-year-old family complaint, the plague [the Jews] dragged with them from the Nile valley, the unhealthy faith from ancient Egypt."[95]

A second reading of Isrulik's madness in *The Nag* situates it within a larger European literary tradition. Abramovitch was not the first to write about a madman or describe the world through a madman's eyes. E.T.A. Hoffmann, Gogol, Dostoevsky, Balzac, and Dickens in the nineteenth century (not to mention Cervantes in the seventeenth) had done this long before him. Isrulik's madness, according to this interpretation, is but a specific (albeit Jewish) example of a much larger theme in European literary history.[96]

Such readings are of course valid. But like the common interpretations of the legend of the Wandering Jew discussed in the introduction to this book, they too threaten to minimize the author's agency and originality; they lack sufficient attention to the exact time and place which gave birth to *The Nag*. Certainly, in composing the novel, Abramovitch drew on literary traditions. But why he chose that particular moment in time and proceeded in this particular manner remains largely unexplained.

The solution, perhaps, is this: the central question with which Abramovitch grapples in *The Nag* is what it means—what it does to the psyche—to want to belong to a society that treats one as less than fully human. Isrulik had great expectations for himself: he left home and applied to university; he wanted to be someone in the world. But reading too many European books, he ended up internalizing the racist, anti-Jewish stereotypes of the society around him, exemplified in both the image of the Jew as less than human and in the theologically charged figure of Ahasverus, the Wandering Jew. His mind turned on itself, as it were, and he went mad. This process is not uniquely Jewish: similar psychological processes have appeared in psychiatric cases of individuals from other groups suffering from racist discrimination, including African Americans in the nineteenth century and colonial subjects in French Algeria in the twentieth.[97] The process was general, but has a particular, time-specific and place-dependent Jewish element in *The Nag*, one that recalls the intra-Jewish debate of the late 1850s about the dangers of Jews reading non-Jewish books (Schulman, Mapu, the Lebensohns). Auerbach had already depicted the appearance of Ahasverus in a Jewish person's dream, but in *The Nag*, Abramovitch describes him not as a thing of the past, as in Auerbach's novel, but as a figure acculturated Jews will inevitably continue to confront in modern European literature. (Freud might have called this phenomenon the "return of the repressed."[98]) In a largely post-Haskalah world, Abramovitch wrote a piece of European literature that took European literature as its target. Prejudices against Jews are baked into European culture. By immersing themselves so deeply in European literature, acculturating Jews run the risk of allowing self-undermining stereotypes to reside in the nethermost parts of their souls.[99]

Epilogue

Acculturation and reading, stereotypes and Jews. At the end of *The Nag*, Isrulik is carried back to his mother's house, unable to recover from the damage inflicted on him by his reading of European histories and novels. The shape of his worldly wanderings is consequently one of downward spiral: from the optimism of youth at his mother's home, into a world that rejects him as a full person, and finally back home again, now a broken man and an utter failure. In its geometry, this shape is distinct both from the one used by the Maskilim, who believed in Jewish progress through education, and the future Zionist movement, which envisaged a linear path leading Jews out of Europe and into a better future in Palestine. Unlike in the Haskalah and Zionism, there is no redemption for *The Nag*'s main character. A curse hangs over him; he's trapped in an eternal, senseless circle.[100]

The years and decades following the publication of *The Nag* continued to see many negative descriptions of the wandering Ahasverus in European literature, politics, and culture. They included the casual use of "Ahasverus" as a denigrating term in European parliaments, for instance, and especially the deteriorating stereotypes of Jews in the media, culminating in the infamous Nazi exhibition, *The Eternal Jew*. It was above all in that exhibition and in Fritz Hippler's eponymous propaganda film that negative representations of Jews in the modern European imagination reached their horrific logical conclusion.

Ever since the nineteenth century, however, there were also positive depictions of Ahasverus among which Abramovitch's was, next to Auerbach's, the earliest Jewish one. Ahasverus might have been born out of anti-Jewish stereotypes. But he could and would be embraced as a sympathetic figure by some Jews. Ben Shoushan's self-identification as Ahasverus in Israel of the 1950s was consequently not a unique occurrence.

More than Ben Shoushan's case and more even than the nag in Abramovitch's tale of 1873, the most extreme appearance of a Jewish Ahasverus took place exactly seventy years after the original publication of *The Nag* and in the same exact city. Two years earlier, in June 1941, the Wehrmacht invaded the Soviet Union, and within a short period it occupied Vilnius. In the following two years, the Germans murdered thousands of the city's Jewish inhabitants in nearby Ponary and drove survivors into a small ghetto in Vilnius's old town. On the eve of their final destruction, a small group of Jewish intellectuals came together and decided to stage a play. Their decision landed on the unlikely topic of the Wandering or Eternal Jew.

In 1906, the Yiddish writer Dovid Pinski had written a play about the Wandering Jew. Building on an early nineteenth-century treatment of the figure by the Irish novelist George Croly, Pinski placed the Wandering Jew at the time of the Second Temple in Jerusalem, portraying him as a Jewish hero.[101] A copy of Pinski's play was nowhere to be found in the Vilnius ghetto, but several activists had seen a production of the play and tried to reconstruct it from memory. An eyewitness, the physician Mark Dvorzhetski, would later describe the scene in his memoirs, recalling how the performance made for hours of elation and filling everyone with a sense of hope. "These were moments of unforgettable light in the midst of the darkness of the ghetto." He writes,

> On stage were presented the last days of Israel's war for its freedom, the sorrow of a single person who did not participate in his people's war, the loss of the people, the birth of the Messiah and the departure of the prophet to an eternal path of seeking the Redeemer. And when from the stage one heard the calls for a final battle with the Romans, the audience understood who the Romans were at this point and who was asked to fight them. The presentation of the Eternal Jew by the Hebrew theater in the ghetto was received by the ghetto youth as a stirring dramatic proclamation of joy and self-defense.[102]

The play Dvorzhetski saw in 1943 Vilnius lacked the sophistication of Abramovitch's Yiddish masterpiece from seventy years earlier. Little wonder: under the circumstances, the time for a multilayered, nuanced treatment of Jewish acculturations through reading was past. (It would emerge again in the wake of the war and in the figure of that modern-day Ahasverus, the mysterious Chouchani/Ben Shoushan.) And yet the symbolism of the play, staged just a few blocks from Žmudski Street in Vilnius, is unmistakable. The idea that germinated in the book printed by Romm Press in 1873 now returned to its birthplace, metamorphosed. According to the great Yiddish poet Abraham Sutzkover, in 1943 ghetto fighters melted the lead stereotypes stored at the nearby building of Romm Press and cast bullets from them with which to fight the Germans ("By the casting of bullets the lead / illumined thoughts—letter after letter melted . . . Jewish bravery once hidden in words / must now strike back with shot!").[103] Ahasverus's figure underwent a similar transformation. Over the course of the nineteenth and early twentieth centuries, the stereotypical Ahasverus was recast as a sympathetic Jew, before becoming part of a concrete embodied reality. Some Jews now identified deeply with, and lived vicariously through, a version of the figure of the Wandering Jew.

3

A True Story That Never Happened (1711)

THE FIRE broke out at half past eight in the evening. It started on the upper floor of the house of Naftali Cohen, a leading rabbi and cabalist who lived across the street from the main synagogue. The date was January 14, 1711, and the place the Jewish ghetto in Frankfurt am Main.[1]

Contemporary accounts describe how the ghetto burned through the night, lighting up the sky over Frankfurt and filling the air with sparks and smoke. The fire bells tolled for nearly twenty-four hours until the early evening of the following day. When the bells finally fell silent, only a single house in the entire ghetto remained standing. All other buildings, even the stonework synagogue, had been burned to the ground.

The combination of high winds and the flammable materials used to construct ghetto houses helped spread the great Frankfurt fire of 1711, but social and religious factors fed it as well. Because Christian hooligans had previously damaged Jewish property in the ghetto, ghetto leaders initially hesitated to seek outside help. They ordered the three gates leading to the ghetto

locked from the inside and refused to let in the city's fire bri-
gade. When the seriousness of the situation dawned on them,
it was too late. Frankfurt's famous *Judengasse* ("Jewish alley"),
home to the largest Jewish community in German-speaking
Europe, had been reduced to a smoldering heap of ashes.

The Frankfurt city council considered the 1711 fire to be such
a spectacular event that it issued a medallion and a broadside
to commemorate it.[2] (See figure 10.) Contemporary Jewish
sources mention the fire as well. For example, Eliezer Lippmann, a Jewish resident of Weinheim, some 50 miles south of
Frankfurt as the crow flies, rushed north as soon as he heard the
news, later jotting down a report "with tears and trembling
hands"[3] about the catastrophe that befell his coreligionists in
Frankfurt. Lippmann bemoaned the wretched state of the survivors, the extent of the property damage, and the destruction
of so many religious books. One thing took him by surprise,
however. "On the following day, I left all my duties and went to
Frankfurt," Lippmann writes in his hurried manner:

> And there's no comparison between seeing something with
> one's own eyes, how the illustrious and beautiful city, the joy
> of all the earth, how its crown had fallen off. Torah scrolls
> and many holy books were burned. Who could gauge [the
> damage]? And who could bear to witness how some had
> saved what they could but many men, women, and children
> were walking around almost without clothes? [And yet] with
> my own eyes I also saw the good deeds performed by the
> gentiles, giving shelter to Jews in their homes and other
> favors. We needed the mercy of the gentiles because of the
> many sins of the Jews.[4]

———

FIGURE 10. Description of the complete destruction of the Jewish ghetto in Frankfurt am Main, 1711. Source: Stadtmuseum Frankfurt am Main, C01698.

One Frankfurt gentile who witnessed the fire of 1711 from up close was Johann Jacob Schudt. Schudt was a scholar of Hebrew and Jewish history who, in the wake of the fire, wrote the most important academic treatment of the legend of the Wandering Jew before modern times. Schudt was a native of Frankfurt, the vice principal at the local gymnasium, and a highly educated man with long-standing interests in classical philology, pedagogical matters, and ancient music.[5] His greatest academic passion, however, was the study of Hebrew and Judaism, with an eye to the possible conversion of Jews. Over the years, this passion led Schudt to spend four years at the University of Wittenberg, where he studied theology with an emphasis on Hebrew, and then to Hamburg, where he studied under one of the greatest scholars of what passed as Jewish Studies (*Judaistik*) in late seventeenth-century Europe. (The academic study of Hebrew grammar and various nonbiblical Jewish texts by non-Jews was about two centuries old at the time.) The attentive reader will remember these two place names from this book's introduction: according to the Kurtze Beschreibung, Paul von Eitzen met Ahasverus in Hamburg, and Eitzen had traveled to Hamburg from Wittenberg, where he was a student at the time. (See figure 11.)

As a child, Schudt grew up in Frankfurt in an apartment given to his parents by the congregation of St. Catherine's Church, where his father served as pastor. Life in the parents' household was not easy: of sixteen children born to the Schudts, only four survived childhood—Johann Jacob and three of his sisters. As a young lad, Schudt attended the local gymnasium, where he acquired a command of Latin as well as rudimentary reading knowledge of Hebrew and Ancient Greek.[6] Just a couple of months before graduation, in the spring of 1680, a hard blow befell the family: Schudt's father died unexpectedly,

FIGURE 11. Map of early modern Germany.

leaving him, in his own words, "without a head, without protection, without any joy in his soul."[7]

The eulogy at Schudt Sr.'s funeral in Frankfurt was delivered by Philipp Jacob Spener, the leading Lutheran pastor in the city and a man who would soon help Johann Jacob obtain a scholarship to study theology at Wittenberg and then Judaistik in Hamburg. Spener knew Schudt's family well. In his funerary oration, he described Schudt Sr.'s many accomplishments, mentioned the deceased's parents, wife, and children by name, detailed his curriculum vitae, and added a short poem in honor of the dead man, describing him as "[my] much beloved colleague."[8] These details matter. Spener was a crucial figure in late seventeenth-century Lutheranism, a theologian of immense influence who would lead his followers to found a religious revival movement within German Lutheranism known as Pietism. Strictly speaking, Johann Jacob Schudt was not a pietist, but he would quote Spener throughout his adult life, always with great admiration, and Spener's views on the Jews clearly informed Schudt's.

Both in Frankfurt and elsewhere, Spener's success made him some enemies. In his major work, *Pia desideria* ("Pious Desires," 1675), Spener emphasized individual piety and personal transformation through inner conversion to Christ. This led to a clash with proponents of Lutheran orthodoxy, who sought to exert much tighter and top-heavy control over their flock. Thus, the same theological faculty in Wittenberg to which Spener helped send Schudt in 1680 would also warn against Spener's teaching and accuse him of no fewer than 264 theological errors. To the modern reader, early modern Lutherans might look like a fairly homogenous group. In reality, however, their internal disagreements were intense, weighty, and at times outright ugly.

Among their many differences, Spener and his opponents in Wittenberg disagreed on the place of Jews in the Lutheran worldview.[9] The most influential proponents of Lutheran orthodoxy in late seventeenth-century Wittenberg ascribed to what is sometimes called the theology of replacement (*Ersatztheologie*) or supercessionism: the ancient Christian contention that following the New Covenant between God and humans mediated by Christ's sacrifice, followers of Jesus Christ replaced the Jews as God's chosen people.[10] This corresponded to Martin Luther's position later in life, when the famed German reformer gave up on the prospect of mass Jewish conversion and used vitriolic language to describe "the Jews and their lies" (1543). Just like Luther a century and a half earlier, Spener was no Philosemite. As Schudt knew all too well, the founder of German Pietism at one point called for the forced uprooting of Jews from many parts of German-speaking lands and their resettlement in less populated parts of central Europe.[11] And yet during most of his adult life, Spener was closer to the moderate, young Luther who reminded his readers that "Jesus Christ was Born a Jew" (1523) than to the later, Jew-baiting one. For instance, Spener called for the protection of Jewish houses of prayer, whereas in 1543, Luther advocated for their destruction,[12] and unlike Luther, Spener not only never relinquished the prospect of converting the Jews but made it a central axis of his theology.[13]

———

A few months after losing his father and supported by the stipend Spener helped him procure, Johann Jacob Schudt left Frankfurt am Main and made his way to Saxony, there to enroll as a student at the famed University of Wittenberg. A century and a half earlier, Martin Luther had walked the same roads in the opposite direction. Luther was then on his way from Wittenberg via Frankfurt (where, according to Schudt, he "without a doubt wandered through the Jewish ghetto")[14] to the city of Worms on the River Rhine. In the early spring of 1521, Luther stood trial in Worms for his heretical views against the Catholic Church, and during the proceedings, he gave one of European history's most famous speeches. Standing in front of the German emperor and the princes and prelates of the Holy Roman Empire, Luther refused to accept any Church teaching that could not be directly supported by Scripture. He concluded his oration, at least according to some subsequent accounts, with the words "here I take my stand, I cannot do otherwise, so help me God."[15]

One hundred sixty years later, Schudt passed through the same physical terrain as Luther before him, moving in the other direction and surrounded by what was now a transformed religious landscape. The Christian reform movement Luther helped unleash after 1517 broke Catholicism's sway over religious life in German-speaking lands but failed to create a new, unified church in its stead. The country's religious composition was consequently fractured, a fact of late seventeenth-century German life that Schudt could observe at every turn along the road from Frankfurt to Wittenberg. Thus, in Frankfurt in 1680, alongside the Lutheran majority, were many individuals who belonged to other Christian confessions and indeed 2,500 local ghetto Jews; in the county of Hanau, just north of Frankfurt, the local count and majority of the population had converted to Calvinism in the late sixteenth century; in the lands of the bishop of Würzburg, farther to the northeast on the way to Wittenberg, the population was still predominately Catholic in 1680; and in parts of Thuringia and finally Saxony, where

Wittenberg was located, a version of orthodox Lutheranism reigned supreme.

———

Schudt arrived in Wittenberg in early June 1680 to join a community of some 500 students and two dozen professors.[16] The entire operation of the university was rather small and concentrated in three main buildings surrounding a courtyard not far from the city's eastern gate. Just a few doors down was Martin Luther's old house, now a dormitory. Following his famous trial at Worms in 1521, Luther became an outlaw outside Saxony, and from then on, lived almost exclusively in Wittenberg—writing, preaching, and serving as a university professor—until he died in 1546 in a nearby town.

It is clear from surviving historical sources that one of Schudt's early teachers at Wittenberg was Johannes Helvicus Willemer, and that in October of his first year as a student, Schudt was supervised by Willemer in a disputation (an academic exercise resembling a debate) that discussed the ancient Jewish sect of the Essenes. Willemer was a rather marginal figure in Wittenberg at the time, arriving at the university only a year before Schudt, publishing little, and leaving after Schudt's freshman year. Much more significant for Schudt's years at Wittenberg were other professors: Andreas Sennert, the *Primarius* (full professor) for Hebrew, and Theodore Dassow, who slowly assumed the teaching responsibilities of the aging Sennert in Hebrew, biblical studies, and rabbinical literature.[17] The two professors' long list of publications and contemporary catalogue of disputations[18] by Sennert's students give the impression of a lively academic community surrounding the two men. Its strong confessional tendencies notwithstanding, this community contributed to the history of Hebrew. For example, one of Sennert's main discoveries (still valuable today), is that the diacritical signs used to signify vocals in Hebrew (known as *nikud* in modern Hebrew) were a relatively late addition to the Holy Tongue.[19] Just two years before Schudt came to Wittenberg, Sennert published a detailed catalogue of books held at the university library.[20] Considering the immense popularity of the Kurtze Beschreibung in seventeenth-century Germany, it is perhaps telling that not a single copy of it existed at Wittenberg's library when Schudt moved to the famous university town.

Despite the important scholarly work by Sennert and many of his associates in other disciplines, the towering figure in Wittenberg during Schudt's sojourn was undoubtedly Abraham Calov. Calov had been teaching as Wittenberg's *Primarius* for theology since 1650 and was at the height of his fame when Schudt arrived at the university. A contemporary report describes how hundreds of students (out of the university's 500) flocked to hear Calov's lectures on a regular basis.[21] Calov's importance in the history of Lutheran theology derives from his extremely popular edition of the Bible as well as his methodical approach to Lutheran theology. His life's aim was the creation of a systematic description of the Lutheran confession's core beliefs with a special emphasis on fighting views (and people) he considered heretical. Indeed, already the committee that hired Calov back in 1650 commented that he "is a scholar who is very experienced in polemics," and that such an expertise is "especially needed at this day and age."[22] Throughout his life, Calov wrote against Calvinists, Catholics, and Socinians (early Unitarians), but also against fellow Lutherans. No wonder some have called Calov "a new Torquemada."[23]

Over many decades, Abraham Calov and his students spilled vast amounts of ink on fighting what they considered heretical views. Sometimes they did so openly, while in other instances they used pen names. For example, fifteen years before Schudt's arrival at Wittenberg, Calov published a collection of dozens of texts in which he dismissed as ridiculous any challenges to his orthodox worldview, and midway through Schudt's stay at Wittenberg, three of Calov's heavy volumes on Christian theology were considered so extreme in their tone and content that permission to publish them was withdrawn.[24] The genres of these polemical works varied. Next to heavy tomes on theology and collections of sermons and letters, there were also polemical pamphlets, caricatures, and even comic plays. In 1676, Calov's son-in-law produced a comedy ridiculing his father-in-law's real and imagined confessional adversaries. In his view, they were little more than buffoons.[25]

Calov's polemical style left a mark on the edition of the Bible (1682) that brought him so much popularity.[26] His strict Lutheran orthodoxy informed the interpretative comments he added to some verses. The same applied to Calov's views of Judaism and the Jews. A proponent of the radical views Martin Luther espoused toward the end of his life, Calov advanced a dark form of antisemitism in his edition of the Bible, the consequences of which can still be felt—and even heard—today.

One year after Schudt left Wittenberg for Hamburg, Johann Sebastian Bach was born in the nearby town of Eisenach, where he grew up in a milieu defined by orthodox Lutheranism of Calov's type. Bach owned a copy of Calov's edition of the Bible and marked important verses to later set them to music.[27] Similar to Schudt's later writings about Jews in general and the Wandering Jew in particular, some of Bach's most popular

compositions—the St. John's Passion foremost among them—
bear the imprint of Abraham Calov's anti-Jewish views.[28]

———

Schudt completed his studies at Wittenberg in four years. He
expanded his rudimentary knowledge of Hebrew and Ancient
Greek and must have also honed his skills interpreting Scripture. Scripture was the cornerstone of early modern Orthodox
Lutheran theology, an infallible text in and of itself which,
thanks to the human proclivity for error, was in need of constant expounding.[29] When elucidating difficult biblical passages, most Wittenberg theologians of Schudt's time preferred
a historical–grammatical approach but also recognized that
next to the *sensus literalis* (literal sense) of the biblical text,
Scripture also had a *sensus mysticus*: a symbolic or mystical message that went beyond historical events per se and related to the
deepest aspects of Christ's sacrifice in relation to humanity, the
Creation, and God.

With an interest in Hebrew and Judaism that dated back at
least to his final year at the Frankfurt gymnasium, Schudt now
faced a stark choice: discard the prospect of converting the Jews
(Calov's position, following the later Luther), or espouse it
(Spener's argument, following the early Luther). That in 1684
Schudt decided to move to Hamburg and study there under
Esdras Edzard makes clear his continued sympathy with Spener's views. Indeed, throughout his life, Spener held Edzard in
particularly high regard.[30]

When Schudt arrived in Hamburg in 1684, Esdras Edzard
was arguably the best teacher of Hebrew in all of German-
speaking Europe.[31] Just like Schudt, Edzard was a pastor's son

who left home to study far away—at Wittenberg, again like Schudt, but then also at Basel in Switzerland and Rostock, on the shore of the Baltic Sea. Independently wealthy, Edzard had no official capacity in academia or in the Church, but in 1667, he established in Hamburg a foundation for the conversion of poor Jews that he directed for the rest of his life. According to Edzard, would-be Jewish converts from the lower classes of society needed special assistance to gain salvation. They suffered from "the vehement hate of their coreligionists," on the one hand, but also from "prevailing local laws," on the other hand.[32] The location Edzard chose for his foundation bore directly on this matter. As Schudt once explained, the part of Hamburg where Edzard's foundation was located was filled with poor Jews for whom "[i]t was a thorn in the eye that such a well-known Jew-converter lived in their midst."[33]

In 1684, the fifty-five-year-old Edzard had already introduced some of the most important Lutheran theologians to the study of Hebrew and rabbinical literature, including perhaps Spener and certainly his most important follower in the emerging pietistic movement, August Hermann Francke. Unlike these two individuals, Edzard was not a prolific writer, a fact that later bothered Schudt so much that he felt compelled to ask Edzard about it. "This would have only made people lazy," Edzard replied to his former student's question, and "writing begets writing" ("*Schreiben macht Schreiben*"). The point was not to hold long discussions *about* Jews; the point was to actively convert them.[34]

———

Even three decades after his sojourn with Edzard in Hamburg, Schudt had vivid memories of his old teacher's busy weekly schedule.

Twice a week, on Wednesday and Sunday evenings, [Edzard] taught the Lutheran catechism to would-be Jewish converts in his private house, and small children and even grown-ups also often attended [these sessions.] On Friday mornings from 9 to 11 or 12 o'clock he also taught there rabbinical literature to a group of students, and every day between 2 and 4 or 5 o'clock in the afternoon he opened the doors of his house to anyone who might be interested in conversing with him: students, young boys and older lads, and even some burghers, each one carrying with him copies of the Old Testament in Hebrew and the New Testament in Greek.[35]

Remembering Ezdard's erudition and dedication, Schudt expressed awe. Reminiscing about his time with him in Hamburg, Schudt called Edzard "the most faithful servant of God, a promoter of Jewish conversion like no other, unparalleled in his erudition of oriental languages and all things related to the Jews. Few Christians could compare with him, and none could be called his master."[36]

Edzard belonged to a long list of Hebraists (Christian experts in Hebrew and rabbinical literature), including Johannes Reuchlin and Edzard's one-time teacher in Basel, Johannes Buxdorff, who interacted with Jews in person, learned Hebrew and sometimes rabbinical literature from them, and occasionally even defended them against their Christian detractors. Reuchlin, for instance, once opposed the suggested confiscation of Hebrew books from the Jews, while Buxdorff rejected accusations of blood libels against them as ludicrous. To be sure, Schudt's attitude toward Jews was more severe than any of these scholars, but like them, he received some of his information about Judaism from actual Jews. Growing up in Frankfurt, the young Schudt must have run into local Jews from the ghetto, and a dedication in a book published in 1712, a year after the great Frankfurt fire, attests to his close ties to at least one ghetto rabbi that year.[37] According to his own testimony, Schudt also had contact with Jews while studying with Edzard in Hamburg. These included would-be converts (Schudt had attended several conversion ceremonies in person), but also regular Jews who lived outside Hamburg's walls, "in Altona [in Danish territory], where they lived among the Christians."[38]

Unlike Luther or Calov, whose interactions with real Jews were all but nonexistent, Schudt was steeped in the art of approaching flesh-and-blood Jews and conversing with them about their religion. How to do so he learned from Edzard. The Hamburg scholar taught his students that potential Jewish converts needed to be addressed gently, and that one should engage them in conversation by way of Scripture and logical reasoning. Edzard recommended tactical flexibility: "[I]n persuading Jews," he once wrote, "one cannot use the same method every time, because while in one case the situation demands that one would begin the conversation in a certain way, in another case one is in need of another method. The rest of [each respective] conversion then follows its own logic."[39] Edzard's methods were also based on Lutheran theology. Already in the early sixteenth century, Luther explained that God's purpose in giving the Old Testament to the Jews was not to deliver them from damnation but to humble them by giving them commandments that proved impossible for them to fulfill.[40] The Torah, serving to demonstrate man's powerlessness to achieve salvation without the grace of God, enhanced one's sense of guilt—a crucial step toward repentance and eventual salvation. Only through God's incomprehensible sacrifice of his one begotten son did he allow humanity to be saved. By refusing to accept Christ as their savior, Jews were stuck in an eternally cursed state.

In a letter to the Lutheran theologian J. F. Mayer, Edzard explained that the key to persuading Jews to convert was understanding (Gr. *Verstehen*): to convert, Jews needed to fully grasp what it meant to live under a curse. Jews could not accept evidence from the New Testament to this effect because they were obviously not yet Christian, and so the Hebrew Bible had to provide the necessary proof. According to Edzard, especially useful in conversing with Jews were biblical verses such as Deuteronomy 27:26 ("Cursed is anyone who does not uphold the words of this law by carrying them out") or Deuteronomy 28:58 ("If you are not careful to do all the words of this law that are written in this book, that you may fear this glorious and awesome name, the Lord your God"). Other biblical passages Edzard liked to cite to would-be converts included certain verses from the prophets Isaiah and Daniel that claim that only the Messiah can fully expiate one's sins. "All humans are sinners,"[41] Edzard liked to say, and Christ alone is the way to salvation. By rejecting the Messiah, God's one and only begotten Son, Jews were damned to continue to live under an impossible law. They were cursed to lead a life of endless hardships and wandering.

———

In September 1688, while Schudt was still a student of Edzard's in Hamburg, French forces crossed the Rhine and invaded the southwestern territories of what is now Germany. The campaign was part of Louis XIV's strategy to fortify his position as the most powerful monarch in Europe and involved razing dozens of castles, villages, and even whole cities on the right (eastern) bank of the Rhine. One of the hardest-hit areas was the German province of the Palatinate, with its capital in

Heidelberg, the seat of an important early modern court and a world-renowned university. French troops sacked Heidelberg twice during the ensuing war, causing wave after wave of refugees to leave the area. Some ended up in faraway places, including London and even New York, while others found shelter in other parts of German-speaking Europe. That was the case of the Hebraist Johann Andreas Eisenmenger, who left Heidelberg in 1688 and settled in Frankfurt, where he stayed for much of the duration of what was later known as the Nine Years' War.[42]

In their scholarship, early modern Christian Hebraists such as Schudt and Eisenmenger were not objective and did not even aspire to objectivity. They studied Hebrew and Jewish writings to shed light on the early history of Christianity or for the sake of converting Jews. Among this group of scholars, Eisenmenger was particularly radical. After studying Judaistik and semitic languages in Heidelberg, the Netherlands, and England, he spent nineteen years, first in Heidelberg and then in exile in Frankfurt, immersing himself in rabbinical literature, which he often studied with local Jews. Uncorroborated rumors had it that Eisenmenger fooled his Jewish interlocutors into studying with him by claiming that he wished to eventually convert to Judaism himself.[43]

During his stay in Frankfurt, Eisenmenger worked on a book that scholars today consider a harbinger of modern antisemitism. The title tells part of the story: *Judaism Revealed, or: a thorough and true description of how the stubborn Jews blaspheme and dishonor the Trinity, God the Father, the Son, and the Holy Ghost.*[44] Each chapter in the book describes a different form of Jewish blasphemy: against the New Testament; against Christians in general; against churches as places of worship and the Church as an institution; and of course against God and His Son. Eisenmenger's text is made up out of countless quotes from Jewish sources torn from their context. A seemingly erudite work of scholarship, *Judaism Revealed* is in fact a libelous scholarly pastiche. Its echoes reverberate throughout the modern period, including in the infamous 1937–38 Nazi exhibition *The Eternal Jew*.[45]

During his sojourn in Frankfurt, Eisenmenger met and befriended Schudt, who in the meantime had moved from Hamburg back to Frankfurt. Many years later, Schudt would describe Eisenmenger as "my life-long faithful friend"[46] and copiously quote from *Judaism Revealed* in the book he published in the wake of the 1711 fire where he also discusses the legend of the Wandering Jew. Schudt was not a systematic theologian; more than one person influenced his thinking about Jews. Next to references to Spener, Luther, Edzard, Lutheran orthodox scholars, and various Christian Hebraists,[47] Schudt's published work also contains unmistakable traces of Eisenmenger's extremely negative "revelations" about Judaism and the Jews.

———

If Schudt had entertained any aspirations of becoming an important academic like Sennert, Calov, or even (in his own way) Edzard, it was clear by the time he completed his studies with Edzard and moved back to Frankfurt, that he had failed. In Frankfurt, Schudt worked as a Hebrew teacher (1691) and vice principal (*Konrektor*, 1695) at the same gymnasium he once attended as a boy. As historian Stephen Burnett observed, in the late seventeenth century, this school enjoyed but a mediocre reputation. One can hear echoes of this in Schudt's published work: in a treatise on Hebrew philology Schudt published in 1700, he noted that "few pay attention to it today," although it "is cardinal for any theologian."[48]

The same year, Schudt began to discuss the legend of the Wandering Jew in writing. The discussion appears in a vast collection of sources about Jewish history that Schudt published in Latin under the self-explanatory title, *A Summary of Jewish history: on the origin, spread and affairs of the Jews, ... chiefly collected from Gentile writers, in which falsities are refuted, doubts are raised, and truths are confirmed.*[49] Compared with his discussion of Ahasverus's legend in the wake of the 1711 fire, in this early work Schudt's language is terse. "It is almost certainly a fable," Schudt writes about the legend of the Wandering Jew, because "neither the sacred history of the Evangelists, nor Luke in the Acts of the Apostles, nor Josephus [Flavius, the first-century Jewish historian], nor any of the ancient Church Fathers ever mention it."[50] That was it. Writing to a scholarly audience in Latin, Schudt didn't feel the need to elaborate on the historical plausibility of the legend of the Wandering Jew.

Three years later Schudt published at his own expense another Latin work on the Jews, this time condemning them in language that resembled his friend Eisenmenger's anti-Jewish diatribes. The book's title sets the tone: *The gravely sinning, punished, Christ-killing Jew, or: a clear and solid demonstration that the killing and rejection of Jesus the Nazarene is the true cause of the present and lasting exile of the Jews and the origin of all their miseries.*[51] In the book, Schudt focuses on the wretched physical state of contemporary Jewry—using the singular form "Christ-Killing Jew" to refer to all Jewish people—then speculates about the divine wrath that must have caused it. "What greater corporal misery can be imagined than the present situation and condition of the Jews?"[52] Schudt asks at the outset. "All over the world, the Jews live miserably among the nations, scattered far and wide, drawing a precarious spirit of fear by their dirty way of living. They are abominable to all, a joke to the whole world, the lowest dregs of all the nations, and an object of slaughter."[53] Schudt wanted to know how could this be the same people who were "once the glory and the first of all the peoples in God's eyes?"[54] In his opinion, the answer was simple, even if the Jews couldn't quite grasp it. ("Whoever tries to converse with Jews about the principles and dogmas of their faith is struck with amazement").[55] Before Jesus's birth, "the possession of the Land of Canaan was the most evident sign (*signum evidentissimum*) that Israel lived under God's grace,"[56] but then the land was taken from them. "The killing and rejection of Christ is [consequently] the direct cause of the long exile of the Jews."[57]

———

Seven years after the publication of *The Christ-Killing Jew* and on a day that coincided with his forty-seventh birthday, Schudt was an eyewitness to the ghetto fire. "It was a terrible spectacle to behold," he recalled, "like watching a small Troy or Rome going up in flames."[58] The speed and intensity of the fire he found astounding. The flames were "so tall and terrifying that not only the whole city and its immediate environs were lit up by them, but also a person twenty miles away could sense their presence."[59] A close friend of Schudt's, "a reliable witness," as he put it, stayed that day in the Wartburg Castle near Eisenach in faraway Saxony. Schudt reports hearing from this man that he "could tell by the sky's deep crimson color that a great fire must be burning somewhere that night."[60]

Up close, the sights were horrendous. "When the fire intensified," Schudt writes, "most of the Jews tried to save their belongings by moving them down to their cellars while others threw their gold and silver into wells or carried them outside the ghetto, leaving them with Christians."[61] The scenes of anguish and loss were heart-wrenching: "Everywhere one heard crying, yelling, wailing, and weeping, especially by women and children; some Jews literally tore off their hair."[62] According to Schudt, several Jews even rushed to the local cemetery, "fell to the ground, and wailed to their [dead] parents '*ach, Tate, ach, Mame, soltest du sehen in was tzore wir stecken!*'" (Germano-Jewish: "Oh, Father, oh, Mother, you should see what catastrophe befell us!"). "One needed a heart of stone not to be moved by so much sorrow or by the sight of the many children running about in the frost and cold."[63]

Schudt's description of the 1711 fire confirms many of the details in Eliezer Lippmann's report quoted in the opening section of this chapter. Both accounts describe how in the wake of the fire, many ghetto Jews found accommodation with Christians in other parts of the city, and Schudt, like Lippmann, reports that local Jews viewed the catastrophe as a direct result of their sins. (Lippmann: "We needed the mercy of the gentiles because of the many sins of the Jews."[64] Schudt: "They bore their misfortune with quiet patience, acknowledging that it was their great sins that led them to this point."[65]) Both accounts also relate that Frankfurt's Jews were shaken by the great loss of property and especially by "the burning of such a large number of Hebrew books, some of them rare and especially valuable."[66] Schudt's account, in other words, is not without value as a historical source.

But Schudt's description of the great Frankfurt fire of 1711, out of which he developed his influential account of Ahasverus, the Wandering Jew, should not be taken at face value either. The issue is not that Schudt was antisemitic—that much is obvious—but rather the particular ways in which his prejudices informed how he wrote about Jews. The very choice to focus on an event that caused so much Jewish suffering (rather than moments of happiness or success) aligned with Schudt's belief that the Jews' harsh exile was an expression of God's anger. That Christians like himself had anything to do with the fire—by enclosing the Frankfurt Jews in a ghetto to begin with, for starters—never crossed his mind. No less telling is Schudt's decision to always speak about *the* Jews rather than about any Jewish individuals, or to highlight how Christian offers of help were at first rejected by Frankfurt's Jewish community. The deep theological overtones of this latter statement could not have been lost on contemporary readers of his work. Christian proselytizers such as the early Luther, Edzard, Spener, and indeed Schudt, had always tried to "help" the Jews, only to realize that the majority dismissively rejected these allegedly benign offers. The Jews' miserable state was the consequence of their alleged stubbornness (*Verstocktheit*) in the face of Christian offers of assistance. Thus, even when Schudt's description aligns with historical reality, it remains tendentious. Schudt tells us a great deal about the 1711 fire, but also about the worldview of Lutheran scholars of his ilk.

————

Though the fire devastated the ghetto in mid-January 1711, Schudt did not sit down to describe it until more than two years later.[67] When he finally did so, the scheme Schudt devised was ambitious, perhaps even grandiose. Nothing in his previous life compared to it; not his student days in Wittenberg with Willemer, Sennert, and Calov, not his time with Edzard in Hamburg, not his friendship with Eisenmenger or his position at the Frankfurt gymnasium, not even *The Christ-Killing Jew* or the other Latin publications. Schudt reports that in the wake of the fire, his intention was simply to write a description of the events in

Frankfurt, not "a chronicle of the entire history of the Jews in Frankfurt, let alone a general history of the Jews."[68] But the more he thought about it, the clearer it became to him that the Frankfurt fire could not be treated in isolation. The tragic events of January 1711 were a direct consequence of the longer history of Frankfurt's Jewish community, which made sense only if one considered it within the history of the Jews as a people. This domino effect led Schudt to expand what could have been a short description of the Frankfurt fire into a four-volume, 2,000-page encyclopedic work for which the 1711 fire seems in retrospect a mere excuse. This work, which Schudt titled *Jüdische Merckwürdigkeiten* ("Jewish Memorabilia") was written in German to attract a wide readership. It consisted of a compendium of noteworthy facts about the history of the Jews.

Schudt's magnum opus began to appear in Frankfurt in late 1714, three and a half years after the fire.[69] The first volume discussed the history of the Jews of Asia, Africa, America, and Europe, respectively; the second treated the history and culture of Frankfurt's Jews; and the third presented primary sources, often in their original language (Hebrew, Yiddish) but many also in German translation, on Jewish life in Frankfurt and other parts of German-speaking Europe. Three years after the publication of the first three parts of *Jewish Memorabilia*, Schudt issued a fourth, complementary volume.

Ever since his youth, Schudt believed that by converting Jews, he was helping them reach salvation. He was doing it for their sake, not his own. In the introduction to *Jewish Memorabilia*, he claims as much while underscoring a crucial difference between himself, an educated person, and what he terms the lower classes of society. "One should not expect of me that I should follow the common Christian custom and use mocking words to degrade or make fun of the Jews," Schudt writes.

Rather, "I speak to them often about their harsh, unjust treatment by the lower classes [and] make it a point not to ascribe the mistakes and sins of individuals to the Jewish nation as a whole."[70] His professions of amity notwithstanding, Schudt's magnum opus is in fact brimming with anti-Jewish prejudices. It reiterates the Jew's allegedly faulty character (Frankfurt's Jews are insolent, presumptuous, and full of self-importance, self-flattery, and false kindness); calls their physical appearance "disgusting"; comments on their alleged lack of basic hygiene; and even devotes a whole section to what Schudt considers the odious Jewish smell.[71] Echoes of the later Luther, Calov, and especially Eisenmenger reverberate throughout these sections. Indeed, the tension in *Jewish Memorabilia* between a professed motivation to help the Jews and a de facto treatment of them as little more than animals is characteristic of early modern Lutheranism. This might have been part of the appeal of Schudt's work. Schudt thought that the cursed state of the Jews was their own fault. By rejecting Christian help—by rejecting Christ as their Lord and Savior—the Jews condemned themselves to a subhuman existence. The Frankfurt fire was consequently not only a particular historical event; it also stood, *pars pro toto*, for Jewish history as a whole.

———

Schudt dedicated one of the longest sections of *Jewish Memorabilia* to the legend of the Wandering Jew. The section contains a full transcription of an early edition of the Kurtze Beschreibung, annotated by Schudt, as well as lengthy discussions of the legend's medieval origins and whether it made sense, theologically or historically. Previously, Schudt's scholarly publications appeared in Latin for a university-educated readership. It is noteworthy that for those readers, Schudt felt no need to elaborate on the question of Ahasverus's historical plausibility. But Schudt wrote *Jewish Memorabilia* in German, catering to the wider reading public. That he decided to include such a protracted refutation of Ahasverus's story suggests that he believed that the general public needed assistance to realize what more educated people could figure out on their own.

Indeed, at the start of his discussion of the legend of the Wandering Jew, Schudt draws a distinction between popular views of the legend, on the one hand, and scholarly opinions, on the other. He notes that in his own day, Ahasverus was such a well-known figure that "[e]ven ordinary people seem to know the story of a certain Jew who is wandering the entire earth . . . and in many a place it is common to hear [such people] use the expression 'He wanders around like the tall Jew'" as a matter of course.[72] Educated people are also aware of the legend, Schudt explains, but the overwhelming majority reject the story as "a tasteless [*abgeschmackte*] legend or fable."[73] There is no shortage of examples to prove this, Schudt writes. To boot,

> Julius Bulinger in his *History of his time*, page 357; Rudolph Botoreus in *Historical Commentary*, volume 2, page 305; the Jewish convert Mr. Diefenbach, chapter 19 page 102; Erasmus Francisci's *The Stage*, part II, p. 305; Gisbertus Voetius's *Disputations*, Part 2, page 104; and August Pfeiffer in his three works *Evangelische Erquick-Stunden*, p. 359, *Disputation about the Messiah*, p. 208, and *The Faith and Superstitions of the Jews*, appendix 3, p. 178.[74]

Throughout the Ahasverus section in *Jewish Memorabilia*, Schudt adds many more names to this list, including those of Jacques Basnage, Johannes Schütze, Johann Sebastian Mitternacht, Gottfried Thilo, Chrisoph Schultz, and others.[75] Also telling is that Schudt never quotes from his own teachers. Luther, Calov, Sennert, and Calov never thought that refuting the legend of the Wandering Jew was worth their precious time.

Several modern scholars have suggested that Schudt's discussion of the legend of the Wandering Jew was new and original compared to what previous scholars had written about it. They often quote a sentence in Schudt's section on Ahasverus, where the Frankfurt gymnasium teacher states that "[w]e ourselves view [the legend] as a mere poem [*Gedicht*]. . . . [Ahasverus] is not a single person but the Jewish people as a whole, which, after the Crucifixion of Christ, spread all over the world and will remain so, according to Christ's testimony, until the End of the World."[76] Certainly, assigning too much originality to this statement is a mistake. As we have seen, Schudt had written in 1700 that because the story of Ahasverus is not attested in Scripture, it is "almost certainly a fable."[77] Three years later, he repeated the old Christian claim that "the killing and rejection of Christ is the direct cause of the long exile of the Jews."[78] In terms of his conclusions, what Schudt did in *Jewish Memorabilia* was to combine his two earlier statements into one elegant formulation, which he then bolstered using a plethora of citations from other scholars' works. Moreover, nowhere in *Jewish Memorabilia* does Schudt claim that his argument about Ahasverus is particularly new or original. On the contrary, he places himself at the end of a list of old, venerable scholars who, while being no friends to the Jews and indeed thinking them a cursed and exilic people, vehemently denied the historical existence of the wandering Ahasverus.

———

Relying at first on other authorities to support his argument that Ahasverus was never a real person, Schudt then turns to specific evidence to support this claim. Just like Luther, Spener, Calov, and innumerable theologians before them, Schudt had no doubt that the Jews were a cursed people and that their exile was a manifestation of God's wrath. Thus, he reminds his readers that as far back as the fourth century, the Roman poet Aurelius Prudentius viewed the general fate of the Jews in this manner. Covered in the blood of the rejected Christ, Prudentius writes (and Schudt quotes), "[i]n uncertain exiles, hither and thither, wanders / The Jew, having been torn asunder from his father's seat / atoning for murder."[79] Once God's chosen people, the Jews turned into exilic wanderers. There was no doubt about *that*.

But during his years of study in Frankfurt, Wittenberg, and Hamburg, Schudt had also learned to pay incredibly close attention to God's Word as expressed in Scripture. Scripture itself, he knew, was inerrant: it could not be contradicted by external (historical) evidence because it was nestled, as it were, within itself. Understood in light of Scripture, the image of Christ, the legend of the Wandering Jew simply didn't make sense to Schudt. How could this story be true, Schudt asks, when "it contradicts the love, gentleness, and patience of our Lord Jesus, who never did any harm to his enemies?" When the disciples James and John offered to harm a village of Samaritans for refusing to extend a helping hand to Jesus, Jesus went to another village instead (Luke 9:51–55). It wasn't that Jesus couldn't curse the villagers; Jesus had once cursed a fig tree that subsequently died, and in another incident, allowed a troupe of demons to enter a herd of pigs. Rather, Jesus never let harm befall another human being. "His whole life he went about doing good, and healing all that were oppressed of the devil; for God was with him" (Acts 10:38). Even during his Passion, when Jesus was led to a denigrating death on the cross, he did not hurt or curse his tormentors. His disciple Peter insisted on it: "When they hurled their insults at him, he did not retaliate; when he suffered, he made no threats. Instead, he entrusted himself to him who judges justly" (1 Peter 2:23).[80] Could Jesus truly have cursed a Jew named Ahasverus on his way to the Calvary?

So important was this Christological point for Schudt that he kept piling on examples to prove it. He reminds his readers that the prophet Isaiah describes the gentleness, patience, and even silence of the Redeemer vis-à-vis his tormentors: "He was oppressed and afflicted, yet he did not open his mouth; he was led like a lamb to the slaughter, and as a sheep before its shearers is silent, so he did not open his mouth" (Isaiah 53:7). And what about those who harmed Jesus physically and not only (like Ahasverus) by their words? "Could Jesus have responded to the few words of the Jew [Ahasverus] with so much zeal whereas he suffered the terrible blasphemies, humiliations, and mocking of his bitter enemies with great patience?"[81] All those "painful blows, the flogging, and the crucifixion he bore with the utmost gentleness," and on the cross, "in the midst of his sufferings, Jesus prayed for forgiveness for his enemies and crucifiers."[82] Here, then, is the main reason why Schudt and earlier theologians rejected the legend of the Wandering Jew as absurd. Even without consulting the historical record, it was clear for them that the legend of the Wandering Jew went against the very spirit of Scripture.

———

Theologians might be content with theology, but for the general readership of *Jewish Memorabilia*, Schudt considered it his role to also speak about history. Already in his *Summary of Jewish History* (1700), Schudt presented himself as an historian as much as an expert in theology, and in *Jewish Memorabilia* he defines himself as an historian over and over again.[83] Just like the Christological aspects of Ahasverus's story, which Schudt so passionately rejected, he felt that the legend of the Wandering Jew rested on hardly any evidence from the historical record. The problem, as Schudt understood it, was not only that the four Gospels and the Acts of the Apostles do not mention the Wandering Jew in a single word—Schudt had already made this claim in 1700—but also that for the next 1200 or 1300 years, not a single historian mentions the Wandering Jew either. This is the case of "Josephus, the Jewish historian, and Philo, Egesippus, Eusebius, Socrates, Thedoritus, Sozomenus, Evagoras, and [even] Nicephoras, who wrote the most minute details about the history of the early Church, including fables sometimes," Schudt claims.[84] Certainly, that written sources do not describe an event or a person does not mean they never existed; the evangelist John even says that "Jesus performed many other signs in the presence of his disciples, which are not recorded in this book" (John 20:30). But had the story of Ahasverus been true, "it is nonetheless credible that the Gospels would not have passed over such a story with silence, for it is such an important thing with which to persuade the unbelieving Jews [of the Christian truth]."[85]

The silence of early sources is only exacerbated by different sources from the Middle Ages onward that constantly contradict one another in describing the person who would later be called Ahasverus or Ahasver. Schudt writes that "Matthew Paris reports that before he was baptized the man's name was Cartaphilus and afterward Josephus, but Botoreus calls him Gregorius and Libavius in his *Praxi Alchimiae* calls him Buttadaeus while [the Kurtze Beschreibung] gives him the name Ahasverus."[86] The 1602 pamphlet further claims that Ahasverus had been a cobbler in Jerusalem and that he lived not far from one of Jerusalem's city gates, but Matthew Paris and Clovers report that he was one of Pilate's doormen. To make matters worse, some sources report that Ahasverus is still a Jew today, others claim that he had converted to Christianity, some say he is in the habit of rejecting Christian offers of money but others claim that he asks for money all the time.[87] How can a story based on such conflicting sources be considered reliable?

Last but not least is the issue of the reliability of the authors reporting on Ahasverus. Take, Schudt suggests, the case of Matthew Paris as an example. This thirteenth-century monk from St. Albans in England "lived in those *barbaris ignorentiae seculis*" (Lt.: barbaric centuries of ignorance) and was consequently prone "to invent wonderful fairy tales."[88] Why take the word of such a man at face value? And what about the so-called eyewitness account from places such as Hamburg (1542) or Lübeck (1604)? "It is curious that in Hamburg no one saw this man except for Doctor Paul von Eitzen, or that in Lübeck no one but a certain Antonius Colerus did the same."[89] When all is said and done, "it is little wonder that one cannot actually find the Jew Ahasverus in any region, land, or city of the world."[90] Ahasverus might represent a theological truth about a cursed Judaism and a triumphant Christianity. But stories about him wandering the world are romances, fabrications, and lies. Only commoners and simpletons would think otherwise.

———

All of this leads Schudt to ask one last—and from our perspective crucial—question. If the legend of the Wandering Jew was a mere fable without any basis in Christology or history, who invented it, under what circumstances, and for what purpose?

Having seriously thought about the issue, Schudt suspected that the inventor of the legend might very well have been a Catholic. Ever since the outbreak of the German Reformation, Luther and his followers described Catholicism as highly superstitious. The cult of the saints, most (if not all) of the sacraments, the selling of indulgences (documents promising the remission of divine punishment), the adoration of the pope—Lutherans perceived it all as foreign forms of idolatry that infiltered the body of the Church, metastasized, and threatened to kill it from within. Schudt echoes anti-Catholic prejudices in his treatment of Matthew of Paris. He conceded that God *could* do anything: God is omnipotent, and had he wanted to, he could have certainly cursed a Jerusalemite cobbler named Ahasverus and made him wander the earth until the Second Coming. "That God can do this is consequently undoubtedly true. Whether he actually did it, however, is the real question."[91] The whole affair must have come from the pen of "petty Catholic writers" (*Katholische Scribenten*), Schudt speculated. "Oh, Dudulaeus [presumed author of the 1602 pamphlet], if this is the basis for your Ahasverus then he is bound to vanish very soon."[92] Not the defeat of religion as such, but the defeat of Catholicism's many superstitions would put an end to Ahasverus, at least according to Johann Jacob Schudt.

A second option Schudt mentions in *Jewish Memorabilia* as a possible source for the Ahasverus legend is common man's naïveté. Sometimes Schudt explicitly raises this issue, whereas elsewhere it is merely implied. Schudt speculated that some sightings of Ahasverus resulted from misunderstandings when uneducated people encountered a wandering madman (*kopfverwirrter Mensch*) or perhaps a deliberate liar and a deceiver (*scheinheiliger Betrüger*) who "travels through the land and deceives the common man with his madness."[93] According to this explanation, the success of the legend is the result of ignorance and class, not the Catholic confession. The common man might believe in such "poems," but it is the scholar's task to set the record straight.

Toward the end of his section on Ahasverus, Schudt raises a final, intriguing possibility regarding the source of the Ahasverus legend that modern scholars have never taken seriously. Relying on the work of the polymath Erasmus Finx (1627–1694)—Schudt, we remember, is much less original than scholars give him credit for—the author of *Jewish Memorabilia* thought it possible that the root cause of the legend's popularity was greed rather than Catholic superstition or common ignorance. Quoting Finx, Schudt writes that the whole affair is perhaps "a pure little fairytale which an overzealous printer or publisher helped produce with this one aim in mind to use this baseless story to make money. People who trade in such smoke screens are after all quite common these days."[94] Early modern print capitalism, Schudt speculates, might be the real culprit behind the invention of Ahasverus.

———

Schudt's *Jewish Memorabilia* is an important document in the history of the legend of the Wandering Jew, even if not for the reason historians have usually cited. Its importance lies less in the originality of its argument than in the way it sums up a theological and historical discussion that largely predated the book. Based on the writings of theologians and other scholars before him, Schudt convincingly shows that the legend of the Wandering Jew makes little sense in terms of Protestant theology or history. He thus highlights a paradox: the 1602 pamphlet was extremely popular in premodern Protestant Europe at the very moment that Protestant theologians rejected its claims out of hand.

Schudt was never a systematic theologian, let alone a successful one. His writings exhibit varied and often conflicting influences and, despite his great ambitions, he never became a university professor. His *Jewish Memorabilia* is a syncretic text, full of prejudices but also suggestive insights, interesting observations but also gaping epistemological holes. Consider, for instance, Schudt's argument that the legend of the Wandering Jew is not supported by Scripture. As Schudt knew all too well, on the first page of the Kurtze Beschreibung, a biblical quote from the Gospel of Matthew appears, in which Jesus tells his disciples, "Truly I tell you, some who are standing here will not taste death before they see the Son of Man coming in his kingdom" (Matthew 16:28). The inclusion of this verse on the pamphlet's first page is supposed to bolster the claim that some contemporaries of Jesus would not die until his Second Coming. And yet it takes only a modicum of biblical literacy to recognize that this verse cannot possibly suggest that Ahasverus was a historical person. According to the Bible, after Jesus said these words, he was crucified, but also resurrected, before finally ascending to heaven. The passage quoted on the first page of the Kurtze Beschreibung has nothing to do with a *second* coming; it predicts events that the Bible actually describes. Schudt should have known better than to overlook this fact. He missed an easy opportunity to further bolster his claim that the Kurtze Beschreibung is based on a faulty understanding of Scripture.

Consider, second, the issue of Ahasverus's very name. Ever since the publication of the Kurtze Beschreibung, no scholar has been able to explain why the anonymous author of the 1602 pamphlet decided to call the Wandering Jew by the name of the

Persian king in the Book of Esther rather than Butadeus, Cartaphilus, or John. It certainly looks odd: why this non-Jewish name? What was the author of the Kurtze Beschreibung trying to do or achieve by it?

The Book of Esther is part of both the Hebrew Bible and the Christian Old Testament. As such, the story it tells about Esther, Mordechai, Haman, and King Ahasverus was well known throughout Christian Europe in Schudt's time. Nicolas Poussin and Rembrandt van Rijn painted famous scenes from the Book of Esther during Schudt's childhood (*Esther before Ahasverus*, 1655, and *Ahasverus and Haman at the Feast of Esther*, 1660, respectively), French playwright Jean Racine wrote a play about Esther just as Schudt moved back from Hamburg to Frankfurt am Main (*Esther*, 1689), and a few years after the publication of *Jewish Memorabilia*, Georg Friedrich Handel even composed the first English oratorio about the story (*Esther*, 1718). Schudt knew the story well enough to frequently quote from it in his various publications: in the *Summary of Jewish History* (1700); *The Christ-Killing Jew* (1703); and especially *Jewish Memorabilia* (1714–17).[95]

As a trained Hebraist, Schudt was familiar with common Jewish depictions of Ahasverus's story in the festival of Purim. In his *Summary of Jewish History* (1700), Schudt gives a brief description of the festival, "that 'Jewish Bacchanalia,'" as he puts it, "in which the Jews celebrate the liberation of their people from the evil advice of Haman."[96] Partly based on a Purim celebration Schudt witnessed in Altona while studying under Edzard in nearby Hamburg,[97] Schudt describes to his readers how, during the festival, Jews "eat, drink, feast, play games, go around masked, and read the Book of Esther in their synagogues."[98] "Whenever they mention the name of Haman," Schudt adds, the Jews "all cry 'may his name be blotted out,' clap their hands, beat with wooden hammers on their benches, and bring forth a great commotion."[99]

Fourteen years after his first scholarly description of Purim, Schudt returns to it for a second time in *Jewish Memorabilia*. Relying on an informant in the Frankfurt ghetto, he describes in detail some of the Purim traditions that were particular to Frankfurt am Main. There, too, Jews eat, drink, and wear masks during Purim, but German Jews also stage comic plays in the ghetto to celebrate the holiday. Schudt discusses two of these plays in detail: one about the biblical story of Joseph and his brothers; the other about King Ahasverus. Schudt reports that despite the challenge of finding copies of the two plays ("as one Jew assured me, the exemplars [of the plays] were later burned so that copies are now rare and hard to come by"[100]), he managed to lay his hands on the text of a 1708 Ahasverus play and fully transcribed it in his book. Schudt found the play as a whole (just like the legend of Ahasverus), "appropriate only for kids, frivolous and tasteless," and he expresses shock vis-à-vis the character of Mordechai, whom he finds "nasty, lewd, and foul-mouthed."[101] "The Jews themselves are ashamed of this Haman- or Ahasverus comedy," Schudt writes.[102]

As with so many other sections in *Jewish Memorabilia*, Schudt's discussion of the festival of Purim is revelatory about both early modern Jewish life and Schudt's prejudices against Jews. On the one hand, the description of the festival contains valuable ethnographic information about the Jews of Frankfurt, including transcriptions of the two earliest known plays in the Yiddish language. Schudt also knew that Purim was the Jewish version of carnival, and he must have also known that in the Jewish tradition, Ahasverus is referred to as Ahasverus-the-fool (Heb.: *Ahashverosh hatippesh*). This is where Schudt's limitations as a scholar are clear, however. Schudt could have lingered on the comic aspects of the Jewish take on Ahasverus, asking whether it had something to do with a story about a Lutheran theologian (Paul von Eitzen) who believed in a character that almost every Lutheran theologian rejected as absurd. This would have perfectly aligned with Schudt's general suspicion about the true intention behind the Kurtze Beschreibung. But even as he furnished multiple pieces of evidence to support such an interpretation, Schudt's pervasive anti-Jewish sentiment made him incapable of seeing it clearly. Anti-Jewish dogma, in his case, was stronger than any empirical evidence; it preceded and shaped his interpretation of reality rather than the other way around. In Schudt's early seventeenth-century Lutheran worldview, the fate of the Jews was an incredibly serious matter, part of a *historia sacra*, the evidence for which could be found in Scripture and only then, if at all, in historical facts. This is why he simply couldn't conceive of Ahasverus's legend as a comedy or farce. For Schudt, the legend of Ahasverus was a historical and theological absurdity that only the lower classes could believe in as a description of an actual person. This is what he meant by calling it "a poem"—essentially a fairytale. The legend was a facile way for uneducated people to perceive, however dimly, a general truth about Judaism and the Jews.

———

Not without reason, scholars assign Johann Jacob Schudt a special place in the reception history of the legend of the Wandering Jew. While he was not the first to suggest as much, Schudt left to posterity an elegant formulation about the legend of the Wandering Jew as both fictive and true. So much of what we've seen in this book's previous chapters follows this line of reasoning. The legend of the Wandering Jew is a true story that never happened. It could be symbolically meaningful although it is theologically and historically absurd.

When read more closely and against the backdrop of Schudt's biography, however, we can see how Schudt's most important contribution to our understanding of the origins of the Ahasverus legend goes well beyond the elegant formulation of an already well-established scholarly view. Following the fire of 1711, and largely unintentionally, Schudt assembled for the modern historian clues with which to start deciphering the motives behind the creation of the Kurtze Beschreibung of 1602. The original pamphlet depicted Paul von Eitzen, a respected Lutheran theologian, believing in what Schudt proved to be Christological and historical nonsense. What's more, the pamphlet's hero—the man Paul von Eitzen allegedly encountered in 1542 Hamburg—was not a Butadeus, Cartaphilus, or John. Rather, he was a character from the Jewish festival of Purim, a man known in the Jewish tradition as Ahasverus-the-fool.

4

The Case of Ahasverus in Hamburg (1602)

IT'S ONLY eight pages long. It's in German. It's printed on low-quality paper. We don't know who wrote it, who printed it, where, or why. There are no identifiable circumstances, no concrete historical context to explain the intent behind the Kurtze Beschreibung, the document that gave life to Ahasverus in 1602. (See figure 12.)

We know, of course, the story the pamphlet tells its readers. Late in life, the distinguished Lutheran theologian Paul von Eitzen recounted for his students an episode from his youth. In 1542, while a student at the University of Wittenberg, Eitzen went to visit his parents in Hamburg. There, on the Sunday following his arrival, he saw a strange man whose name, it turned out, was Ahasverus. Eitzen approached Ahasverus, inquired about what brought him to Hamburg, and learned that he had been born a Jew in Jerusalem more than fifteen hundred years earlier. Ahasverus was once a shoemaker and had a wife and child. But because he joined the crowd at Pilate's palace calling for Jesus's execution, and especially because he didn't

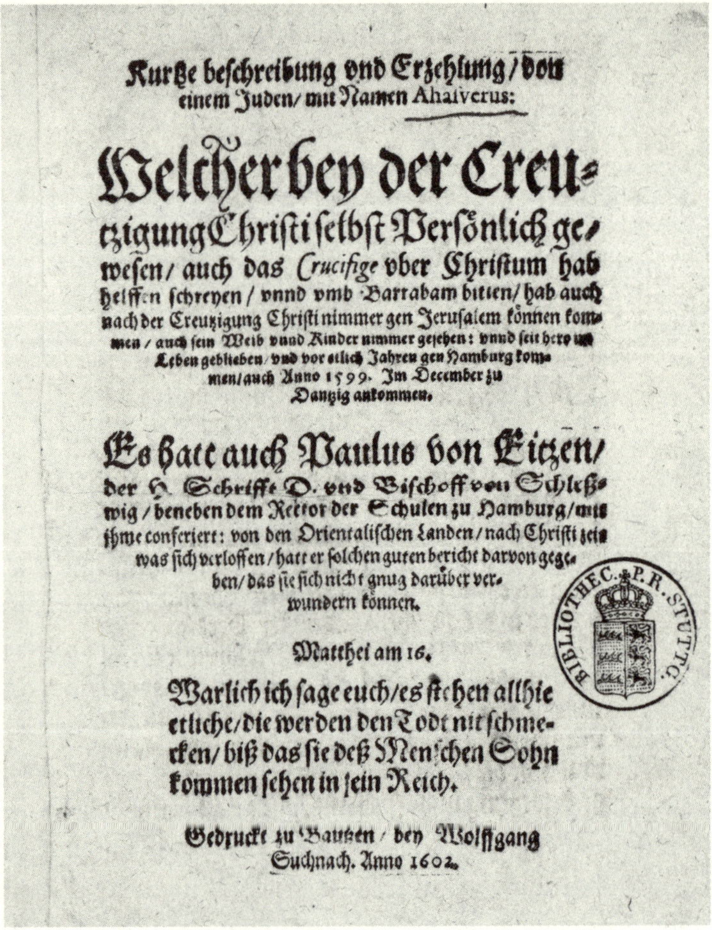

Kurtze beschreibung vnd Ertzehlung / von
einem Juden / mit Namen Ahasverus:

Welcher bey der Creutzigung Christi selbst Persönlich gewesen / auch das Crucifige vber Christum hab helffen schreyen / vnnd vmb Barrabam bitten / hab auch nach der Creutzigung Christi nimmer gen Jerusalem können kommen / auch sein Weib vnnd Kinder nimmer gesehen: vnnd seit hero vñ Leben geblieben / vnd vor etlich Jahren gen Hamburg kommen / auch Anno 1599. Im December zu Dantzig ankommen.

Es hat auch Paulus von Eitzen /
der H. Schrifft D. vnd Bischoff von Schleßwig / beneben dem Rector der Schulen zu Hamburg / mit ihme conferiert: von den Orientalischen Landen / nach Christi zeit was sich verloffen / hatt er solchen guten bericht darvon gegeben / das sie sich nicht gnug darüber verwundern können.

Matthei am 16.

Warlich ich sage euch / es stehen allhie etliche / die werden den Todt nit schmecken / biß das sie deß Menschen Sohn kommen sehen in sein Reich.

Gedruckt zu Bautzen / bey Wolffgang
Suchnach. Anno 1602.

FIGURE 12. Title page of N². Source: Württembergische
Landesbibliothek, Kirch.G.qt.595.

give Jesus respite when the latter passed by his shop on his way to Golgotha, Jesus cursed Ahasverus to wander the earth until the Second Coming. This is why, in Eitzen's story, Ahasverus was still alive in 1542.

Strewn throughout the Kurtze Beschreibung are more details about Ahasverus. The pamphlet informs us that this wandering or eternal Jew was able to corroborate his astonishing tale to Paul von Eitzen by answering the latter's learned questions about the circumstances of the Crucifixion, the history of the Orient, and the lives, sufferings, and deaths of the Apostles. His story included details that "neither the evangelists nor historians report."[1] The pamphlet also describes Ahasverus as a particularly tall person who speaks German with a Saxon accent and is proficient in many other languages. It claims that although many eyewitnesses did not give credit to the Jew's story, Paul von Eitzen was persuaded by it.

Next to its content, we also know a thing or two about what happened once the Kurtze Beschreibung saw the light of day. The pamphlet came out in at least twelve different German editions in 1602 and in dozens more, both in German and in other European languages, by the end of the seventeenth century. As Johann Jacob Schudt would demonstrate in *Jewish Memorabilia* in the early eighteenth century, practically all early modern Lutheran theologians dismissed the legend of Ahasverus as theologically and historically absurd. Schudt called it a mere allegory or poem ("Gedicht"), claiming that only common people would take it seriously. Modern scholars have largely followed Schudt's lead. With but a few exceptions, they have read the Kurtze Beschreibung as a fictional text with little, if any, bearing on historical reality.

———

At first, thinking about the Kurtze Beschreibung as a text or a story can seem unproblematic. Strictly speaking, however, it is something else. The Kurtze Beschreibung is first of all a physical object—a pamphlet—made out of paper and ink. Pamphlets of this sort were very popular in early modern Europe. In English, they are often called "chapbooks" ("chapman" is an old term for itinerant dealers), but other languages have different names for them, and around 1600, they were not known under a single appellation in any language. The term chapbook defines the form of a printed material, not its content or genre; it applies to short and often low-quality booklets one could buy at early modern fairs, in a special section of a bookstore, or at street stands.

The content of early modern chapbooks was anything but uniform: some chapbooks described the birth of misshapen creatures and the life stories of witches and executed criminals, others contained folk tales, ballads, and romances, and even more consisted of news reports (*Zeitungen* in German) and poetical and even theological tracts. Many early modern chapbooks have passed into oblivion, but others came to occupy a pride of place in the history of European literature. The sixteenth-century French satirist François Rabelais based his uproarious series *Gargantua and Pantagruel* on a chapbook; William Shakespeare drew inspiration from chapbooks and included a description of a chapman in *The Winter's Tale* (Autolycus, Act 4); and the story of Faust, featured several times in the pages of this book already, came out in print for the first time in an anonymous 1587 chapbook.[2]

———

Early modern European chapbooks are fascinating material objects. They are made of paper of varying quality that was printed on and then folded, cut, and bound to form a booklet. The ink on their pages, of uneven quality and occasionally of more than one color, forms individual letters, words, and whole lines of text, which an artisan or his assistants laid out on the page according to a deliberate typographical design. Individual chapbooks often came out in more than one edition and did not always show consistency in terms of orthography or ornamental elements such as letters, separators, and images. The original author of the Kurtze Beschreibung might have been a single individual; in the production of different editions of the 1602 chapbook, however, he was certainly not acting alone.

Today, copies of the first editions of the Ahasverus chapbook exist in a handful of European libraries.[3] The first impression they make is not particularly impressive. The inventor of the printing press, Johannes Gutenberg, probably started his career by publishing chapbook-like materials, though the low quality of such publications means that none has survived the ravages of time. When it came to printing his famous forty-two-line Bible, however, Gutenberg was much more careful. He used vellum for about a quarter of his Bible's 180 copies, fine paper for the rest. On each side of these sheets, Gutenberg made a careful imprint of two pages, using galleys made of beautiful cast letters he had helped cast. (Gutenberg originally trained as a goldsmith.) After pressing the ink-covered galleys onto the paper, Gutenberg and his associates hung the wet sheets to dry, folded each one in half to create two leaves or four pages, and later sewed the folded sheets together and bound them into a codex. (See figure 13.) Even at its infancy, this revolutionary process for the production of books was far more efficient than anything that preceded it. A medieval scribe might take a whole year to finish a single (well made)

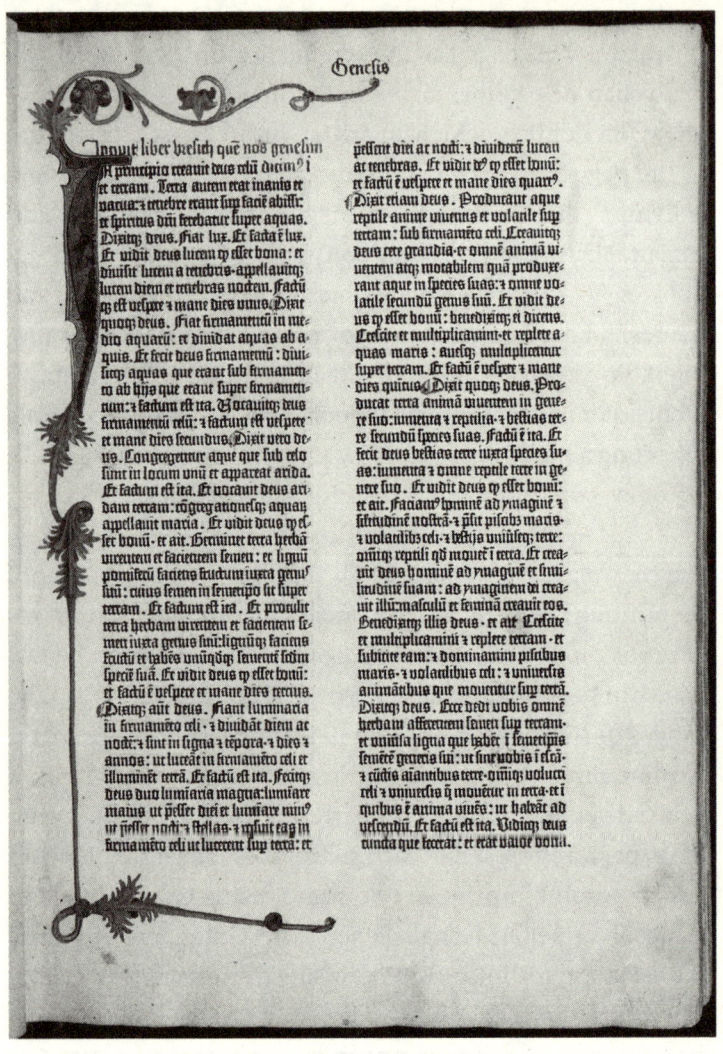

FIGURE 13. A page from the Gutenberg Bible, ca. 1455. Source: Special Collections, Princeton University Library, https://dpul.princeton.edu /gutenberg/catalog/7d278t10z.

copy of the Bible; Gutenberg and his collaborators managed to print almost two hundred magnificent exemplars in just a couple of years.[4]

Though the Kurtze Beschreibung was the product of a printing press not unlike the one Gutenberg used for his Bible, the chapbook's surviving copies are decidedly inferior to the remarkable products by the famous printmaker from Mainz. Their paper is rough and granular, and the unknown workers who covered the galleys with ink did not always perform their job carefully. For example, in one of the earliest extent copies of the Kurtze Beschreibung, the workers overinked the galleys, in another they underinked them, and in a third, a careless worker left an imprint of his inky fingers on one of the chapbook's pages.[5] Further proof of the low quality of the Kurtze Beschreibung's early copies is the utterly ordinary nature of their overall design and the font of the moveable types used to compose their respective texts. Typographically speaking, copies of the Ahasverus chapbook are nothing to write home about.[6]

Last but not least on the list of the ordinary physical traits of the Kurtze Beschreibung is the folding of the printed sheets into leaves and pages. Unlike the Gutenberg Bible, whose sheets were folded once (creating in the process a large book format known as a folio), the unknown printer of the early copies of the Kurtze Beschreibung folded its sheets twice, producing in the process more individual pages that were also smaller in size (a quarto edition). Unlike other contemporary quarto editions, such as early copies of Shakespeare's plays or the Faust chapbook of 1587, the production of the Kurtze Beschreibung demanded no sewing since its eight pages of text fit neatly onto a single sheet of paper, printed on both sides.

What all these technical details mean in practice is that the printing of the Kurtze Beschreibung was inexpensive and probably done in haste. The mundane aspects of early copies of the Kurtze Beschreibung also indicate that trying to identify an author or printer based on typographical considerations alone is highly impractical. The list of possible suspects would be simply too long in this case.

———

Enter Leonhard Neubaur (1847–1917), a gymnasium teacher in Elbing (modern-day Elbląg in Poland) who studied theology at Königsberg and received a doctorate in philosophy from the University of Halle in 1875. Now completely forgotten beyond a small circle of Ahasverus scholars, Neubaur is one of the great heroes in the history of the study of the Ahasverus legend.[7]

Neubaur's life coincided with the heyday of the legend of Ahasverus in European culture. Like Ludwig Philippson, who commented on the innumerable "different literary treatments of Ahasver's legend in the past several decades,"[8] Neubaur was deeply impressed by the widespread nature of the legend of Ahasverus in his day. He also found these treatments quite confusing. And so Neubaur pulled up his sleeves and went to work. From 1882 nearly until his death thirty-five years later, this independent scholar collected and analyzed every copy of the Kurtze Beschreibung and other Ahasverus-related materials on which he could lay his hands. Neubaur traveled to Dresden, Munich, Strasbourg, Stuttgart, Tübingen, Berlin, and even Copenhagen in search of early copies of the chapbook and other relevant materials, and he communicated by mail with many archivists and librarians across Europe he couldn't meet in person. Neubaur's idea was to create a catalogue of all known exemplars of the Ahasverus pamphlet, including the Kurtze Beschreibung of 1602, but also later (and many non-German) ones. He wrote six important publications on the topic (one in 1884, two in 1893, and one each in 1911, 1912, and 1914[9]) that are still worth reading today. Indeed, in many respects, Leonhard Neubaur is the author of some of the best work ever published on the legend of Ahasverus.

———

Neubaur's main conclusion from his meticulous work spanning several decades was that the early editions of the 1602 chapbook, while related, also show key differences. The title of the Ahasverus chapbook changed over time, the content of the story expanded, the spelling of particular words in different pamphlets wasn't consistent, and ornamental elements, including visual representations of Ahasverus's figure, also evolved. Most important for Neubaur was to show that in comparing the texts of different editions, they could all be traced to a single source. This ur-text (which Neubaur located in the Bavarian National Library in Munich) he identified as the original Ahasverus pamphlet: it was, he believed, the textual basis for every subsequent version. Based on this discovery, Neubaur suggested a way to chronologically order all extant copies of the 1602 pamphlet. He created a list of these copies, which he updated as he discovered new editions over time.

For the sake of brevity, it is useful to call different editions of the Kurtze Beschreibung by their placement on Neubaur's chronological list. Thus, the earliest edition Leonhard Neubaur identified will be referred to as N^1 from now on, the second oldest will be N^2, and so on. Of the first ten editions that Neubaur identified, four in particular are noteworthy:

- N^1 (see figure 1, chapter 1) is the earliest surviving edition of the Kurtze Beschreibung, according to Neubaur, and consequently the likely ur-text for all subsequent editions of the pamphlet. The first page includes a quote from Matthew 16:28 ("Verily I say unto you, There be some standing here, which shall not taste of death, till they see the Son of man coming in his kingdom"), and the imprint at the bottom reads: "Printed in Leyden [Leiden] by Christoph Creutzer, 1602." Only one copy of this edition survives. It is now located at the Bavarian State Library in Munich.
- N^2 (see figure 12) is the second oldest edition of the Kurtze Beschreibung. Copies exist in Stuttgart, Darmstadt, Tübingen, and Strasbourg. Before World War II, a fifth copy, now extinct, existed in Berlin. This edition contains the same text as N^1 with two notable exceptions: the German word "Zweyer" (two) is misspelled on page eight of the pamphlet, and the imprint on the first page reads, "Printed in Bautzen by Wolffgang Suchnach, 1602."
- Of N^4 (see figure 14) only one copy survives, also in Munich. It contains almost exactly the same text as N^2 and N^1 but differs in terms of typographical design. On the first page appears the first visual representation of Ahasverus we know of: previous editions of the pamphlet featured none.
- Finally, surviving copies of N^{10} (see figure 15) are in Leipzig and Breslau/Wrocław (present-day Poland). This edition bears a different title from all previous ones.

Kurtze Beschreibung vnd Erzehlung von einem
Juden / mit Namen Ahaßverus /

Welcher bey der Creutzi-

gung Christi selbst persönlich gewesen / auch das
Crucifige über Christum hab helffen schreyen / vnd vmb Barrabam bitten / hab auch nach der Creutzigung Christi nimmer gen Jerusalem
können kommen / auch sein Weib vnd Kinder nimmer gesehen / vnd seithero im
Leben geblieben / vnd vor etlich Jahren gen Hamburg kommen / auch Anno 1599. im December zu Dantzig ankommen.

Es hat auch Paulus von Eitzen / der H. Schrifft
Doctor vnd Bischoff von Schleßwig / beneben dem Rector der
Schulen zu Hamburg / mit jhme conferirt von den Orientalischen Landen /
was sich nach Christi zeit verloffen / hat er solchen guten bericht davon gegeben /
daß sie sich nicht gnug darüber verwundern können.

Matthei am 16.

Warlich ich sage euch / es stehen allhie etliche / die werden den Todt nicht
schmecken / biß daß sie deß Menschen Sohn kommen sehen inn
sein Reich.

Gedruckt zu Bautzen / bey Wolffgang
Suchnach / Anno 1602.

FIGURE 14. The title page of N⁴. Source: Bayerische
Staatsbibliothek 4 Diss. 1417#Beibd.22.

FIGURE 15. The title page of N[10]. Source: Leipzig
Universitätsbibliothek Lit.germ.B.1657:1/1.

The text describing Eitzen's meeting with Ahasverus is quite different from what it was in N^1, and for the first time in the history of the Kurtze Beschreibung, the imprint contains the name of a presumed author: a Chrysostomos Dudulaeus Westphalus. The visual representation of Ahasverus on the first page of this chapbook is also new.

————

The order in which Neubaur listed early editions of the Kurtze Beschreibung has important scholarly ramifications. For instance, the identification of N^1 as the earliest copy of the Ahasverus pamphlet means that identifying the original author and publisher of the legend requires starting here. N^2 is significant inasmuch as the printer changed the imprint from "printed in Leyden by Christoph Creutzer" to "printed in Bautzen by Wolffgang Suchnach." The reason for this change is unknown. Neubaur noted that in both cases, we are dealing with false identities since no such printers are known to have worked in Leiden (in the Netherlands) or Bautzen (Saxony) in 1602.[10]

N^4 and N^{10} demonstrate an evolution in the visual representation of Ahasverus. In N^4, Ahasverus is depicted as a typical Jew (note the typical Jewish hat and the round Jewish badge), but by the time we arrive at N^{10}, the image of Ahasverus lacks clear Jewish characteristics. Moreover, and as already mentioned, for the first time in the history of the pamphlet this edition of the Kurtze Beschreibung contains an author's name: Chrysostomus Dudulaeus Westphalus. Just like the respective names of the (pseudo) printers Christoph Creutzer of Leyden and Wolffgang Suchnach of Bautzen, there is no evidence that a person by that name ever lived. As several scholars have already noted, "dudeln" means mumbling or humming (a tune) in German. As in so many other instances recounted in this book—Ben Shoushan/Chouchani and Mendele Mokher Sefarim immediately come to mind—Dudulaeus, in all likelihood, is a playful pseudonym.[11]

———

Neubaur's achievements over a century ago are indisputable. Even scholars such as George K. Anderson, who wrote a very different book about the Wandering Jew in which he paid no attention at all to the Kurtze Beschreibung's physical aspects, sang his praises. And yet the many years Neubaur spent collecting, analyzing, and comparing different editions of the Kurtze Beschreibung did not yield a conclusive answer to the questions with which this chapter began. N^1 might have been the earliest edition of the pamphlet. But lacking an identifiable author or publisher, it leaves our investigation stuck at square one.

Luckily, some of the stylistic elements in the early editions of the Kurtze Beschreibung escaped even Leonhard Neubaur's meticulous attention. Neubaur knew, of course, that the first page of N^1 contains a quote from the Gospel of Matthew. This is the same quote discussed in the previous chapter, albeit briefly, in the context of the work of Johann Jacob Schudt. What Neubaur overlooked is that instead of the German word "nicht" (not), which is standard German today and was common in the early modern period to most German dialects, the biblical quote on the first page of N^1 uses the word "nit." (This would be corrected in later editions, for example, in N^4, as can be seen in figure 14.) This word is atypical to most German dialects but prevalent along the Rhine Valley, thus in Mainz, for instance, or farther upstream in Strasbourg.

The quote on the first page of N^1 is interesting for another reason, too. During the Reformation, Martin Luther famously translated both the Old Testament and the New Testament into German. By the time the Kurtze Beschreibung was published in 1602, Luther's translations had acquired an almost sacred status among Lutherans. All major Lutheran theologians of the day, including Dr. Paul von Eitzen, used only Luther's translation in their printed work. It is of note, therefore, that the translation used on the first page of N^1 is not by Luther's hand. The same is true with respect to Catholic translations of the Bible into German, of which, contrary to common belief, there were many both before and after the outbreak of the Reformation. The quote on the first page of the early editions of the Kurtze Beschreibung is demonstrably not from any of these Bible translations. By process of elimination, one can posit that the cited passage is likely from an unknown Reformed (Calvinist) edition, or perhaps the work of the chapbook's author. Either way, one can be reasonably confident that the author of N^1 was neither a strict Orthodox Lutheran nor a Roman Catholic.[12] It is also not unreasonable to assume, albeit with the necessary caution, that he might have come from the Rhine Valley ("nit" instead of "nicht").

Curiously, there is also the following discovery, unknown to Neubaur. The chapbook's anonymous author claims that Paul von Eitzen came to believe in the story that the Jew Ahasverus told him in a Hamburg church, but he adds that he remains uncertain in his judgment (a word N^1 spells in Latin, "*iudicium*"). An early modern reader of one of the earliest known copies of the Kurtze Beschreibung documented his strong objection to this claim. In the margin of the first page of his copy (now housed in the library of Bamberg University in Germany), this unknown reader expressed his conviction that the story the chapbook recounted was a malicious fabrication: "*Est mendacium, meo Iudicio*"—"In my *iudicium*, it is a lie."[13] (See figure 16.) This negative assessment by an educated (because

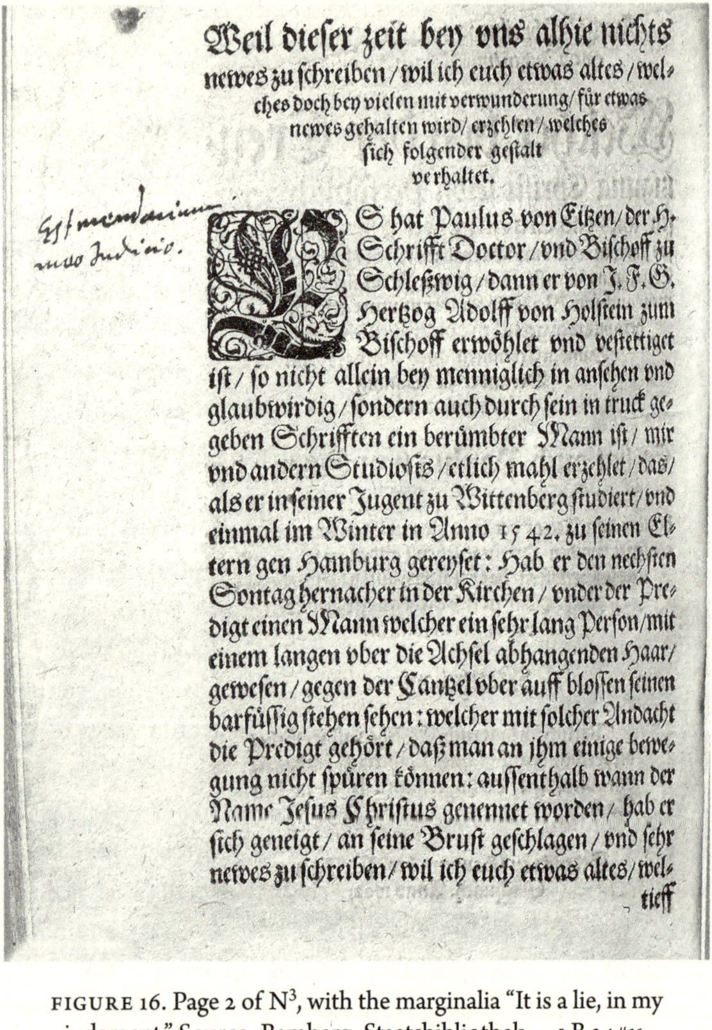

Weil dieſer zeit bey vns alhie nichts
newes zu ſchreiben / wil ich euch etwas altes / welches doch bey vielen mit verwunderung / für etwas
newes gehalten wird / erzehlen / welches
ſich folgender geſtalt
verhaltet.

Eſt mendacium
meo Iudicio.

ES hat Paulus von Eiten / der H.
Schrifft Doctor / vnd Biſchoff zu
Schleßwig / dann er von J. F. G.
Hertzog Adolff von Holſtein zum
Biſchoff erwöhlet vnd veſtettiget
iſt / ſo nicht allein bey menniglich in anſehen vnd
glaubwirdig / ſondern auch durch ſein in truck gegeben Schrifften ein berümbter Mann iſt / mir
vnd andern Studioſis / etlich mahl erzehlet / das /
als er in ſeiner Jugent zu Wittenberg ſtudiert / vnd
einmal im Winter in Anno 1542. zu ſeinen El-
tern gen Hamburg gereyſet : Hab er den nechſten
Sontag hernacher in der Kirchen / vnder der Predigt einen Mann welcher ein ſehr lang Perſon / mit
einem langen vber die Achſel abhangenden Haar /
geweſen / gegen der Cantzel vber auff bloſſen ſeinen
barfüſſig ſtehen ſehen : welcher mit ſolcher Andacht
die Predigt gehört / daß man an ihm einige bewe-
gung nicht ſpüren können : auſſenthalb wann der
Name Jeſus Chriſtus genennet worden / hab er
ſich geneigt / an ſeine Bruſt geſchlagen / vnd ſehr
newes zu ſchreiben / wil ich euch etwas altes / wel-
tieff

FIGURE 16. Page 2 of N³, with the marginalia "It is a lie, in my judgment." Source: Bamberg, Staatsbibliothek—.5 B 24#11.

Latin-speaking) reader is significant. As Johann Jacob Schudt would demonstrate a century after the publication of the first Ahasverus pamphlet, practically every Lutheran scholar dismissed the historical credibility of the Kurtze Beschreibung out of hand.

———

Leonhard Neubaur pointed out that the two earliest editions of the Kurtze Beschreibung (N^1 and N^2, respectively) are almost indistinguishable. Indeed, they are typographically identical but for two minute details: a changed spelling of a single word on page eight ("Zweyer" in N^1 is misspelled "Zcheyer" in N^2), and their respective imprints (Christoff Creutzer of Leyden in N^1, Wolffgang Suchnach from Bautzen in N^2).[14]

Buried in Neubaur's earliest treatment of the legend of the Wandering Jew is an even bolder claim about the two earliest editions. The two are so similar, Neubaur argues, that "they must have been printed with the same letters."[15] Neubaur was certainly correct, as a comparison between N^1 and N^2, on the one hand, and N^4, on the other, reveals. (See figure 1, chapter 1, and figures 12 and14.) N^1 and N^2 were printed in the same workshop, by the same printer, and with the same tools. They are not two separate editions at all, but a split edition: the workers began printing the pamphlet with one imprint and one spelling of the word "Zweyer," then stopped to change the imprint and the spelling before locking the printing frame into place again and printing the other copies.

One might ask which of the two imprints came earlier: did the printers start with the name Creutzer (N^1) and switch to Suchnach (N^2), as Neubaur assumed, or did they print this split edition in the reverse order? Logic dictates that there's no

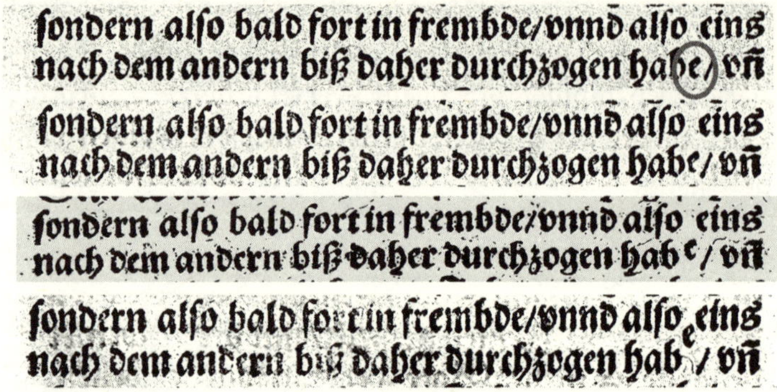

sondern also bald fort in frembde/vnnd also eins
nach dem andern biß daher durchzogen habe/vñ

sondern also bald fort in frembde/vnnd also eins
nach dem andern biß daher durchzogen habe/vñ

sondern also bald fort in frembde/vnnd also eins
nach dem andern biß daher durchzogen hab e/vñ

sondern also bald fort in frembde/vnnd also eins
nach dem andern biß daher durchzogen hab e/vñ

FIGURE 17. The movement of the letter "e" (bottom line, penultimate word) on page 7 of the Kurtze Beschreibung. Sources, from top to bottom: Universitätsbibliothek Tübingen, Gh 732.4-OR (N^2 type); Württembergische Landesbibliothek Stuttgart, Kirch.G.qt.595 (N^2 type); Médiathèque protestante du Stift, Strasbourg, 17-1370/4 (N^2 type); Bayerische Staatsbibliothek München, Rar. 825 (N^1 type).

reason to change a correctly spelled word (N^1) to an incorrect spelling (N^2). Consequently, N^2 came before N^1. Another piece of evidence corroborates this hypothesis. On line twenty-three of the fifth page of N^1, the letter "e" appears above the line. (See figure 17.) This phenomenon happens when a particular type letter is not fully secured in the printing forme, and under the immense pressure of the printing press it loses its location and starts to wander. The original position of this letter can be seen in three separate copies of N^2. N^2 was consequently printed before N^1. Wolffgang Suchnach of Bautzen (N^2) was the first imprint our anonymous printer used, together with a misspelled "Zcheyer." During the printing process, the operation was halted at some point, "Zcheyer" (N^2) was corrected to "Zweyer" (N^1), and Suchnach (N^2) replaced by Creutzer (N^1). Otherwise, the two editions were printed by the same master printer, one after the other, possibly on the very same day.

These details might seem overly technical, but they do matter. The publication of the Kurtze Beschreibung was a milestone in the modern history of the legend of the Wandering Jew. Schudt interpreted it as an allegory about Judaism and the Jews, and later antisemites, including the Nazis, used the figure of Ahasverus in their hateful propaganda. It is understandable that scholars have understood the Ahasverus chapbook primarily through the lens of the long history of Christian anti-Judaism. As long as the first edition of the 1602 pamphlet bore the name Christoff Creutzer, this hypothesis seemed compelling. For native German speakers, the pseudonym Christoff Creutzer of Leyden evokes the passion of Christ: Kreutz means cross in German, and Leiden, though a very real city in the Netherlands, also means "suffering" in German. The pseudonym Christoff Creutzer in Leyden, which scholars assumed, following Neubaur, to be the original imprint of the Ahasverus chapbook, can be translated into German as "Christ of the Cross in Suffering." The Ahasverus chapbook seems to be about theology.[16]

Now that we know that N^2 came before N^1, the picture looks different. The name "Suchnach" in German comes closest to the English imperative "look for!" or "go inquire!" Translated into English, Wolffgang Suchnach approximates "Jack-go-figure," or perhaps, "Joe-go-and-find-out!" This command isn't dark or theological, but playful.[17] The strange and admittedly uncomfortable possibility raised by these technical details is that the Kurtze Beschreibung was not just a hastily put together, cheap, and perhaps deliberately mendacious description of a fictitious encounter between Paul von Eitzen and the Wandering Jew in 1542. Taken together, "the mumbler Westphalus," "Christoff Creutzer of Leyden," the strange name "Ahasverus," and especially the pseudonym, "Wolffgang Suchnach," suggest a certain

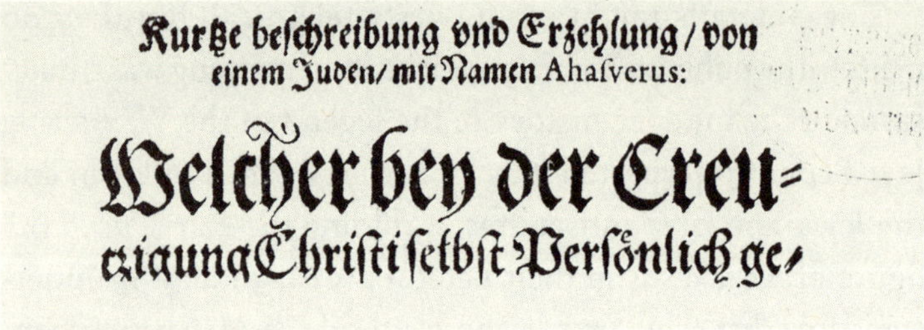

Kurße beschreibung vnd Erzehlung / von
einem Juden/ mit Namen Ahasverus:

Welcher bey der Creu=
tziaung Christi selbst Persönlich ge∕

FIGURE 18. Detail from the title page of the Kurtze Beschreibung ($N^{1/2}$). Note the damaged top arm of the letter "h," third line from the top. Source: Bayerische Staatsbibliothek München, Rar. 825.

light-heartedness and even humor on the part of our (Rhenish? Calvinist?) author.

But there is more. Unlike the name Christoff Creutzer, which does not appear on any known early modern print other than the Kurtze Beschreibung, the name Wolffgang Suchnach had appeared before 1602 in a book published by the printer Bernhard Jobin of Strasbourg—a city, we remember, where the word for "not" in the local dialect is "nit" and not "nicht."[18] Jobin's most famous author was the great German satirist Johann Fischart who not only dabbled in creating fake news stories but also invented the word for it that Germans still use today (*Geschichtsklitterung*, or "hodge-podge history"). Jobin died eight years before 1602, but one of his assistants, Martin Jost, was demonstrably the original publisher of the Kurtze Beschreibung. The smoking gun is once again a small technical detail: the first page of the split edition $N^{1/2}$ contains a capital H missing an arm. (See figure 18.) It is the product of a damaged cast metal piece used by the printer. (Compare an undamaged type of the same font in figure 19.) This same type can be seen in another work printed by Martin Jost, originally of Jobin's workshop, but by 1602, an independent printer in Strasbourg. (See figure 20.) The split edition $N^{1/2}$ was thus printed by Jost. We

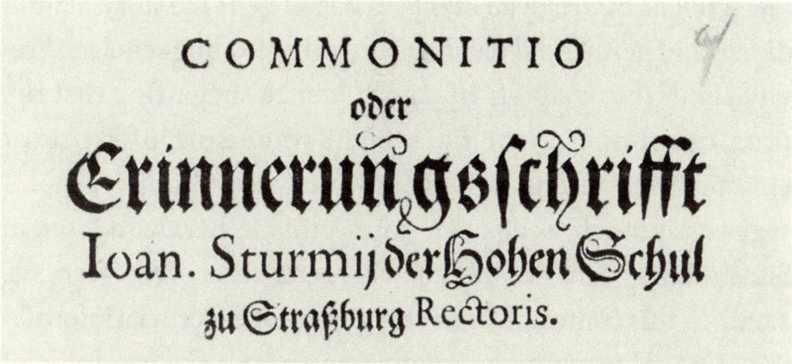

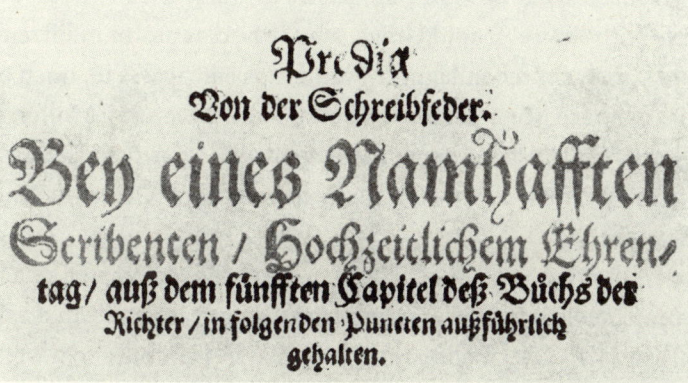

COMMONITIO
oder
Erinnerungsschrifft
Ioan. Sturmij der Hohen Schul
zu Straßburg Rectoris.

FIGURE 19. Detail from the title page of Johannes Sturm, *Commonitio oder Erinnerungsschrifft Ioan. Sturmij . . .* (1581). Note the undamaged "h" in line 3. Source: Bayerische Staatsbibliothek, 4 H.ref. 688.

Predia
Von der Schreibfeder.
Bey eines Nambafften
Scribenten / Hochzeitlichem Ehren-
tag / auß dem fünfften Capitel deß Büchs der
Richter / in folgenden Puncten außführlich
gehalten.

FIGURE 20. Detail from the title page of Thomas Birck, *Predig Von der Schreibfeder* (Straßburg: Martin Jost, 1594). Note the damaged "h" in line 3. Source: Bayerische Staatsbibliothek—Hom. 2086. m.

even know the street address: Strasbourg's Vieux-Marché-aux-Grains, not far from the city's famous cathedral.

———

Considering the importance of the Kurtze Beschreibung for the history of the legend of the Wandering Jew, it is surprising that few scholars have delved into Paul von Eitzen's life story. Schudt didn't, and neither did Neubaur and other leading scholars. Previously in this chapter, we saw evidence suggesting that the 1602 chapbook might have been some sort of satire or Geschichtsklitterung—the name Suchnach ("look for me!") suggests as much, as does the connection to Bernhard Jobin in Strasbourg and the common Jewish perception of Ahasverus as a fool. In this context, Eitzen's biography offers crucial information. Other literary forms might comment on the condition of humanity in a general manner, but satire, almost by definition, takes concrete situations and people as its subject.

There are only two archive-based biographical accounts of Eitzen, both dating to the eighteenth century. Their two respective authors are Arnold Greve, who served as pastor in Eitzen's old parish church in Hamburg and thus had access to much of his predecessor's correspondence; and Johannes Moller, a German–Danish Lutheran theologian with a particular interest in the history of Lutheranism in northern Germany and Scandinavia.[19]

In many ways, Moller's and Greve's respective works are complementary: Greve writes at great length about the first half of Paul von Eitzen's life, from his birth in Hamburg to a well-established family in the early 1520s, through his formative years in Wittenberg and early career in Hamburg, to his decision to leave the city of his birth in 1562 and move to the Danish province of Schleswig. Where Greve leaves off, Moller takes up the story. He covers the second half of Eitzen's life, when the protagonist of the Kurtze Beschreibung served as the general superintendent (Lutheran bishop) of Schleswig. Significantly, both Greve and Moller categorically reject the plausibility of the Ahasverus story. The German–Danish Moller minces no words in condemning the 1602 chapbook, claiming that

Ahasverus was an impostor or a figment of someone's frantic imagination. "The emptiness (*vanitas*) of this most obscene tale is such that it is not even worth refuting,"[20] he writes. Arnold Greve agrees with this damning judgment but uses different tactics. Although he undoubtedly knew about the Ahasverus legend (not least because Moller shared a complete draft of his Eitzen biography with him before publishing it),[21] Greve decided to completely ignore the Kurtze Beschreibung in his detailed description of Paul von Eitzen's Hamburg career. It's as if, facing a piece of "fake news," the two authors used opposite strategies: Moller went low, attacking the anonymous author with vitriol, while Greve went high, deciding not to engage with him in the first place.

During his long career as a Lutheran pastor and superintendent, Eitzen published several works on theology. Dozens of his personal letters are still extent. Together with the works of Greve and Moller, these materials help us paint the general outlines of his biography against the backdrop of sixteenth-century German Lutheranism.[22] Eitzen was born in Hamburg in 1521, or perhaps a year later, and spent his childhood and youth in the city of his birth. This location matters: sixteenth-century Hamburg was a flourishing trade center and one of Northern Europe's most important cities. Located on the banks of the River Elbe, it dominated commerce between much of Central and Northern Germany, on the one hand, and the Baltic Sea basin, on the other. Indeed, because Luther spent almost his whole adult life in Wittenberg, and because Wittenberg was located on the banks of the Elbe (though farther upstream than Hamburg), many of the Saxon reformer's ideas traveled northward quite literally by way of the Elbe and Hamburg. Thus, when Catholics sought a disparaging nickname for Luther, they often called him "the Elbe Pope"[23]—the joke, of course, being that Luther equated the Pope with the Antichrist.

After attending gymnasium in Hamburg, in 1538, Eitzen traveled up the river to Wittenberg, where he studied theology under Luther's close associate and friend, Philipp Melanchthon. When Eitzen arrived in the small university town, the Reformation movement was about twenty years old and its figurehead, Martin Luther, still very much among the living. The prominent place of Melanchthon in Luther's intimate circle of friends and the university's modest size make it certain that Eitzen knew Luther and many of his associates in person. The same is also true for Eitzen's connections to Melanchthon's other students, who all spent time (and occasionally even resided) in their teacher's elegant three-story house next to the main university lecture halls.

Twenty years before Eitzen's arrival in Wittenberg, Luther published his famous ninety-five theses in this very town, and his message soon spread throughout German-speaking Europe. That Luther was so successful in so many places was due in no small part to the Saxon reformer's astonishing skill at using the novel medium of print—a hallmark of Reformation propaganda—but there was also, and not least, the content of his evangelical theology. Luther believed that man's salvation depended on the grace of God alone, and he criticized the Roman Church for claiming that human beings could exert any influence on it through individual actions ("good works"). The problem with the papacy, Luther insisted, was the novelties it introduced to Christian worship over the centuries. "The Romanists have built, with great skill, three walls with which they have so far protected themselves," he explains in a famous tract he published in 1520, "so that no one could reform them, whereby all Christendom has fallen terribly."[24]

Next to personal faith and the centrality of God's grace and grace alone, a third and most important article of faith for Luther was God's word as expressed in Scripture. This was the decisive issue Luther defended in the famous Diet of Worms (1521), and which almost cost him his life. Additions to Scripture or innovative interpretations thereof Luther found scandalous. Christians had to return to the original, uncorrupted meaning of Christ's message. What the Bible plainly stated and not what the medieval doctors of the Catholic Church claimed it did—only this had to be the basis for a reformed, evangelical community of believers.

From the biographies by Greve and Moller, we know that Paul von Eitzen had always been a staunch supporter of Luther's ideas. Indeed, we know that he often chastised others (including, at one point, even his very own Wittenberg professor, Philipp Melanchthon) for not being Lutheran enough. Against this backdrop, two curious aspects of the Kurtze Beschreibung stand out: first, as previously mentioned, the chapbook's anonymous author did not use Luther's translation of the Bible in composing the chapbook; and second, the Kurtze Beschreibung ascribes to Eitzen a theological position that is diametrically opposed to one of Luther's most cherished beliefs. According to the 1602 chapbook, a Jew persuaded Paul von Eitzen of the truthfulness of a fantastical story by reporting various incidents from Christ's Passion that "neither the evangelists nor historians relate."[25] When read against the life story of Paul of Eitzen, this passage cries out with mocking irony: it puts words in Eitzen's mouth that he could never have uttered himself.

Neither Greve nor Moller tell us how long the young Paul von Eitzen stayed in Wittenberg. What is clear from Eitzen's extant correspondence and the two eighteenth-century biographies is that in 1543, he took a job as a didactics teacher at a Berlin gymnasium,[26] that a few years later he moved to a similar job farther north in the city of Rostock, and that he found his way back to Hamburg after a couple of years, first working as a pastor in a local parish church, and then serving in the local cathedral chapter before assuming the position of superintendent for all religious affairs in the city.[27] Six years after reaching this exalted position, Paul von Eitzen was offered the job of general superintendent in the neighboring Danish province of Schleswig and left Hamburg. In Schleswig, Eitzen became entangled in several theological disputes (more about them momentarily), but also spent time on more mundane tasks such as the reorganization of church bureaucracy and the founding of a local Latin school where he later taught. Some editions of the Kurtze Beschreibung open with a frame story that identifies the pamphlet's author as one of Eitzen's students. ("Paul von Eitzen, doctor of Holy Scripture and Bishop of Schleswig . . . on many occasions told us and other students that in his youth, when he was studying in Wittenberg . . .")[28] Whether this was true we do not know. What is clear is that the pamphlet's author had some familiarity with the story of Paul von Eitzen's life.

As general superintendent of Schleswig, Eitzen had a long, interesting career, not every aspect of which is relevant to the present investigation.[29] Like all Lutheran pastors, Eitzen preached on a regular basis; preaching was at the heart of his pastoral mission above his other occupations and responsibilities. Late in life, Eitzen collected some of his favorite sermons and published them in a book for the public's use and edification.

Literary scholars of the Wandering Jew long ago identified two seemingly related biblical passages. The first is a passage we have already encountered twice. Taken from the Gospel of Matthew, it is quoted on the first page of the Kurtze Beschreibung: "Verily I say unto you, There be some standing here, which shall not taste of death, till they see the Son of man coming in his kingdom." The second is a verse from the Gospel of John: "If I will that he [John] tarry till I come, what is that to thee?" (John 21:22). It is interesting to note, then, that Paul von Eitzen included a short sermon about the latter verse in his sermon collection, but that here, too, there is no reference whatsoever to the story of the Wandering Jew.[30] Schudt was right: there is no evidence that Eitzen ever said in fact what is attributed to him in the Kurtze Beschreibung.

One final and key observation about Paul von Eitzen's curriculum vitae is in order here because it elucidates a crucial aspect of the Kurtze Beschreibung that left previous scholars of the case completely in the dark. From N[10] onward, copies of the Ahasverus pamphlet name Chrysostomos Dudulaeus ("the mumbler") Westphalus as their author. Until now, no one has been able to explain why.

The key to solving the riddle is to be found in Eitzen's biography. After leaving for Schleswig in 1562, Eitzen's successor as superintendent in Hamburg was Joachim Westphal (in Latin: Joachimus Westphalus). Westphal was one of the fiercest Lutheran critics of John Calvin in the second half of the sixteenth century and indeed the man who gave the derogatory nickname "Calvinists" to followers of Calvin. (It was derogatory because it made them look like a personality cult instead of a serious evangelical movement.) Chrysostomos literally means "golden mouth" in Greek, and Dudulaeus seems to be related to humming or mumbling. "Gold-mouth, mumbling Westphalus" should consequently be read as a derogatory *and humorous* description of Joachim Westphal. Indeed, the visual representation on the first page of N^{10} might very well be of Westphal and not Ahasverus. (Compare figures 3 and 4.) This would explain, for instance, why the figure has no recognizably Jewish characteristics, unlike the image on N^4.

———

As pastor and superintendent in Hamburg (starting in 1548) and later as general superintendent of Schleswig (after 1562), Paul von Eitzen made himself a long list of enemies. The evidence suggests that they were predominantly Protestant, not Catholic; some were Lutheran, others Calvinist.

Ever since the outbreak of the Reformation in 1517, theological disagreements and personal disputes were as common within the reform movement as they were between reformers and Catholics. Part of the issue was structural. Opposing the papacy in the first half of the sixteenth century was not an organized church but a loose movement with no official head (not even Luther) and few disciplinary mechanisms. This movement consisted of a superabundance of groups, subgroups, and sects, including Wittenbergians (as Luther's strict followers were commonly known in the sixteenth century), Sacramentarians (Zwinglians), Karlstadtians, Sabbatarians, Anabaptists, Oecolampadians, Schwenkfelders, Osianderists, Majorists, Picards (Hussites), and many others, with or without distinct names. Disagreements between these factions revolved around many points of faith, foremost among them, the Eucharist. As one recent study emphasizes, the issue of the Eucharist was of cardinal importance to sixteenth-century theological debates because it revolved around a series of fundamental relationships that defined Christians as such: "between their persons and Christ; between objects of the mundane world and God; and among what they did in worship, their faith, and God Incarnate."[31] At stake in the Eucharist, in other words, was salvation itself.

By the sheer force of his charismatic personality, Luther managed to hold large parts of the reform movement together after 1517. When he died in 1546, however, and especially after the promulgation two years later of an imperial religious law known as the Interim, internal fissures within the Saxon Reform party multiplied. The Interim's aim was to re-Catholicize central Europe, a feat deemed possible in the late 1540s because Protestantism had just suffered a devastating military defeat at the hand of the Catholics. Lutherans reacted to this pressure in one of two ways. On one side were supporters of Philipp Melanchthon, Luther's successor in Wittenberg (and Eitzen's—as well as Westphal's—old teacher), who in the wake of the Interim were willing to make tactical concessions in their quest for religious peace. On the other side stood Luther's more radical followers, who feared a dilution of their dead teacher's evangelical message and vowed to continue a stubborn fight for their beliefs. Who belonged to which of these two camps within Lutheranism was not always clear, and these positions became even more complex when adherents of John Calvin of Geneva entered the picture. (Calvin's theology diverged from Luther's in many fundamental respects, but his conception of the Eucharist was not far from that of Philipp Melanchthon.) Still, the analytical distinction is valid: late sixteenth-century Lutheranism was marked by internal opposition between Philippists (followers of Philipp Melanchthon), on the one hand, and Gnesio-Lutherans ("authentic Lutherans"), on the other.

The fracturing of German Lutheranism into two opposing camps is important for the case of Ahasverus in Hamburg because Paul von Eitzen first made a name for himself as a Gnesio-Lutheran. In a series of documents, some published even when Luther was still alive, the Melanchthon party formulated deliberately vague doctrinal statements to allow different theological views to coexist within the wide tent of the reform movement. Gnesio-Lutherans such as Joachim Westphal, Paul von Eitzen, and especially the theologian Matthias Flacius attacked this conciliatory approach. All three had once been Philipp Melanchthon's students in Wittenberg. Flacius, who incidentally was familiar with Matthew Paris's version of the legend of the Wandering Jew, even taught in Wittenberg alongside Melanchthon for a while.[32] In the wake of the Interim, however, the students turned against their teacher, attacking his position on the nature of the Eucharist, free will, predestination, and the so-called *adiaphora* (what is essential to faith and what is not). So heated were these mid-sixteenth-century disagreements that Flacius and his followers called Philippists by a long list of derogatory names, including bedfellows of the pope, thieves, liars, and even murderers of Christ.[33] Melanchthon, on his part, did not remain idle either. He once wrote about Flacius that "we have nourished a snake in our midst."[34]

As attested by his extant letters to Melanchthon, Paul von Eitzen never used Flacius's offensive language against his old teacher,[35] and at one point, he and Westphal even traveled in person to Wittenberg aiming to reconcile the two parties. (When the surprised Melanchthon saw them at his doorstep, he became so agitated he almost had a heart attack.)[36] Moreover, although Eitzen and Westphal tried to carry out their dispute with Melanchthon in a polite manner, some in Melanchthon's camp pelted them with every conceivable insult, including in two satirical poems. The first claimed that Eitzen and Westphal simply "crawled from Flacius's ass,"[37] while the other, only slightly more nuanced, compared the Gnesio-Lutheran group as a whole to a flock of idiotic birds. Flacius, in this account, was literally a cuckoo, while Paul von Eitzen was an Eisvogel—common kingfisher—apparently because of the similarly sounding names (Ei-tzen, Eis-vogel) and because of the kingfisher's small head.[38]

Such satirical descriptions might make us smile, but for contemporaries, they were more than merely laughing matter. What was at stake in the Reformation was the question of salvation and, by extension, the necessity to fight anyone who jeopardized it. This was also true in the case of Paul von Eitzen's writings. Thus, the man who allegedly believed the fantastical story told by a Jew in a 1542 Hamburg church once wrote in a letter to Flacius that "it is undoubtedly true that these are the end of days about which it is written that many false apostles shall rise, leading many true believers astray."[39] Humor was one way of exposing and undermining aberrant beliefs; it wasn't incidental to the Reformation, but a quintessential part of it.

————

Eitzen confronted Philippists and other "false prophets" throughout his adult life, but these confrontations came to a head especially on two occasions. The first took place during a failed reconciliation attempt with Melanchthon, when attacks against Eitzen also occurred in Hamburg. "It is well known," an exasperated Eitzen wrote to the city council at the time, "that this good city is experiencing a growing and angry discord . . . which hinders the spread of the Gospel and which—God forbid!—might also lead to the corruption of our churches and government."[40] Eitzen conceded that he bore part of the blame for the escalating discourse, but the lack of support from the city council left him no choice: "It is better that I go from here than that I compromise my conscience."[41] As everyone knows, "I, among others, have been constantly attacked [*iniuriiret*] in a most scandalous way" by various preachers in the city, and though "they do not mention me by name, everyone with even a little intelligence knows immediately that I am the aim of their attacks."[42]

After Eitzen's move to Schleswig in 1562, the situation came to a head a second time. The cause was the so-called Formula of Concord of the 1570s: the last attempt in the sixteenth century to forge a doctrinal compromise on which all followers of Luther could agree.[43] "We must speak according to our conscience and disregard the authority of men," Eitzen writes in response to the Formula, "and we must say that some articles are set forth [in the Formula] in such confusion, and they are so defective, that we cannot regard and approve them as correct, clear, and plain."[44] The rejection of the Formula by Eitzen had wide-reaching consequences because as general superintendent of Schleswig, he stood particularly close to the Danish crown. Greve reports that "persuasions, exhortations, or arguments" were of no avail against Eitzen's determined position. "All the way up to his death, Eitzen made known that his mind was hostile as much toward the Formula of Concord as toward its authors."[45] Not only did Eitzen refrain from signing the Formula himself, but "he also claimed that errors were promulgated in it and persuaded others not to sign it. It is primarily though his agency that the Formula of Concord was not accepted in Holstein, Denmark, and beyond."[46]

———

If his Philippist enemies weren't enough, Eitzen also acquired a long list of Calvinist adversaries. It all started with the work

of Eitzen's colleague and friend, Joachim "the mumbler" Westphal. The latter, just like Eitzen, was a native of Hamburg, a
former Melanchthon student, a leading Gnesio-Lutheran, and
eventually also superintendent of Hamburg after Eitzen left the
city for Schleswig in 1562. Starting in 1552, Westphal published
a series of poignant ad hominem attacks against John Calvin
that were considered extreme even according to the standards
of the radical polemical language of the period. In his publications, Westphal questioned Calvin's conception of the Eucharist, ridiculed his alleged philosophical proclivities, and termed
Calvin's movement "Calvinism" for the very first time. "They
could attach us no greater insult than this word, Calvinism,"
Calvin himself once wrote about Westphal. "It is not hard to
guess where such a deadly hatred comes from that they hold
against me."[47] Moreover, and in what the reader will already
recognize as a typically Lutheran move, Westphal used satire in
his work, complete with the obligatory accompanying puns.
Calvin, for Westphal, was "the calf of Geneva," and his close
Swiss associate Heinrich Bullinger "the Bull of Zurich."[48] John
Calvin, usually cool and level-headed, did not remain calm in
the face of such personal attacks. He described Westphal and
his associates (including Eitzen) as "barbarous and tyrannical"
and found these characters to be "mere apes" of Luther.[49] "With
regard to Westphal and his followers," Calvin later admitted, "it
was difficult for me to control my temper."[50]

Eitzen did not keep out of the fray either, and in fact got involved in the dispute between John Calvin and Joachim Westphal early on. He faulted Calvin and "Calvinists" for their lack
of biblical literalism—a claim that Calvin of course vehemently
denied—and especially for what he perceived to be their use of
logic and abstract philosophy in interpreting Scripture. Eitzen
was under the erroneous impression that Calvin and his

followers deemed Christ's physical body a subject to the laws of physics. This is why, he believed, they rejected the idea that in the Eucharist, the body of Christ could be in more than one place at the same time.[51] Eitzen dismissed such notions out of hand. In 1518, Luther had already taught that faith is inherently paradoxical. "Although the works of humans always seem attractive and good," he opened one of his famous disputations, "they are nevertheless likely to be mortal sins; although the works of God are always unattractive and appear evil, they are nevertheless really eternal merits."[52] Many decades later, Eitzen reiterated the same point. The question, he opined, is not what philosophy or logic teach us, but what Holy Scripture states in no uncertain terms. In the things that look impossible to the human senses, the revealed word of Scripture remains inerrant. Thus, "many things in philosophy might seem most clear and evident, but in fact they are most wrong [*falsissima*] according to Christian theology."[53] Echoing those Church Fathers (like the second-century author Tertullian), who highlighted the incommensurability between faith and reason, Eitzen claimed that the Christian faith is not based on human thoughts, but on the grace of God alone. Calvin's (alleged) emphasis on science and logic was dangerous in his eyes. Philosophy might make sense in India, Eitzen summed up his position, "but in Germany no one would believe in that."[54]

Much in the way that satire played an important role in Philippist–Gnesio Lutheran disputes, the rhetorical war of attrition waged between Lutherans and Calvinists often involved irony, satire, and parody. Perhaps later Calvinists would lose their sense of humor; in the second half of the sixteenth century, that was certainly not yet the case. Alongside their sophisticated and indeed profound works of theology, late sixteenth-century Calvinists incessantly poked fun at their opponents.

The most important German-speaking satirist of the sixteenth century, Johann Fischart (whose publisher, we remember, was Bernhard Jobin of Strasbourg) came from their ranks. Fischart not only translated the French satirist François Rabelais into German but also published many original satirical pieces under various pseudonyms. The same is true in the case of Theodore Beza, Calvin's successor in Geneva and the most important Calvinist theologian of his generation. Beza wrote several biting satires targeting opponents of Calvin's movement, including one poem against the Jesuits he composed on his very death-bed, and two directed at Joachim Westphal, an old enemy. So deep was the personal enmity between Westphal and Beza that the former called the latter "a son of a priest's concubine," and the latter continued to calumny the former even after Westphal's death.[55]

This crash course in the history of sixteenth-century Protestant polemics isn't easy, but it is important for any understanding of the case of Ahasverus in Hamburg. It demonstrates that anonymous, mocking attacks against Paul von Eitzen, Joachim Westphal, and other sixteenth-century Lutheran theologians had taken place long before the 1602 Kurtze Beschreibung. Such attacks stemmed both from the heated Philippist–Gnesio Lutheran disputes of the second half of the century and from a nasty exchange of blows between Joachim Westphal, Paul von Eitzen, and their circle, on the one hand, and John Calvin and Theodor Beza, on the other.

The history of Protestant theology is important for the case of Ahasverus in Hamburg also because it helps us narrow the pool of potential authors for the 1602 chapbook. Our author was still alive in 1602, but since he recalled the fiery debates of the mid-sixteenth century, he must have also been rather old. Furthermore, although he could be Philippist or Calvinist, it is arguably more likely that the author of the Kurtze Beschreibung was one of John Calvin's German supporters. At least three pieces of evidence underpin this conjecture: (1) the biblical quotation on the first page of the Ahasverus chapbook, which is not by Luther's hand; (2) the works of Orthodox Lutherans that, as Schudt would later demonstrate, deemed the Ahasverus story absurd; and (3) the crucial role played by Joachim Westphal in the conflict with Calvin in the second half of the sixteenth century.

The reader will remember that the imprint of the first (split) edition of the Kurtze Beschreibung calls on its readers to "look for" or "search" for its creator in Bautzen ("Wolffgang Suchnach in Bautzen"). Who could it be, then? A very likely candidate is Caspar Peucer (1525–1602). Peucer was a mathematician, astrologer, and physician who studied in Wittenberg alongside Eitzen and Westphal, married Philipp Melanchthon's daughter Magdalena in 1550, and later served as professor and even rector of the University of Wittenberg. At one point in his life, Peucer seems to have clandestinely converted to Calvinism, which led to accusations against him that landed him in a Saxon prison for twelve years. After his release and for the rest of his life, Peucer authored many works (including satirical ones) and corresponded with followers of Calvin in Germany and elsewhere. He died in September 1602, just in time for us to consider him a possible author of the Kurtze Beschreibung.

What makes Peucer such a good candidate for the authorship of the 1602 pamphlet are several considerations. Peucer possessed the knowledge to write the Kurtze Beschreibung—he knew Eitzen and Westphal in person—as well as experience in satirical writing. Because of his long incarceration, Peucer also had a strong motive to calumny his Lutheran enemies, and since they were all dead by 1602, there was no one left to fight him back. Finally, Peucer was born in Bautzen and indeed was his native city's most famous son at the time of the publication of the 1602 pamphlet. For all these reasons and then some, the name Caspar Peucer might very well be the answer to the imperative "look for [me] in Bautzen," which appears in the imprint of the earliest edition of the pamphlet about the Wandering Jew.

———

This chapter began by reminding the reader of the content of the 1602 pamphlet and continued with an examination, respectively, of the physical copies of the Kurtze Beschreibung, its text, and the life story of its main protagonist, Paul von Eitzen. These steps helped us identify the print shop that produced the earliest (split) edition of the Kurtze Beschreibung and develop the hypothesis that the pamphlet was originally meant as a satire or Geschichtsklitterung against Paul von Eitzen and his circle of Gnesio-Lutherans by a Calvinist author. The biblical quote on the first page of the pamphlet, the pseudonyms Suchnach ("look for!"), Creutzer, and Christoff Dudulaeus Westphalus; the connection of the Strasbourg publishing house to Fischart and Geschichtsklitterung; and the unflattering depiction of a gullible Paul von Eitzen who believes in a theologically nonsensical story told by a Jew all point in the same direction. The 1602 chapbook was originally a work of sixteenth-century confessional satire (also known as Grobianism, after one of its famous practitioners), not a dark or even particularly anti-Jewish Romantic piece about Judaism per se (Schudt).

But what about Ahasverus? Why this name, and why in conjunction with Eitzen, Westphal, or Hamburg? If the Kurtze Beschreibung is a satirical work, who or what is being ridiculed in the figure of Ahasverus?

If the argument this chapter has advanced so far is true, it stands to reason that like Eitzen and Westphal, Ahasverus is more than a mere symbol. His name might be a reference to a real person. If so, we already have a police-like profile of him: Ahasverus studied in Wittenberg (he "spoke Saxon like a native"—that is, Luther's language, literally and figuratively); he was a man of the generation of Eitzen and Westphal, and just like them, was a Gnesio-Lutheran; he was a well-known opponent of Calvinism, thus attracting the ire of the pamphlet's author; he was particularly tall; and something about his behavior and perhaps his very name would make the reference to Ahasverus (an anagram?) obvious to people who knew him. This last point is crucial: the point of writing is to communicate a message to an audience. Our anonymous author must have provided his readers with enough clues to figure out for themselves (Suchnach!) both what he meant by composing the Kurtze Beschreibung and who he was. A century earlier, Luther made this point when discussing an anonymous ad hominem attack he had authored. "I made it so that I would be recognized. And whoever reads it and has ever seen my thoughts or quill will have to say, 'This is Luther!' "⁵⁶ Eitzen, too, participated in this game. About his detractors, we remember, he once said that "they do not mention me by name, but anyone with even a little intelligence knows immediately that I am the aim of the attacks."⁵⁷

The group of major figures in the Gnesio-Lutheran movement of the late sixteenth century isn't large. It includes, among others, Matthias Flacius, the man "from whose ass Eitzen crawled." If Ahasverus is a reference to Flacius, it is not immediately clear why this name was assigned to him, or why he was portrayed in this particular manner. The group of potential suspects also includes Johannes Aepinius who was, like Eitzen and

Westphal, superintendent of Hamburg. Other Gnesio-
Lutherans come to mind: Nikolaus von Amsdorf; Kaspar
Aquila; Nikolaus Gallus; Tilemann Heshusius; Simon Mu-
saeus; Johann Wigand; and others.

Even on the basis of their names alone, one person in this
group stands out as a likely candidate for Ahasverus's role.

————

The most rabid anti-Calvinist Lutheran of the second half of the
sixteenth century was Tilemann Heshusius (pronounced Hess-
HOU-syus). Originally from the Rhineland, Heshusius spent
time studying under Melanchthon in Wittenberg before em-
barking on an ecclesiastical career that took him to many places
and earned him an especially long list of confessional enemies.
Like the description of Ahasverus in the Kurtze Beschreibung,
Heshusius was especially tall, donned long dark clothes, and
wore his hair long. Theodor Beza, Calvin's lieutenant and future
successor, describes Heshusius in 1561 thus: "he is thirty-four
years of age, tall, thin, jaundiced, with a quick and angry temper,
full of arrogance, impertinent, pompous, and vain, stubborn
and obstinate above and beyond all reason in his [theological]
claims."[58] A contemporary portrait corroborates at least some
aspects of this description. (See figure 21.)

A leading historian of the Reformation maintains that Heshusius "set himself apart from other Lutheran preachers" in his
lenient attitude toward Jews.[59] He was also known as the author
of a book on why the Jews blaspheme the name of Christ in
their prayers.[60] A passage in the Kurtze Beschreibung, where
Ahasverus is described "beating on his breast" and "sighing very
deeply" whenever Christ's name is mentioned seems like an
allusion to Heshusius's book.

FIGURE 21. Tilemann Heshusius. Source: Hans
Haase and Günter Schöne, Die Universität
Helmstedt 1576–1810. *Bilder aus ihrer Geschichte*
(Bremen: Jacobi-Verlag, 1976), 45.

In his description of Heshusius, Theodore Beza portrayed
him as particularly unpleasant. Indeed, he often made fun of
him, including in a little treatise with the not-so-subtle title *The
Ass Logician* (1561), which calls Heshusius a buffoon and a
dunce, before addressing him directly with the words "tu
manebis asinus per omnia secula seculorum" ("You shall remain an ass for all eternity").[61] Heshusius, on his part, did not
refrain from similar tactics, calling the reformed theologian
Wilhelm Klebitz, "Kleinwitz" (simpleton) on one occasion, for
instance.[62] Little wonder, then, that the man who served as the
main object of ridicule in the Kurtze Beschreibung was chased

from place to place throughout his adult life: chased from the city of Goslar and chased from Rostock, chased from Magdeburg and from Heidelberg, chased away from Jena, and shown the door at the distant East Prussian city of Königsberg, before finding a temporary haven in Zweibrücken, which he eventually was asked to leave as well. His life was truly one of unceasing wanderings. Heshusius's last domicile was the Lower Saxon town of Helmstedt, where he died in 1587. On his Helmstadt gravestone, one can still read these words:

> The most venerable and famous man Tilemann Heshusius, Doctor of Holy Theology, died peacefully and in firm faith at the age of sixty years and eight months on September 25th in the year of our Lord 1589, after glorifying Christ through the preaching of pure doctrine over a period of thirty-five years, in eight different churches and schools, and suffering seven times a hard exile. He held the rank of professor primarius at this university for eleven years.[63]

A nineteenth-century biography, *The Seven Exiles of Tilemann Heshusius*, confirms and expands on the gravestone inscription which is itself unique among all similar Reformation monuments in its emphasis on exile.[64] Tall, peripatetic, and always dressed in his long, dark robes, Tilemann Heshusius acquired many enemies. He knew Eitzen in person and was very close to Joachim Westphal. Like so many of his contemporary Lutherans, Heshusius turned against his old Wittenberg teacher Melanchthon after the latter had allegedly grown too soft on doctrine, but he also had a nasty falling out with Matthias Flacius, whom he attacked repeatedly both in person and in his books. Most important, perhaps, are Heshusius's many anti-Calvinist campaigns. John Calvin knew Heshusius well, as did Calvin's successor in Geneva, Theodore Beza. The latter's surviving correspondence, for instance, mentions Heshusius's name many dozens of times, and almost always in a most denigrating fashion.[65]

Alongside Paul von Eitzen and Joachim Westphal, Tilemann Heshusius was an ideal person to ridicule in the anti-Lutheran, Calvinist piece of fake news known as the Kurtze Beschreibung.

––––––––––

Scholars like to speak about the Kurtze Beschreibung in abstract, disembodied terms. They claim that it was an expression of the spirit of the Reformation age, or perhaps even an allegory about the general fate of humanity. Such approaches to the history of the 1602 pamphlet gloss over the fact that like all printed materials before or since, the Kurtze Beschreibung began its life as a physical object, authored by an actual person and fashioned by very real artisans. Parts of its story are now clear for the first time: the original printing in Jost's shop in Strasbourg, or the way the print workers changed the imprint on the first page midway through the process. This chapter also shed light on the reasons for the names Suchnach and Westphalus, on the genre—Geschichtsklitterung—and on the probable connection to Caspar Peucer of Bautzen and especially Tilemann Heshusius of Helmstedt. In a manner typical of the Reformation, Heshusius was accused of being "Jewish," though strictly speaking, he wasn't a Jew.[66] Like the links of a chain, none of these pieces of evidence can carry the weight of the entire argument. Together, however, they form what I hope the reader will agree is a powerful historical interpretation.

Habent sua fata libelli, quipped the ancients—books have their own fates or lives. Created as a kind of inside joke or piece of "fake news" in a specific, and to modern eyes all but completely obscure, anti-Lutheran context, in the years after its publication the Kurtze Beschreibung acquired a life of its own. Indeed, even while its first copies came hot off the printing press, Jost changed the imprint from the particular joke about "Suchnach in Bautzen" to the more generic (and theologically charged) "Christoff Creutzer in Leyden." From then down to the present day, the legend of Ahasverus became the subject of changing interpretations, including influential ones by Schudt and the Nazis, but also Jewish authors such as Abramovitch, Pinski, and even Chouchani/Ben Shoushan. No interpretation is ever completely stable because all readings are also misreadings: books change their readers, but readers also always change the way books are read. That the case of Ahasverus in Hamburg sheds light on the original, historical Ahasverus moment does not diminish in any way the power of later interpretations of the story of Ahasverus in Hamburg. Rather, it highlights the great creativity with which future writers and readers interpreted and reclaimed a story the origins of which have been largely hidden from view up to now.

5

I, Ahasverus (2025)

I'd become convinced in recent years that every narrative should include, within itself, the adventure of its own writing, what gives it form.

—ELENA FERRANTE[1]

MORE THAN four centuries after the original publication of the Kurtze Beschreibung, a Jewish scholar sits in his New Jersey home and browses old backup folders on his computer. He takes his time. Slowly but surely, he starts seeing a pattern emerging in what he reads. The image of the Wandering Jew is stamped, like a watermark, on much of his life.

It begins when he reads an excerpt from an old notebook, pathos-filled and a little humorous, or at least that is how it seems to him when he looks at it now. It read as follows:

> It is true what they say: I was born in Jerusalem. I also grew up in Jerusalem and went to school in Jerusalem, made life-long friends in Jerusalem, and acquired self-awareness there. I also got married in Jerusalem and saw self-proclaimed

messiahs in Jerusalem and witnessed the sufferings of others there. I no longer live in Jerusalem; it's been many lifetimes since I lived in the city of my birth. But on occasion I visit Jerusalem, and Jerusalem is constantly on my mind.

Most of the people I knew growing up in Jerusalem moved away or passed on. Family members, friends, classmates, and other acquaintances are also buried in Jerusalem. The physical city is much as I left it, with streets bearing old Jerusalemite names, houses baking in the hot Jerusalemite sun, and Jerusalemite street cats still licking their Jerusalemite paws on top of black Jerusalemite garbage bins filled with Jerusalemite trash. And yet a city is much more than the sum of its physical parts; above all else, it is a community of people. And so, returning to Jerusalem, it seems to me a desolate place. It is no longer the Jerusalem in which I remember growing up.

Other things people say about me are true as well: I have traveled a great deal. Too much, if you ask me. Across oceans and continents, visiting dozens of countries and cities, meeting people as many as the sand on the shore. I don't speak much but when I do, I converse in many languages. I know my history, including the life of Jesus and the Apostles, and of course the story of my own people, the Jews. I am often alone and almost always contemplative, and I feel an uncanny affinity to Germany and know much about its past. In just a few years, I'll turn fifty. I don't believe in God but I talk to him constantly. My favorite literary character is Goethe's Faust.

———

A second occurrence appears in an email he once sent to Veronika, a close German friend from the time he spent in

Munich. It's dated August 2001. "When I lived in Jerusalem," it begins,

> my two brothers and I used to ride the bus to school. Line 4, from the Beit Elisheva Community Center in the direction of Katamonim, better known as "hashkhuna" ("the hood"). I can easily conjure the scene: the doors open, and we climb up to enter the bus, handing the driver our multijourney ticket, which he punches with a handheld perforator. The three of us stumble toward the back, where two red benches, each with two seats, face each other. Cigarette smoke fills the air. Children jeer and shout in the background. My older brother cracks open a window. We sit down.
>
> When we arrive at the stop on Shimon Bar Yochai Street, near the bank, the three of us get off the bus and climb the steep stairs up the hill, toward the elementary school. A black gate, red bricks, water fountain, the pungent smell of urine, then more stairs, we say goodbye to one another, and I enter the classroom. Shalom Ariel and Nimrod, shalom Racheli and Noga. Here are also Dodani, Haim and Hezi, Eyal and Michal, Amir, Bentzi and Noah. The bell rings, and the teacher enters the classroom, asking us to open our Bibles and study a new chapter. Later, during recess, we play stanga (a version of soccer). We are typical Jewish-Israeli children with typical Jewish-Israeli names having typical Jewish-Israeli childhoods in the early 1980s.
>
> The school we attend had been established a few years earlier by an association of parents alarmed by the right-wing Likud Party's victory in the 1977 general elections. That was the first time something like this happened in the short history of the State of Israel. The country was founded by mostly left-wing (socialist) Eastern European Jews, but

following the disastrous Yom Kippur War of 1973, socialist-Ashkenazi hegemony was broken, the leader of the liberal-nationalist Likud party, Menachem Begin, formed a coalition government, and the ministry of education fell into the hands of a right-wing religious politician by the name of Zevulun Hammer.

Hammer's career was complex, and his political positions changed over time.[2] But in 1977, Hammer still exemplified to my parents and other founders of my elementary school the changes that the religious-Zionist movement Hapo'el Hamizrahi had undergone in the previous decade. No longer was the majority of religious Zionists politically and theologically dovish. On the contrary, many now espoused a messianic ideology, inspired by Rav Kook, that saw in the Jewish resettlement of areas occupied by Israel in the Six-Day War a sign for the coming of the Messiah. My parents and their social milieu vehemently rejected such an interpretation of modern Jewish history. Classical Zionism was pragmatic, not fundamentalist and certainly not messianic.

The political upheaval of 1977 threatened to turn the lives of people like my parents upside down. They fought it through education, at least in part. The school they helped found had two interrelated goals: educating children according to socialist-Zionist principles; and bringing children from stable Ashkenazi families to the difficult neighborhood in southern Jerusalem where the school was located. The idea was to foster social integration to help reconnect local inhabitants, most of whom were Likud supporters, to the Zionist labor movement.

As a child, my classmates seemed utterly ordinary. We played stanga at recess, got into fights and made up, and exchanged love letters with the girls in our class. Only in retrospect do I now recognize that as ordinary Jerusalemite kids, we had family histories that were all extraordinary. Our family names, palimpsest-like, bore witness to extended wanderings. Halevi and Cohen were the names of ancient Jewish tribes, Abudrahm and Shukron were typical of Jews from Morocco (and before that, Spain). Marvadian was Kurdish, Seton Jewish-Syrian, Orstav (originally Ostrovsky) Polish, Mintzker Lithuanian.

———

The connection the young boy has to the world beyond Jerusalem is limited, with the past mediated through spectral objects and rituals.

In third grade, he and his classmates had their annual fieldtrip to Tel Aviv. They first took a bus to the old train station in the German Colony neighborhood of Jerusalem, then boarded the train and started the slow descent down the mountain passes toward the coastal plain. Tel Aviv felt to them like a foreign country. Wasn't it funny that people there spoke Hebrew as well? They went to the skyscraper Migdal Shalom ("the tallest tower in the Middle East," the teacher said), where they viewed the gray city and blue sea from the observation deck before taking the elevator down to the Israeli Wax Museum. The figure of Herzl was on display, as were other Zionist leaders. But they were more attracted to foreign figures like Johnny Weissmuller in the role of Tarzan and Marie Antoinette next to the guillotine.

They returned to Jerusalem by bus, chatting, singing songs, and pulling pranks on the girls. Just before the final climb to Jerusalem, perched on a mountainside, they saw the deserted houses of the Arab village of Lifta, whose population was displaced during Israel's war of independence in 1948. It was an eerie sight. Lifta's houses, made of white limestone and with hollowed cavities where doors and windows used to be, reminded him of skulls and bones. He never said a word about this to anyone.

———

On other occasions they traveled in time. At nursery school and elementary school, they celebrated the Jewish holidays through reenactments. On Hanukkah they were the Maccabees, fighting their Greek oppressors; on Shavuot they dressed in white and pretended to bring grain offerings to the Jewish Temple. When they studied Genesis in Torah class in second grade, the teacher told them to "make tohuwabohu [chaos], like before the creation" (a direct quote from the class newsletter, 1983; see figure 22), so they turned the tables and chairs upside down and poured all the contents of their backpacks on the floor. Already as a three-year-old, he dressed up as King Ahasverus (figure 23), and in 1983, he and his classmates made a model of Ahasverus's palace in Shushan in their classroom, complete with the figures of Ahasverus, Esther, and the court Jew Mordechai. The party was over when two of their friends broke into the palace dressed as American cowboys. They shot at Ahasverus and Esther with their cap guns, then ran away, giggling.

Holocaust Remembrance Day they celebrated in a solemn mood, but the principle—acting out the past—was similar. They didn't simply study history; they revived and relived it. At eleven o'clock in the morning, they stood at attention as a two-minute siren brought the entire country to a halt. Later, during the school-wide ceremony, they sang songs. They were victims and fighters, survivors and prophets. They identified with

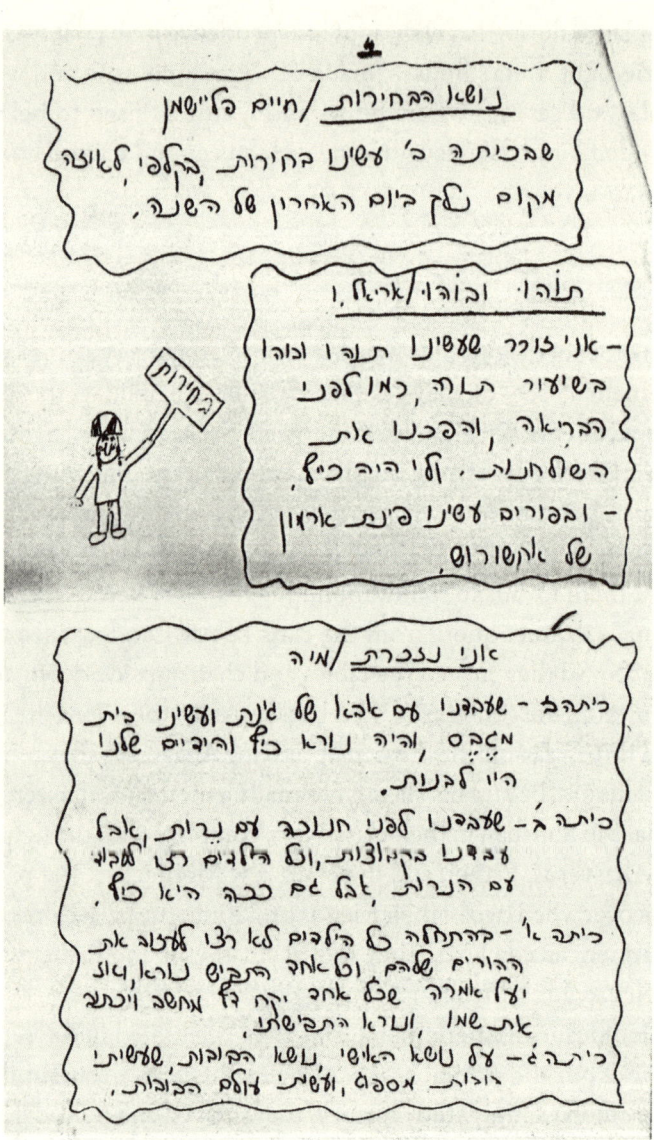

נושא הבחירות / חיים גליקסמן

שבכיתב ב' עשינו הבחירות, הקלפי לעזרה
אקום כך ביום האחרון של השבוע.

תודה! ובזבוז / אריאל ו.

- אני גוזר שעשינו תודה ובזבוז
  השיעור תודה, כאו לפני
  הבריאה, והבכנו את
  השלחנות . זה היה כיף.
- והבזורים עשינו כינט ארון
  של הינזורוט

אני נזכרת / אנה

כיתה ב - שהגענו עם אובול של כינה ועשינו בית
  מבבס, והיה נורא כיף והביבים שלנו
  היו לגענת.

כיתה ג - שהגענו לפני חנוכה עם נרות, ואובל
  ובפע גדולות, וכל הולכים רק לעבוד
  עם הנרות, וזה לא כבה היו כל.

כיתה ד - מהתחלה ה הילדים לא רצו לעבוד את
  הבזורים שלהם, וכל אחד הכין נורא, עוד
  ואז לאחר שכל אחד זכה יהה זה אחסה ויכתב
  את שאו, ונורא התפיסתי.

כיתה ה - אל נעשא האושי, נעשא הבזורות, עשיתי
  נודגה, אספם, ועשיתי יולא הבזורות.

FIGURE 23. The author dressed as King Ahasverus, ca. 1979.

Hanna Szenes, the Jewish poet from Mandatory Palestine who was parachuted into occupied Hungary only to be executed by the Nazis in November 1944. (Szenes's poem, "A Walk to Caesarea," has been part of almost every Israeli Holocaust remembrance ceremony ever since.) They blamed the world for not helping their murdered brothers and sisters by invoking the prophetic words of Mordechai Gebirtig who wrote about the looming disaster in 1936. ("Our town is burning . . . and you do not help!") They were partisans in the woods, singing the Hebrew version of the Yiddish fighting song *Zog nit keyn mol* ("Do not say this is your last way"): "Our promised hour shall soon come / our marching steps ring out: we are here!" Many years later, he will learn that this song was written in the Vilnius ghetto in May 1943, the same time and place where Dvorzhetski helped stage a version of Dovid Pinski's play *The Eternal Jew*.

———

On vacations and occasional weekends, the Mintzker family drove to Haifa in its Renault 4. The mother's parents, Dov and Sarah Langberg, lived there in a four-bedroom apartment atop Mount Carmel. To the child Yair, the elderly couple looked almost like twins. Both had Polish accents in Hebrew, both snow-white hair. He also knew that both had immigrated to Mandatory Palestine from the same shtetl in Poland, though to the best of his recollection they never mentioned it by name.

While a shared past brought the elderly couple together, silence about it kept them apart. The grandfather's silence about his family's history was made up of resignation and anger. After immigrating to Mandatory Palestine in 1921, this penniless shlemiel tried to reinvent himself as a productive laborer, working on construction projects in the north of the country. For several years, he saved his pennies to help the rest of his family join him in Palestine, but when he finally sent the money, they spent it on a vacation at the hot springs in Carlsbad. As far as the grandfather was concerned, he had done everything in his power to help his family escape Europe. That they perished in the Holocaust wasn't his fault.

The grandmother's story could not have been more different. True, she came from the same Polish shtetl, but her family owned a bakery on the town square, making them quite well off. Because the parents were busy running the family business, and because she was the family's eldest sibling, it fell primarily to her to tend to household chores and take care of her two younger sisters. She was particularly attached to her younger sister Manya, who she mostly raised by herself.

In 1934, when she was twenty-five, the grandmother met her future husband. He came from Palestine to visit his parents and fell in love with her almost at once. She was just so beautiful, talented, and intelligent. He wooed her, then asked her father for her hand in marriage, and the latter, at first reluctant, eventually caved. After the wedding, which the whole town attended, the couple traveled to Palestine, to raise a young new family there.

Four years later, Sarah made one last trip to Poland. The year was 1938, and she had a three-year-old toddler, Nira, to whom she wanted to introduce everyone in her hometown. It was spring now, Poland was verdant and beautiful, and the reunion with her family was wonderful in all respects but one. Manya, the little sister, decided that she too wanted to live in Palestine, but her father rejected the idea out of hand. "I had already lost one daughter to the Zionist movement," he reportedly told his two daughters, "if another one leaves me, my life is at end." There was kvetching in the house, then crying and shouting, to which the father responded by locking himself in his room. The two sisters eventually relented, and Manya stayed behind in the shtetl in Poland. The two sisters would never see each other again. Together with everyone else, Manya perished in the Holocaust.

Meanwhile, in Mandatory Palestine, life continued. The couple had two more daughters and later there would also be many grandchildren. Despite the tragedy that befell her family in Poland, the grandmother had much to be proud of, much to enjoy and even celebrate in this life. But instead of feeling elated, she was weighed down by her decision not to insist that Manya also leave Poland. The result was a deafening silence consisting of muted cries of guilt and anguish. It was a silence that defined her for the rest of her life.

———

Still a child and still in Jerusalem, Yair had dreams about traveling abroad. For many years, they did not materialize. Apart from a three-week journey to the Low Countries and France when he was three—his father was in Europe for professional reasons, so they joined him with some family friends for a trip up the Rhine—he did not leave Israel before turning eighteen. This was typical in his social milieu. In the 1970s and 1980s, Israel's precarious geopolitical position and continuous economic crisis made international travel difficult, if not impossible, for many families like his.

Following the 1948 War, Israel had only temporary ceasefire agreements with its Arab neighbors. There was no permanent peace. The country's main gateway to the world was its single international airport with its single terminal, not far from Tel Aviv. Even when Israel finally signed a peace treaty with an Arab country (Egypt, 1981), the peace was "cold." Few Israelis traveled to Egypt, and those who did put their lives at risk. The proof is a short booklet published by his school in late 1985. That year, his classmate Dina traveled to the Sinai Peninsula in Egypt with family friends. Near a place called Ras Bourka, an Egyptian soldier opened fire on them, killing Dina and six other travelers on the spot. After that, traveling to Egypt was no longer an option for most Israelis. As one of Dina's teachers wrote in the booklet: "I have never been to the Sinai, and now in Sinai I will never be. . . . I stretch my hands to hug you [Dina], but you are gone."[3]

No less decisive for his lack of international experience was the economic crisis that hit Israel in the early 1980s and rendered trips abroad too expensive for families like his. The roots of the economic crisis dated back to the expansion of the Israeli army following the 1973 Yom Kippur War and the populist policies pursued by the Begin government after it came to power in 1977. It was not until the late 1980s that the economy finally rebounded and ordinary Israelis could afford international travel.

Because so many Israelis couldn't travel internationally, the word *chutzla'aretz* ("abroad" in Hebrew) exerted almost magical power over him and his friends. Chutzla'aretz was Spain and its treasures, London with its Big Ben, Italy and its art collections, France, Belgium, and the Netherlands. It is curious to think about it now, but what chutzla'aretz usually meant for Jewish Israelis at the time was Western Europe and perhaps the East Coast of the United States. These were places with which Ashkenazi Jews had identified long before the founding of the State of Israel. A few decades of Zionism couldn't erase that.

There was another wrinkle in his fascination with chutzla'aretz. In the 1950s and 1960s, when Israel was still a young country, many had to travel abroad to pursue professions for which a course of study in Israel did not yet exist. Thus, his father learned architecture in Israel but later specialized in monument restoration in Italy and France, and his mother aspired to become a landscape architect, but without any options for study in her home country, spent more than six years learning landscape architecture in the Netherlands. Chutzla'aretz was a real place *and* an aspiration or a dream both in the lives of his parents and, as we shall see, also in his.

———

While reading about the stories of Ben Shoushan and Mendele, Schudt, and the anonymous author of the Kurtze Beschreibung, one might wonder about when each first heard of the legend of the Wandering Jew. In all four cases, we simply do not know; we have no access to that part of their respective biographies. Writing about one's own life, however, the situation is different. The memoirist has direct access both to private documents and, what is more, to his own memory.

The young me was then a student at a boarding school in Jerusalem, living in a dorm with several dozen students from across the country, Jews and non-Jews alike. (In his elementary and middle schools there were no Arab students.) The students were a group of smart but mostly self-absorbed individuals that included accomplished young musicians and artists, future scientists, and aspiring industry leaders, writers, and engineers. When he first set foot in the school in September 1990, all but one of his fellow students were complete strangers. The exception was another Jerusalemite kid. His name was Itai.

Tall, broad shouldered, and with his trademark curly hair, Itai's special talent was chemistry. He was so good at it that in tenth grade he already attended advanced chemistry courses at the university. In a cohort of competitive and often selfish kids, Itai was unusually generous, kind, and sensitive to his surroundings. His fascination with chemistry, he explained, stemmed from his realization that nature, though endlessly complex, could also be described by using relatively few mathematical formulae. How amazing was that? What is more, the study of science was a good metaphor for life, at least in Itai's view. All the forms of injustice he witnessed in Israel—most visibly, the plight of Palestinian Arabs—could be studied, Itai believed, and logically solved. If you understand how something works, you will also be able to fix it when it's broken. What was true in science and engineering was also true for social and political life.

Like so many other characters associated with the legend of the Wandering Jew—Chouchani and Abramovitch, Eitzen, Luther, and Schudt—both Itai and Yair were voracious readers. The latter read history, philosophy, classical literature, and works on religion, while Itai read books on chemistry, physics, and mathematics, but also the poems of Berthold Brecht, the novels of Franz Werfel, and Yerofeyev's *Moscow-Petushki*. Such important works and authors notwithstanding, during their shared high school years, the book Itai most admired was East German author Stefan Heym's novel on the Wandering Jew. The book, originally published in 1981 and translated into Hebrew two years later, was a wild mix of myth, history, and theology that revolved around Ahasverus's story. In Heym's rendering, Ahasverus is a fallen angel who, banished from heaven alongside Lucifer, never gives up on the idea of ameliorating the fate of an imperfect humanity.

The two boys' correspondence attests to the way they read Heym's novel for the first time. The way the novel seamlessly moves between mythical and historical time, and between different historical periods, they both found extraordinary. The novel contains conversations between Ahasverus, God, and Reb Joshua (Jesus), between Luther, Melanchthon, and Paul von Eitzen, and a long epistolary exchange between 1980s academics in Israel and East Germany. Because of the intensity of their academic environment, Itai and Yair were drawn to the academic aspects of Heym's story. They giggled at the imaginary correspondence between the Israeli professor Jochanan Leuchtentrager of the Hebrew University in Jerusalem and his East German colleague, Prof. Siegfried Beifuss of the Institute of Scientific Atheism in East Berlin. Another passage they both admired was the advice Lucifer gives to Paul von Eitzen on the eve of the latter's oral exam in theology: "you either know your answers when the time comes and they ask you or you don't know them, and your best bet is just to say something and keep on talking, your whole theology is but a lot of words, and any good quote from any authority will fill the bill."[4] It reminded the two boys of their own academic experience, for example, when they were asked obscure questions by their teachers in subjects like Bible studies or philosophy.

All these aspects of Heym's novel notwithstanding, the most arresting part, at least as far as the young Yair was concerned, was how closely the personality of Heym's fictional Ahasverus resembled that of the flesh-and-blood Itai. They both admired nature while challenging the justice of God's Creation, and they both, in the face of injustice, categorically refused to idly sit by. In a passage from Heym's novel that Itai later used in the school yearbook (figure 24), God and Ahasverus have the following exchange:

And again the voice rose and spoke: The world is full of wonders from morning to evening. Even a single molecule is

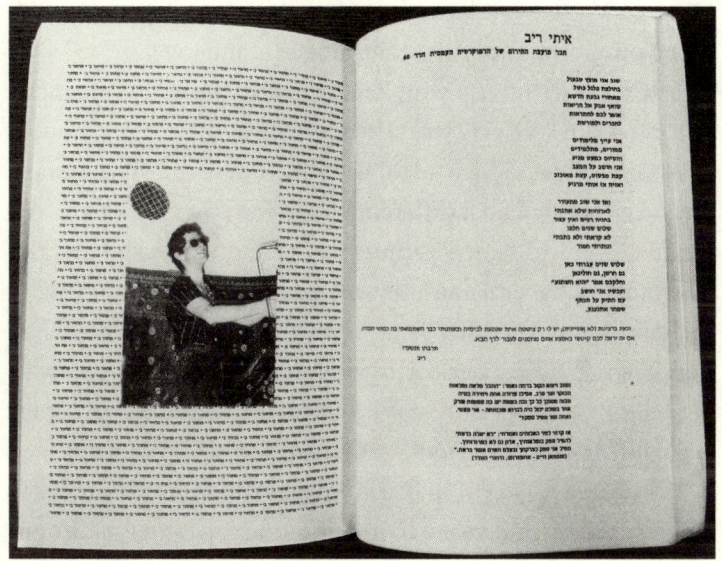

FIGURE 24. Itai's page in the yearbook, 1993.

structured in so complex a manner, while its idea is so ingenuously simple, that it could have only one creator, namely me. Seeing this, how can you still have doubts?

But I bowed down deeply before God and said: Far be it from me to doubt your miracles, O Lord, or your little molecules; my doubts concern your divine justice and the claim that man, whom you made, was actually created in your image.[5]

Nature and creation, molecules and the fate of humanity. Itai set the example, and his friend followed suit. He loved Itai, and because of him, learned to know and love the story of Ahasverus. This is the origin of his fascination with the story of the Wandering Jew.

One last word about Jerusalem, dear reader, and one last word, with your permission, about wanderings and love.

Just as his friendship with Itai deepened, the young me met a girl and fell in love. She was also a student at their high school in Jerusalem, and although all three of them were Ashkenazi Israeli Jews, her family had a different story from theirs. Born in the United States to Israeli parents in the late 1970s, she was the daughter of a classical musician who had moved to New York City to pursue her career. After living in the United States for more than a decade, the mother decided to move back to Israel, together with her reluctant husband and two young daughters. Despite her international success, the mother was still an ardent Zionist.

When he met her at high school, her family had been in the country for several years, living in a stunning three-bedroom apartment overlooking one of Tel Aviv's main squares. The apartment had that unmistakable air of chutzla'aretz he had always found so seductive. Stepping inside was like being transported to a foreign country. The place was filled with foreign art objects, books, and the constant background music of the mother playing the violin.

His infatuation with her was unrelenting. For the better part of a decade, they led a delicate if often painful romantic relationship mediated through literature and the arts. She read to him T. S. Eliot (Prufrock) and John Donne ("I wonder, by my troth . . ."), and he replied with Rilke's *Duino's Elegies* and an old Hebrew translation of *Faust*. She played Fauré's "Clair de lune" and Schumann's "Dichterliebe" on the piano, and he described to her his favorite paintings by Masaccio and Poussin. Not by accident, the motto they chose for their love story was taken from a work of literature: their relationship, they agreed, was "pure and complicated" (J. D. Salinger).[6] Fiction and reality, as always, were deeply, inexorably entwined.

When talking about their relationship, she used language that conflated literature and life just as often as he did. Unlike him, however, she was cognizant of the dangers. In particular, she accused him of putting her on a pedestal; of turning her, quite literally, into a work of art. "I have hands, you know," she writes in an early email (he was then dating another girl), "and legs and hips and lips. Have you ever noticed? No—hands and lips are things that only other girls have." Or this: "Do you think that I'm even a real person? Who gets up in the morning with disheveled hair and bad breath, stumbles down the hallway to the bathroom while scratching her butt, squinting at the world through eyes that have yet to get accustomed to daylight? But you don't want to sleep with me, to get up with me, to have breakfast with me. You are not interested in my daily routine. Because I'm an image, I'm a legend, I'm a story in your mind."

The estranged lover leads a life of exile, constantly on the lookout for a way back to a lost (real or imaginary) home. In the spring of 1998, while he was a university student, she was admitted into a prestigious music program at Northwestern University near Chicago. She made up her mind to accept the offer even if it meant putting their relationship at risk. The decision left him breathless. On a warm August evening she boarded a plane at the Tel Aviv airport. She promised things would eventually work out between them. Alas, they did not.

———

The story of how he eventually left Israel isn't unique. This is partly a question of numbers. Since the founding of the State of Israel in 1948 until his emigration in the late 1990s, the country's Jewish population grew more than tenfold, from approximately half a million in 1948 to slightly more than 5,000,000 in 2000.

Much of this growth was due to Jews from around the world immigrating to the young Jewish state. Less well known but equally important is that during the same period, approximately 750,000 Israelis left the country to settle someplace else.[7] Many of these emigrants had made aliyah just a few years earlier, couldn't find their place in Israel, and decided to move on. (Exhibit A: Ben Shoushan.) Another group consisted of native Israelis seeking social mobility and professional and personal opportunities they couldn't find at home. Until the mid-1980s, the official state attitude toward Israeli emigrés was overwhelmingly negative. Prime Minister Yitzhak Rabin once called them "a fallout of wimps," the journalist Yehuda Gothelf viewed them as "deserters," and the writer Yehoshua Bar-Yosef wrote that the Israeli expatriate (*"yored"*) is "an extremely pathetic figure."[8]

This societal attitude began to shift after the shock of the Yom Kippur War in 1973—Israel, it turned out, was not a safe haven for Jews after all—and even more so after the rise of the Likud Party to power in 1977 and the Lebanon War it launched in June 1982. (The same process repeats itself today, following the formation of Benjamin Netanyahu's far right-wing government in 2022, the Hamas attack of October 7, 2023, and the ensuing war in Gaza and in the Middle East more generally.[9]) These processes ushered in the country a political shift to the right that made many in the old socialist-Zionist-Ashkenazi elite doubt whether Israel was still home. To further complicate matters, starting in the mid-1980s, Israel became integrated into the global economy, which opened up new educational and professional opportunities for members of Israel's declining Ashkenazi-socialist elite. A particular form of neoliberal ideology also became widespread, helping fragment any sense of Israeli collectivity. Thus, what used to be a stigma became over time almost a badge of honor. Thousands of educated Jewish Israelis have preferred to build their lives abroad, primarily in the United States, turning "back" into wandering Jews.

For some Israeli expatriates, the encounter with diaspora Jews (let alone non-Jews) has been revealing, even revelatory. Though many diaspora Jews are enthusiastic supporters of Israel (indeed, tens of thousands of them make aliyah every year), others are critics of Israel's policies toward the Palestinians, and others still are so shocked by Israel's actions that they doubt whether a state that defines itself as Jewish should even exist. This group includes not only disaffected college students, as is commonly believed, but also such luminaries like the Talmud scholar Daniel Boyarin at UC Berkeley, or the Harvard Divinity School professor Shaul Magid. But there is more. The migration of educated Israelis to Europe and the United States created communities of Israeli expatriates who think and write in Israeli Hebrew even though some (not all) are no longer Zionists. In the United States, prominent expatriate Israelis include the musicians Daniel Barenboim and Itzhak Perlman, novelists like Maya Arad and Rubi Namdar, the Hebrew literature scholars Chana Kronfeld and Hannan Hever, the historian Omer Bartov, the journalist Noa Aviv, and many others. Not surprisingly, these Israeli expatriates often write about diasporic existence, displacement, Jewish and Israeli identities, and wanderings.[10] On occasion, some of them also refer to the story of the Wandering Jew.

Even many years after Yair's own emigration, he viewed his personal story as unique. What inspired his many peregrinations, he felt, was the allure of chutzla'aretz, his family's history, and his high school sweetheart, whom he followed to Chicago in a failed attempt to win her back. Only with time did he start realizing that his personal biography, including his growing fascination with the story of the Wandering Jew, was perhaps less extraordinary than he had surmised. Thousands of fellow Israelis left Israel for similar reasons just when he himself left Israel behind.

———

In the meantime, his wanderings in the physical world expanded also his temporal horizons. Past events he never experienced in person and people he never did (or could) meet face-to-face became part of his innermost personal recollections. Three examples, all taken from his digital archive, shed light on these experiences.

The first example is related to the constant consumption of literature and the incessant seeping of literary figures into his mind. When, in 1999, he stepped into a bookstore in the Schwabing neighborhood of Munich, he read Faust in German for the first time. Already in the opening scene, he discovered a fictional figure that reminded him of himself:

I have pursued, alas, philosophy,
Jurisprudence, and medicine
And, help me God, theology,
With fervent zeal through thick and thin.
And here, poor fool, I stand once more,
No wise than I was before.
They call me Magister, Doctor, no less,
And for some ten years, I would guess,
Through ups and downs and tos and fros
I have led my pupils by the nose—
And see there is nothing we can know!
It fair spears my heart to find it so.[11]

He read further. Like him, Faust was a fugitive and a wanderer, and just like him obsessed with love and doom. Thinking about his love-object, Gretchen, Faust asks:

> What use her love's celestial graces?
> As I grow warm in her embraces
> Do I not always sense her doom?
> Am I not fugitive, the homeless rover,
> The man-beast void of goal or bliss,
> Who roars in cataract from cliff to boulder
> In avid frenzy for the precipice?[12]

Melancholy, scholarship, wanderings, love. In Faust, he recognized a dim image of his own life story. The more he sees himself in the figure of the restless, melancholic Ahasverus, the more he also identified with Goethe's Faust.

––––––

A second mechanism that expanded his temporal horizons in the years since leaving Israel operated through objects and places rather than texts. Famously, Toni Morrison called this mechanism rememory. In her novel *Beloved* (1987), she writes how "[a] picture floating out there outside my head . . . right in the place where it happened . . . if you go there—you who never was there—if you go there and stand in the place where it was, it will happen again; it will be there for you, waiting for you."[13] In his own attempts to understand what was happening to him in the early 2000s, and still unaware of Morrison's work, he returned time and again to Marcel Proust, writing, for instance, in an email to a beloved childhood friend who would soon die by suicide: "An insight during a train ride today: the European train is to the modern Wandering Jew what the petite madeleine was for Proust—the past trapped in a place and an object. When you touch or visit it, you are transported into the past." He then continues:

> The experience begins at the train station. A few years ago, on my first trip through Poland, I found myself looking at the departures and arrivals board at the Breslau/Wrocław train station. So many familiar place names: Warsaw, Łódź, Krakau, Lublin. Such a strong feeling of déjà-vu. According to Zionist ideology, you and I are supposed to be "New Jews," persons who cut their ties with diasporic existence [*galut*]. But my own powerful sense at this moment is that I've been to these Polish cities before. Have I not already been *there*, at least for a while? Then my heart skips a bit as I look at the bottom right-hand corner of the board and see the destination "Przemyśl." My maternal grandparents' old shtetl was located just a short distance from there. With every fiber of my body, I feel the spectral presence of my ancestors.

Later in the same email he adds the following:

> Dear Gady [his friend's name], there is also sound: the chugging, clanking, even the conductor's announcements on the PA system. . . . Last year, when I boarded the RER from Charles de Gaulle to visit you in Paris, I entered a train car that was quiet, clean, half-empty. Then we passed the Drancy station [the site of an infamous transit camp for French Jews during World War II], and for a moment I was as if transported to a crowded cattle car in the 1940s.

———

One can live vicariously through literary figures, and a traumatic collective memory can later burst into the open during an encounter with an object, a person, or a place. Sometimes, however, the process of expanding one's mnemonic horizons takes a different, more deliberate and overtly ideological shape.

In a speech before the German Bundestag in 1996, a clip of which he kept in his files (it appeared on the first page of the leading Israeli newspaper *Yediot Ahronot*), Israeli President Ezer Weizman compared his own biography to the life story of the Wandering Jew. "I am no longer a wandering Jew who migrates from country to country, and from exile to exile," Weizman said, "but all Jews in every generation must regard themselves as if they had been there, in previous generations, places, and events. Therefore, I am still a wandering Jew, but not along the far-flung paths of the world. Now I migrate through the expanses of time, from generation to generation, down the paths of memory":

Memory shortens distances. Two hundred generations have passed since my people first came into being, and to me they seem like a few days. Only two hundred generations have passed since a man named Abraham rose up and left his country and birthplace for the country that is today mine. Only two hundred generations have elapsed from the day Abraham purchased the Cave of Makhpela [Cave of the Patriarchs] in the city of Hebron to the murderous conflicts that have taken place there in my generation. Only one hundred fifty generations have passed from the Pillar of Fire of the Exodus from Egypt to the pillars of smoke from the Holocaust. And I, a descendant of Abraham, born in Abraham's country, have witnessed them all.

For Israelis to understand themselves, Weizman insisted, they must embrace the memory of the past rather than cut their ties from it. "I am a wandering Jew," Weizman modifies his opening statement by the end of his Bundestag speech. "With the cloak of memory around my shoulders and the staff of hope in my hand, I stand at this great crossroads in time, the end of the twentieth century. I know whence I have come, and with hope and apprehension I attempt to find out where I'm heading."[14]

———

Even before leaving Israel in the late 1990s, Yair had resolved to become a historian. "From the many possible answers to the question 'why,' " he writes to his love in 1996, "it is history that is providing me with the most intriguing and compelling answers. It is the study of history, therefore, that will guide me through my intellectual journey, and it is the passion and devotion to the study of the past that I will strive to convey to my own students one day."

Studying the past cannot be done in isolation. One needs mentors, colleagues, publishers, students, readers. But in the end, he thinks, we learn by ourselves and for ourselves: because we are curious, or driven, or because we seek assistance from others in answering our deepest questions and concerns. (One of his favorites quotes, by Ralph Waldo Emerson, is that in the great works of the past, "we recognize our own rejected thoughts; they come back to us with a certain alienated majesty."[15]) After a few years of wanderings in the United States and Europe, he became a historian by profession, and on his university campus, he's known as a caring, if also rather demanding, teacher. But he hopes that he doesn't overwhelm his students with information or pretend to know everything about the past. Rather, he strives to find the "rejected thoughts" of his students and readers, helping them phrase and address them using the historian's toolkit. He seeks to inspire, to create an intellectual space where questions, uncertainty, and even errors—including his own—are legitimate. To err is human, in the double sense of the word.

Because he's a reader of Nietzsche's famous treatise on history, he knows that the past is often a double-edged sword: without the past one cannot understand the present, but by overemphasizing the past, one cannot overcome it. The study of history for him is consequently a cornerstone in any liberal arts education but should not be considered an end in itself. He constantly reminds himself that he must place human beings at the center of his stories, that he needs to emphasize change and otherness, and that he ought to help his readers rediscover their own "rejected thoughts" in what he relates.

———

Sitting in his study one evening several years ago, he discovered his own discarded thoughts in several backup folders on his computer. The spectral image of the Wandering Jew haunted them all. So he set himself the task of understanding this image not as an act of self-aggrandizement, but in order to understand how, even after Haskalah and Zionism, the Wandering Jew remains such an existential problem for modern Jews like him. His life story is for him but a prism through which to explore topics much more important than his personal self: the larger shifting landscapes of Jewish existence and the incurable problem of Jewish (and non-Jewish) homelessness.

Over the course of several years, he then explores the history of the Wandering Jew with the help of the historian's toolkit—the only one he truly knows. He does it in reverse chronological order, delving ever deeper into what Thomas Mann memorably called the bottomless well of the past. Teleologies invade one's writing when the end point of the story, its *telos*, is predetermined. By going back in time, into a past that looks ever more alien, he hoped to avoid falling into this trap.

He started with the case of Monsieur Chouchani, whose name he once heard at a book launch party in Jerusalem. The joke behind his name was apparent to him at once, but the full story of why and how this lonely man embodied Ahasverus in 1950s Israel revealed itself only slowly and with deep archival research. Here was a remarkable example of Ahasverus's spectral nature: the Wandering Jew could be real and imaginary at the same time, an actual person with a real-life story but also a ghost from the past. It quickly became his belief that the entire story of the Wandering Jew could best be told as a story of a series of apparitions: Ahasverus is a spirit, for sure, but also one that does live among us.

Straining his eyes, he then looked deeper into the pit, seeking to identify the sources of Chouchani's decision to identify so fully with the story of Ahasverus. How could it be, he asked himself, that a figure that originally had strong anti-Jewish overtones was reclaimed by modern Jews? It so happened that Sh. Y. Abramovitch's *The Nag*, which he had admired since his university days, was the earliest example he could find of a sympathetic description of Ahasverus in a work of Jewish literature and indeed a description of the psychological mechanism that allowed his reclaiming process to take place in the first place. One aspect of Ahasverus's ghost-like nature in *The Nag* is that his figure haunted the imagination of nineteenth-century European Jews. Some have chosen to repress or reject it (Auerbach, Philippson, the early Zionists), while Yiddish writers came to identify with what started as the Christian, anti-Jewish figure of the Wandering Jew (Abramovitch, Pinski). His deep fascination with *The Nag* had at least two other sources. As this very book demonstrates, the Russian doll–like structure of Abramovitch's novel can serve as a model for history writing more generally, because historical events are ensconced in contexts within contexts. Moreover, the texture of all our personalities are sewn together from fragmentary mnemonic parts. This, too, is beautifully exemplified in Abramovitch's remarkable retelling of Ahasverus's story in *The Nag*.

On his journey into the deep past, he then stopped in the early eighteenth century. Previously, he had read that the idea expressed by Johann Jacob Schudt—that Ahasverus's legend was merely a poem and yet symbolically and theologically true—began there.[16] Ahasverus's ghost-like nature took a different form in Schudt's *Jewish Memorabilia*. The Wandering Jew was both real and imaginary not because some saw him while others didn't (Chouchani), and not even because he appeared in a dream (Auerbach, Abramovitch). The very fabric of God's creation consisted of individual threads or stories *and* larger patterns like the stories of whole peoples. The literal sense of Scripture and the layers of its symbolic–theological meanings, though related, were not identical. The circle could be squared: Ahasverus was a historical fabrication at the same time that the curse cast on the Jews as a people was a Christian-theological fact.

When he reached the deepest point of his journey, 1602, he was ready to ask not only what the universal meaning of Ahasverus's story was, and what the "zeitgeist" was that gave birth to it at a specific moment in time, but also and especially who deployed his figure, why they did so, and in response to whom or what. This proved to be the most challenging part of his investigation, full of dead ends and red herrings. But through a detective investigation of the material aspects of the 1602 pamphlet, as well as the forgotten life stories of the Kurtze Beschreibung's main protagonists (Paul von Eitzen, Joachim Westphal, Tilemann Heshusius), he discovered that even in 1602, Ahasverus refused to be pinned down, slipping into a preexisting context like the ghost he was. To make fun of Heshusius as a modern-day Wandering Jew presupposed a prior knowledge of his legend; Ahasverus simultaneously did and did not exist because his presence was often *implied*. In that respect, his suggested solution to the 420-year-old mystery behind the Kurtze Beschreibung proved a larger point. No matter where or when in the past we look for the one true Wandering Jew, his specter withdraws from us. Thus does the observer become the observed, and a scholarly examination of the story of others turns into an algorithm of self-exegesis. When you chase the ghost of Ahasverus long enough, you becomes a wandering figure yourself.

———

Let me switch now, finally, definitively, and not without trepidation, from the "he" of the past back to the "I" of right now. At a particular moment in my life, because of my family history, the place I grew up, and the people I came to know and learn from and love, I became fascinated by the legend of the Wandering Jew. Many years later, after accidently rediscovering discarded files on my computer, I sensed that Ahasverus left a kind of watermark on much of my life. I consequently began scrutinizing my Ahasverus archive, contextualizing the pieces historically, then stitching them together to form a larger narrative-collage. The result is a book that is suffused with my

personality and personal editorial choices at the same time that
it reflects the social milieu in which I grew up and larger, perhaps universal, themes or tropes. Indeed, a fundamental argument of this book has been that apparitions of Ahasverus
have always been made up of this particular mixture. Ahasverus is universal, literary, *and* time- and place-specific. In this,
I confess my deep debt to the wonderful French writer Annie
Ernaux.

This insight has acquired a particularly personal meaning for
me in the last three years. First was the formation, in November 2022, of a new Israeli government led by Benjamin Netanyahu. Netanyahu, the long-time leader of the Likkud party, has
been a staunch opponent of any territorial compromise between Israelis and Palestinians and a particularly ruthless (if
also shrewd) politician. When he took office, Netanyahu was
standing trial for a long series of alleged crimes, including em-
bezzlement of public funds and accepting bribes. He faced a
long jail sentence. In an attempt to escape justice, Netanyahu
formed an extremist coalition government that sought to undermine the rule of law. Nothing like this had ever existed in the
annals of the State of Israel. Next to the Likkud party, Netanyahu's government included representatives from two ultra-
Orthodox, anti-Zionist and anti-democratic Jewish parties: the
semi-fascist political party *Otzmah Yehudit*, led by the convicted
criminal Itamar Ben-Gvir (whom Netanyahu appointed minister of police, no less); and a religious Zionist party, *Hatsiyonut
Hadatit*, whose members were predominantly messianic Jewish
settlers. What place, if any, could a country led by such people
offer Israelis of my background? More than ever before, the
elections of 2022 made me feel that I could never go back to my
home country. I was, and would probably forever remain, an
exile, a Wandering Jew.

Worse still was October 7th, 2023, and its aftermath. I was in Montreal that day, attending an academic conference, when I saw a barrage of text messages from Israeli family members and friends on my phone. They reported in real time the details of the day's barbaric terrorist attacks. Shaken by the news and anxious beyond measure for the lives of loved ones, I witnessed mythical aspects of Ahasverus's old legend becoming real once again. They included an image of a God too distant to be bothered with the fate of his chosen people (Ben Shoushan's point); pictures of houses on fire and people displaced both in the past (Schudt, Abramovitch) and at present (Gaza, parts of Israel); a realization that attacking Jews and Judaism is often but a proxy for other wars (the Kurtze Beschreibung of 1602, encampments in American campuses in 2023–2024); and a flood of publications by secular, educated Israelis who, Ahasverus-like, categorically reject any form of messianism and take practical steps to leave Israel behind.

In the wake of October 7th, my familiarity with Ahasverus's story also helped me see with particular clarity some of the deep temporal structures behind contemporary attitudes toward Jews. I now realize, for instance, that attacking Jewish-Israelis for their alleged lack of empathy for the sufferings of others is an old accusation associated with Ahasverus (Karl Gutzkow in his 1838 essays, for instance), or that American academics who call Israeli-Jews "settler colonialists" replicate some of the worst aspects of the legend of the Wandering Jew. At its core, Ahasverus's legend depicts Jews as eternal strangers no matter where they are or what they do. But in light of postcolonial discourse, one has to wonder: if Jews aren't indigenous to what they call the Land of Israel, where exactly *are* they indigenous? In America? Poland? Scandinavia? Jews, according to postcolonialism's binary ideology, are always and everywhere alien; their fate is to forever remain wandering Jews.

All this is not to say that Ahasverus should be perceived as a wholly negative figure. On the contrary, as Galit Hasan-Rokem claimed many years ago, the legend of the Wandering Jew was often a Christian–Jewish coproduction, and as the present book has demonstrated, the figure of the Wandering Jew has frequently served, at least since the late nineteenth century, as a model of identification for many Jews. They didn't just passively accept it; they reclaimed, reshaped, and deployed it. They used it to express their sense of wonder vis-à-vis God's creation, but also a defiant stance against an indifferent God (Wiesel, for instance); to imagine identity less as a theological or biological fact (for example, Schudt, modern antisemitism) and more as a literary collage or a series of performances (Abramovitch and Ben Shoushan, respectively); and to discuss Zionism without rejecting Jewish self-determination by way of a Romantic praise for exile (Daniel Boyarin, Shaul Magid), while also avoiding embracing Zionism as the sole solution to modern Jewish political life (Pinsker, Hertzl). Finally, there's a way of identifying with the figure of the Wandering Jew that calls into being a vision of the Jewish future that is inseparable from a deep appreciation, and indeed playful reenactment, of the past (Weizman, Ben Shoushan). For all these reasons, I now embrace the figure of Ahasverus. To boot: I now proudly choose him to be a model for political life.

I conclude my memoirs as a present-day Ahasverus with one final thought or suggestion. It concerns the relationship between literature and history. This is a theme that has cut through each of the book's chapters and framed it as a whole—figuratively and literally. In retelling Ahasverus's story as my own and my own story as a new iteration of Ahasverus's, I sought to downplay allusions to universal archetypes or abstract zeitgeists in favor of the concrete, sociological, and time- and place-specific ways that make an engagement with a fictional character meaningful in a particular person's life. Understood in this way, I hope my readers will find in this book an inspiration to examine their own life stories and look for fictional characters in them, too. To a lesser or greater extent, aren't all our lives bound in intimate bonds of fiction? If so, who are the fictional characters that live vicariously through you?

PRINCETON, NEW JERSEY, JUNE 2025

Appendix

THE KURTZE BESCHREIBUNG, ANNOTATED

Author's Note:

The following is based on the earliest known copy of the Kurtze Beschreibung which, as I explain in chapter 4 of this book, must be the one currently located in Tübingen (Universitätsbibliothek Tübingen, Gh 732.4-OR). Every translation is an act of interpretation, and the present one is no different. This is partly a matter of the language of the Kurtze Beschreibung, which is replete with archaic word choices, the typical German overuse of the passive voice, and excessively long sentences. The issue is further complicated by our distance from the first appearance of this important pamphlet in both time and space. To alleviate the last issue, I included some footnotes that are based on the research presented in chapter 4 of this book. It is also worth mentioning that while I learned a great deal from George K. Anderson's English translation of the Kurtze Beschreibung in *The Legend of the Wandering Jew* (1965), the following is my own original work.

A short description and tale of a Jew named Ahasverus[1]
Who was present in person at the Crucifixion of Christ and
also yelled the *crucifige*[2] and pleaded on behalf of Barabbas,[3]
and after the Crucifixion of Christ could never go back to
Jerusalem and never saw his wife and child again; and since
then, remained alive, and a few years ago came to Hamburg.
Also, in December of the year 1599, he arrived in Danzig.
Paul von Eitzen,[4] Doctor of Holy Scripture and Bishop of
Schleswig, next to the rector of the schools in Hamburg,[5]
conversed with him about what happened in the Orient
after the time of Christ, and he gave them such a good
report thereof that they couldn't be more astonished.
Matthew 16:
Verily I say unto you, there may be some
standing here who shall not taste of
death until they see the Son of Man coming
into his kingdom.[6]

1. Ahasverus is the name of the Persian king in the Book of Esther. Modern scholars identify him with Xerxes I (518–465 BCE). In the present context, the name
seems to be an anagram of the name of anti-Calvinist Lutheran theologian Tilemann
Heshusius (1527–1588).

2. Latin for "Crucify him!"

3. According to the New Testament (John 18:14; Mark 15:7), Barabbas was a
murderer and a robber. When given the choice of releasing him or Jesus, the crowd
at Pilate's Palace preferred to free Barabbas.

4. A historical person. Born in Hamburg in 1521 or 1522, Eitzen served as Lutheran
bishop (Superintendent) in Hamburg and later in Schleswig (Denmark). He died in
1598, four years before the publication of the Kurtze Beschreibung.

5. In 1542, this man was Matthäus Delius (1500–1565). Not much is known about
Delius apart from the fact that, like Eitzen, he was a native of Hamburg, a Lutheran,
and a graduate of the university of Wittenberg.

6. The original translation of this biblical passage is idiosyncratic and cannot be
traced to any known German translation of the New Testament, including Martin
Luther's.

Printed in Bautzen[7] by Wolffgang
Suchnach.[8] 1602.

———

Because at this time there is nothing new to report, I
will tell you something old which by many is received with
wonder and held for something new. It takes the following
form:

Paul von Eitzen, doctor of Holy Scripture and Bishop of
Schleswig (he was elected and confirmed by His Grace Duke
Adolf of Holstein[9] to serve as bishop), is famous not only as
a trustworthy and reputable man but also for his printed
works. On many occasions, he told us and other students[10]
that in his youth, when he was studying in Wittenberg,[11] he
once in the winter of 1542 journeyed to his parents in Hamburg. And there, at church on the following Sunday, he saw

7. A town in Saxony known in the early modern period as the birthplace of Caspar Peucer (1525–1602), a personal acquaintance of Eitzen's, Westphal's, and Heshusius's from their time as students in Wittenberg and Philip Melanchton's son-in-law.
Peucer died in September 1602, in time to be considered a possible author of the
Kurtze Beschreibung.

8. Suchnach means "look for" in German. As the (false) name of a publisher, it
was used already in 1580 by the satirist Johann Fischart (1545–1591) of Strasbourg.

9. A historical person. Duke Adolf of Holstein-Gottorp (1526–86) was the youn-
gest son of King Frederick I of Denmark and brother of King Frederick II. Together
with his brother, in 1562 Duke Adolf appointed Paul von Eitzen as bishop of
Schleswig and Holstein.

10. In later editions of the Kurtze Beschreibung, the pamphlet's author is identified as one Chrysostomus Dudulaeus Westphalus. This name is a thinly veiled reference to Joachim Westphal (1510/11–74)—Ioachim Westphalus in Latin—a close
associate of Paul von Eitzen's and the latter's successor as Superintendent of Hamburg. Westphal was known as a staunch critic of John Calvin.

11. Eitzen is attested in Wittenberg starting in 1539. How long he stayed in Wittenberg, and whether he was still there in 1542, is unclear.

next to the preacher's lectern a very tall man[12] with hair flow-
ing over his shoulders, standing barefoot against the pulpit.
[And this man] listened so attentively to the sermon that one
could not detect any movement in him other than when the
name of Jesus Christ was mentioned, upon which he bowed,
beat on his breast, and sighed deeply. He had no other clothing in that cold winter other than pants stretching to his feet,
an outer garment reaching to his knees, and over that a coat
down to his feet. Otherwise, he looked about 50 years old.
And when [Paul von Eitzen] inquired about him, because of
[this man's] clothing and behavior, who he was and what was
his business, he was told that he had been in Hamburg for
several weeks during that winter and told people that he was
born a Jew in Jerusalem and that his name was *Ahasverus* and
that his vocation a cobbler. He was present in person at the
Crucifixion of Christ and since then had remained alive and
traveled through many lands. He supported these claims by
reporting many circumstances which happened to *CHRIST*
after he was caught and led in front of Pilate and then
Herod[13] before being crucified. These circumstances neither
the evangelists nor historians relate.[14]

———

Also [this man] had good knowledge of similar stories and
political developments which transpired in the several hundred years after the Passion of Christ, as well as [the stories]

12. The height of the Jew is noteworthy. Tilemann Heshusius was known as a
particularly tall man.

13. Pontius Pilate was the governor of the province of Judea in the early first
century CE. Herod Agrippa was the last king of Judea (ca. 11 BCE–44 CE).

14. A stunning claim about Paul von Eitzen and his companion, both staunch
Lutherans. Adherence to Scripture is one of the basic tenets of Lutheranism.

of the Apostles, where each one lived, taught, and eventually suffered martyrdom. When Paul von Eitzen heard all of this, he was all the more amazed by it and sought an opportunity to converse with [this man]. When he did, he queried him earnestly, and the Jew gave him a detailed account of how he was a resident of Jerusalem in Jesus's time and was angry with the Lord Jesus, whom he held for a heretic and a seducer, because he didn't know any better and also because he wasn't taught any better by the priests and scholars.[15] So he did his best to destroy this seducer, as he thought him to be. And eventually he also caught him, led him to the High Priests and Pilate, accused him, called *crucifige* against him and asked for the release of Barabbas, all of which contributed to [Jesus] being condemned to death.

———

Once the sentence was pronounced, he rushed to his house, because Lord Jesus was supposed to pass by it, and told this to his entire household so they too would be able to see [Jesus]. He himself held his small child in his arms and stood in front of his house so they could both see the Lord. When then Lord Jesus passed by carrying the cross, he leaned a little on the house, and this enraged [the Jew] even more, and so he told him with invectives to pack and betake himself to where he belonged. Jesus then looked at him sternly and told him forcefully: I WILL STAY AND REST BUT YOU MUST GO.[16] And immediately [the Jew] put

15. "Schrifftgelehrten," which doesn't have an exact English equivalent, had often negative connotations in the post-Reformation age.

16. This sentence, as well as many other details in the Kurtze Beschreibung, is taken from medieval chronicles. At least one of them, Matthew Paris's *Flores*

down his child and couldn't stay in his house, but joined [the crowd] and saw how [Jesus] was executed. After all this was done, it was impossible for him to go back to Jerusalem and indeed he didn't go back there; he didn't see his wife, child, and household servants again, but immediately traveled abroad and journeyed[17] to [one land] after the other and although he came back several centuries later, he found the land desolate and Jerusalem destroyed and couldn't recognize it.

————

He did not know what God planned to do with him, why he let him lead such a miserable life for so long, and whether God intended that he would perhaps remain alive until the Last Days as a living testimony to the Passion of Christ for the sake of the godless and unbelievers. He himself wanted to suffer until God would call him away from this vale of tears. He later continued to converse with Paul von Eitzen, as well as with the rector of the Hamburg schools (an erudite man and knowledgeable in books of history) about all kinds of events that took place in the Orient after Christ's death. His descriptions were so detailed that [the two men] couldn't be more amazed by them. In general, he was quiet and withdrawn, not speaking to anyone unless addressed first, and when he was invited as a guest he would show up without eating or drinking much, and when offered money he wouldn't take more than 2 schillings which, however, he

————

Historiarum, was readily available in print at the time of the Kurtze Beschreibung's publication.

17. In the original German: "durchzogen habe." It is the "e" at the end of "habe" here that would wander farther and farther up the page in the course of the first, split edition of the Kurtze Beschreibung. See chapter 4, p. 148.

would then give immediately over to the poor, saying that he didn't need it and that God would take care of him. During the time he spent in Hamburg, no one saw him laughing. No matter which land he comes to, he speaks its language, and while [in Hamburg], he spoke the Saxon dialect of the German language as if he were a native Saxon himself.

———

Doctor Eitzen also reported that many people from many lands and faraway places went to Hamburg to see and hear [this man],[18] and that many passed hard *iudicia*[19] over him. The majority held that he had a wandering spirit which revealed itself in this way. But [Paul von Eitzen] did not share this opinion, because [the Jew] not only liked to hear God's word and spoke about it, and not only because whenever he mentioned God's name he did so with great reverence and deep sighs, but also because he wouldn't tolerate any curses, and when he heard someone cursing by evoking God's passion and wounds he would physically shake and retort with much passion: "you pitiful man, you pitiful creature, why do you misuse the name of God and his martyrs? Yes, you should have seen and heard—as I have—how painful were Jesus's wounds to him, which he suffered on your behalf and mine. Had you seen it, you would have preferred to let yourself be tortured before mentioning his name." All of this and much more did Paul von Eitzen tell me and many others in person,[20] which since then I have heard affirmed by many

---

18. Not a single source confirms this claim as Johann Schudt, among others, had confirmed already in the early eighteenth century. (See chapter 3.)

19. In Latin also in the original, meaning "judgments."

20. There is no trace of this story in all of Paul von Eitzen's massive oeuvre, or any other pre-1602 source, for that matter.

old burghers here in Schleswig, who in part had also seen this man back then and conversed with him.

———

This past year [15]75,[21] Secretary Christoph Ehringer and Magistrate Jacobus[22] were sent as legates to the King of Spain. They were to make inquiries about money owed our lord Duke Adolph of Holstein for his participation, alongside his soldiers, in the Duke of Alba's campaign in the Netherlands in 1572. When these two men came back to Schleswig, they reported that they saw this same man in Malduit [Madrid], with the same build, clothing, gestures, and age as before, that they conversed with him alongside other people who understood him, and that he spoke good Spanish.

Each can pass their own *iudicium* about this man. God's works are wonderful and inscrutable and will be revealed only slowly, the more so the closer we are to the Last Judgment and End of the World. Happy the man who understands and recognizes this and doesn't long inappropriately after [such knowledge].

DATED SCHLESWIG, 9 JUNE, 1564.[23]

21. The provenance of this anecdote is unclear. Its inclusion in the Kurtze Beschreibung seems to attest to the rushed manner in which it was created.

22. The backstory to this section is historical. In 1912, Leonhard Neubaur managed to show that Christoph Erich and Jacobus Berglin were indeed historical figures, and that the Spanish general Fernando Álvarez de Toledo y Pimentel, 3rd Duke of Alba (1507–1582), owed Duke Adolf of Schleswig a large sum of money for military assistance during his campaigns in the Netherlands.

23. The significance of this date, so out of place in the Kurtze Beschreibung, is unknown.

This man or Jew is reported to have such thick callouses on the soles of his feet that one could measure them with two[24] fingers across. They are hard as horns due to his many wanderings and travels. It is also reported that he was seen in Danzig in 1599.

End.

24. Misspelled in the original as "Zcheyer" rather than "Zweyer," this typo would be corrected halfway through the first, split edition of the Kurtze Beschreibung.

ACKNOWLEDGMENTS

WHILE RESEARCHING and writing this book, I have incurred a debt of gratitude to many persons and institutions. Deborah Harris was the first to tell me about Ben Shoushan, and Lior Lavid and Hila Baharad helped in uncovering a set of remarkable documents about the man's stay in Israel. My very heartfelt thanks also go to the Bachrach family, both for a wonderful dinner in London a few years ago and for sharing with me a set of very personal letters by Zvi Bachrach Z"L. David Bell, Shmuel Feiner, Phil Nord, Daniel Rodgers, and Starry Schor read closely the first draft of chapter 1, as did in 2020 the participants of Princeton's Davis Seminar for Historical Studies. Also very valuable for my understanding of Ben Shoushan's story were conversations I had with Solomon Malka, Claude Sitbon, and especially Joel Rappel. I am grateful to the editors of *Jewish Social Studies* for fast-tracking the publication of my 2023 piece on Ben Shoushan/Chouchani, to the two anonymous readers of the journal, and to Susannah Heschel, who suggested I publish the piece in JSS in the first place. A few months after the publication of my article, which forms the basis for chapter 1 in this book, Michael Grynzspan's extraordinary documentary on Chouchani came out. Though we have different interpretations of Chouchani/Ben Shoushan's life and oeuvre, I have the utmost respect for Grynszpan's work and recommend it very warmly indeed to all who are interested in Ben Shoushan's story.

For three years, William Dingee tutored me patiently in Latin in preparation for the research on Paul von Eitzen and his circle. He then also helped with parsing out difficult passages in some of Eitzen's Latin works. During the same time, William Theiss assembled dozens of scans of different editions of the 1602 pamphlet while also serving as a crucial interlocutor as I was analyzing them. Eric White of Princeton's Firestone Library identified the smoking gun connecting the Kurtze Beschreibung to Martin Jost in Strasbourg, and Christopher Boveland of the Herzog August Bibliothek in Wolfenbüttel, Germany, helped explain the significance of the "wandering e" I noticed on page 8 of the chapbook.

A long, long list of colleagues and friends, both at Princeton and elsewhere, shared their vast knowledge with me over the years in which I researched and wrote this book. The errors that remain are of course wholly my own. I would like to mention especially Peter Burschel, Robert Evans, Tony Grafton, Galit Hasan-Rokem, Matthias Pohlig, Sally Poor, Lyndal Roper, Alexander Schunka, Moulie Vidas, and Mordechai Zalkin. Hannan Hever proved an invaluable interlocutor when I was trying to make sense of Abramovitch. At various points along the way, Ginat Ben-Dar, Victoria Bergbauer, Bianca Centrone, Marcus Hultmark, and Sonja Thäder lent a helping hand with specific issues. Many thanks also for Tsering Wangyal Shawa for preparing the maps.

The research for this book was supported by a special director's fellowship at the Herzog August Bibliothek in Wolfenbüttel, Germany, as well as several grants by Princeton University's Committee on Research in the Humanities and Social Sciences. Research in the humanities depends on such grants. I am very grateful for all this generous support.

Right before I sent the manuscript to the publisher, I had eleven remarkable Princeton students read and comment on it in a seminar I co-taught with my colleague Joel Lande. Talia Czuchlewski, James Healy, Eve Hepner, Aaryan Jagtap, Pippa LaMacchia, Anna Salvatore, Sofiia Shapovalova, James Sowerby, Jacob Unger, Riley Yowell, Laura Zhang, and Joel himself posed probing questions that made this book better. Rachel Kadish, Daniela Blei, and Jennifer Harris made many valuable stylistic comments on different versions of the manuscript, and Daniela was also kind enough to agree to compose the index. I would also like to thank my agent, Don Fehr, and my editor, Priya Nelson, for all their help and encouragement.

Several family members read parts of the manuscript and shared their thoughts with me along the way. They include my mother, Hannah Mintzker, my brother Yishai Mintzker, my late father, Yohannan Mintzker Z"L, and my partner Mikhal Dekel. My daughters, Naomi and Lydia, teach me new things every single day. I am also deeply grateful to their mother, Katie, for all her support over the years.

I dedicate this book to my beloved friend Itai Ryb. This book is his as much as it is mine.

LIST OF ABBREVIATIONS

BSB:	Bayerische Staatsbibliothek, Munich
CR:	Corpus Reformatorum, 101 vols., Haale/Saale, 1834–
CZA:	Central Zionist Archive, Jerusalem
Elie Wiesel Archive:	Elie Wiesel Collection, Boston University, Boston, MA
HAB:	Herzog August Bibliothek, Wolfenbüttel
ISA:	Israel State Archives, Jerusalem
IStG:	Institut für Stadtgeschichte, Frankfurt am Main
JMF:	Jüdisches Museum Frankfurt am Main
LA Schleswig-Holstein:	Landesarchiv Schleswig-Holstein
LW:	Luther's Works, 55 vols., Minneapolis and St. Louis, 1957–1986
NLI:	National Library of Israel, Jerusalem
RA Copenhagen:	Rigsarkivet Kopenhagen
SNA:	Swedish National Archives, Stockholm
Stabi Bamberg:	Staatsbibliothek, Bamberg
StA Hamburg:	Staatsarchiv, Hamburg

UA Halle-Wittenberg:	Universitätsarchiv Halle-Wittenberg
UB Tübingen:	Universitätsbibliothek Tübingen
VD16:	Verzeichnis der im deutschen Sprachbereich erschienenen Drucke des 16. Jahrhunderts
VD17:	Verzeichnis der im deutschen Sprachraum erschienenen Drucke des 17. Jahrhunderts
WB:	*D. Martin Luthers Werke: Kritische Gesamtasgabe*, Schriften, 72 vols. Weimar, 1903
WLB:	Württembergische Landesbibliothek Stuttgart
ZIM Archive:	ZIM Archive, Haifa

NOTES

To the Reader

1. Augustine, *Confessions*, 10.8. Famously, Petrarch quotes this passage in his *Ascent of Mount Ventoux* (1350). Petrarch, *Epistolae familiares*, 4.1.

Introduction

1. The Latin name for the houseplant commonly known as the Wandering Jew is *Tradescantia zebrina*. One recent example for the use of the term "Wandering Jew" on social media is Jonathan Judaken, Facebook, April 5, 2023, https://shorturl.at /tvzEG. The musical reference is to Paul Simon, "Hearts and Bones," on *Hearts and Bones* (Warner Bros., 1983), LP.

2. *Kurtze Beschreibung und Erzehlung von einem Juden, mit Namen Ahasverus, welcher bey der Creutzigung Christi selbst persönlich gewesen . . . und seit hero im Leben geblieben, und vor etlich Jahren gen Hamburg kommen . . .* (Leyden: Christoph Creutzer, 1602), 2. For the full translation of the pamphlet, see the appendix to this book.

3. *Kurtze Beschreibung,* 8.

4. *Kurtze Beschreibung,* 2.

5. *Kurtze Beschreibung,* 4.

6. "Kurtze Beschreibung und Erzehlung von einem Juden, mit Namen Ahasverus, welcher bey der Creutzigung Christi selbst persönlich gewesen . . . und seit hero im Leben geblieben, und vor etlich Jahren gen Hamburg kommen." For a full discussion of the different editions of the chapbook, see Leonhard Neubaur, *Die Sage vom ewigen Juden* (Leipzig: J. C. Hinrichs, 1884), as well as chapter 4 of this book.

7. Almost every author who wrote about the 1602 pamphlet tried to speculate about the circumstances of its publication. Good examples for the inconclusiveness of such attempts are Jürgen Beyer, "Jürgen und der Ewige Jude: ein lebender Heiliger wird unsterblich," *Arv. Nordic Yearbook of Folklore* 64 (2008): 125–40; George K. Anderson, *The Legend of the Wandering Jew* (Providence, RI: Brown University Press, 1965), 43; Arno

Schmidt, *Das Volksbuch vom Ewigen Juden: ein Beitrag zur Entstehungsgeschichte des Buches* (Danzig: Druck von A.W. Kafemann, 1927).

8. Anderson, *The Legend of the Wandering Jew*, 53–69. About the name Ahasverus, see David Daube, "Ahasver," *Jewish Quarterly Review* 45 (1955): 243–44, and Galit Hasan-Rokem, "Ahasver—The Enigma of a Name," *Jewish Quarterly Review* 100, no. 4 (Fall 2010): 544–50.

9. Martin Gilbert, *The Routledge Atlas of Jewish History*, 8th ed. (New York: Routledge, 2010), 65. On the spotting of the Wandering Jew in upstate New York, see Rudolf Glanz, *The Jew in the Old American Folklore* (New York: Waldon Press, 1961), 30–42. Some examples from nineteenth-century Germany include apparitions in Ertingen and Hohenstatt (Württemberg), Glantz (Saxony), and Buchen (Odenwald). Anton Birlinger, ed., *Volksthümliches aus Schwaben*, vol. 1 (Freiburg im Breisgau: Herder, 1861), 211–12; Richard Kühnau, *Schlesische Sagen*, vol. 4 (Leipzig: B. G. Teubner, 1910), 304; and Wendelin Duda, *Sagen des Odenwaldes und westlichen Baulandes von Buchen und Walldürn nach Adelsheim und Neudenau* (Freiburg in Breisgau: Echo Verlag, 2007), 18. I am grateful to Hermann Schaeffner for these references.

10. Thus in *Verhandlungen des Reichstages 35. 1874/75* (Berlin: Verlag der Buchdruckerei der Norddeutschen Allgemeinen Zeitung, 1875), 1437. About medical reports on late nineteenth-century "wandering Jews," see Jan Goldstein, "The Wandering Jew and the Problem of Psychiatric Anti-Semitism in Fin-de-Siècle France," *Journal of Contemporary History* 20, no. 4 (October 1985): 521–52.

11. József Eötvös, *Die Emancipation der Juden*, trans. Zeev Zwi Klein, 2. verm. Aufl (Pest: Gustav Heckenast, 1841), 1–2.

12. Wolfgang Benz, *"Der ewige Jude": Metaphern und Methoden nationalsozialistischer Propaganda* (Berlin: Metropol, 2010).

13. Emmanuel de Las Cases, *Memorial de Sainte-Hélène*, edited by André Fugier, vol. 1 (Paris: Garnier, 1963), 893.

14. The literature on Ahasverus is vast. No attempt will be made to list all, or even most, of it here. The two most quoted modern works on the topic are Anderson, *The Legend of the Wandering Jew*, and Galit Hasan-Rokem and Alan Dundes, eds., *The Wandering Jew: Essays in the Interpretation of a Christian Legend* (Bloomington: Indiana University Press, 1986).

15. Some examples are Anderson, *The Legend of the Wandering Jew*, 1–10; E. Isaac-Edersheim, "Ahasver: A Mythic Image of the Jew," in *The Wandering Jew: Essays in the Interpretation of a Christian Legend*, ed. Galit Hasan-Rokem and Alan Dundes (Bloomington: Indiana University Press, 1986), 511–28; and S. Hurwitz, "Ahasver, the Eternal Wanderer: Psychological Aspects," in *The Wandering Jew: Essays in the Interpretation of a Christian Legend*, ed. Galit Hasan-Rokem and Alan Dundes (Bloomington: Indiana University Press, 1986), 211–26.

16. Alexandre Dumas, *Isaac Laquedem* (Bruxelles: Meline, Cans et Cie, 1853), 183.

17. Hannah Arendt observed once that some theories constitute an "escape from the area of ascertainable facts." Based on "non-specific, abstract, hypothetical assumptions—from the Zeitgeist down to the Oedipus complex—[they] are so general that they explain and justify every event and every deed: no alternative to what actually happened is even considered and no person could have acted differently from the way he did act." Hannah Arendt, *Eichmann in Jerusalem: A Report on the Banality of Evil*, rev. and enl. ed. (New York: Penguin Books, 1994), 297.

18. Treatment of literary and artistic representations of Ahasverus include, among many others, Marie-France Rouart, *Le mythe du juif errant dans l'Europe du XIXe siècle* (Paris: J. Corti, 1988); Lisa Lampert-Weissig, *Instrument of Memory: Encounters with the Wandering Jew* (Ann Arbor: University of Michigan Press, 2024); and Richard I. Cohen and Mirjam Rajner, "The Return of the Wandering Jew(s) in Samuel Hirszenberg's Art," *Ars Judaica* 7 (2011): 33–56.

19. A summary of previous researchers' findings is Anderson, *The Legend of the Wandering Jew*, 11–37.

20. Aristotle, *Poetics*, 1451^a.

21. Robert Darnton, *The Great Cat Massacre and Other Episodes in French Cultural History* (New York: Basic Books, 2009), 5. The low quality of some historical speculations about Ahasverus's origins combined with the dominance of symbolic and literary interpretations of his legend led Galit Hasan-Rokem to poke fun at the very possibility of raising historical questions about him. Hasan-Rokem, "Ahasver—The Enigma of a Name," 544.

22. Galit Hasan-Rokem, "Der Ewige Jude in Europa—Eine Jüdische-Christliche Koproduktion," in *Jüdischer Almanach: Grenzen*, ed. Gisela Dachs (Berlin: Jüdischer Verlag, 2015), 75–83.

Chapter 1. The Apparition (1952)

1. József Eötvös, *Die Emancipation der Juden*, trans. Zeev Zwi Klein, 2. verm. Aufl (Pest: Gustav Heckenast, 1841), 2.

2. An earlier version of this chapter appeared as Yair Mintzker, "I, Ahasverus: Monsieur Chouchani in Israel, 1952–56," *Jewish Social Studies* 28, no. 1 (2023): 49–78, https://dx.doi.org/10.2979/jss.2023.a882888.

3. Avraham Ariel, " 'Kolot ha-yama'im': behirot la-histadrut ba-oniyah Artsa, nosakh 1955," *Maritime Heritage Watch*, Jan. 25, 2016, http://www.moreshetyamit.net ‎/תווצו-םיגיהנמ/א-הינאב-תורדתסהל-תוריחב-םיאמיה-תולוק/.

4. Information about *Artsa* is taken from Erich Gröner, *Die deutschen Kriegsschiffe, 1815–1945*, vol. 4 (München: Bernard & Graefe, 1982), 54–56. Also valuable are

"Photographs of *S.S. Artsa*, 1949–1963," KH\404484–404487, CZA, Jerusalem; Photographs of *S.S. Artsa*, NSC\117532–117543, CZA; "Arẓah," 1949–63, ZIM Archive, Haifa.

5. Alexander Manor, *Dyokano shel rav-ḥovel ʿivri* (Tel Aviv: Alef, 1963).

6. "'Im haflagat ha-meʾah," *Toren: dapim le-beyt Zim* 7 (1955): 18–19, at 18.

7. "Poem—A Toast to the Artsa," *Toren* 7 (1953): 17.

8. "Havraḥot be-Arẓah," *Ḥerut*, Sept. 16, 1952; "Melẓarit ʿarka mi-Arẓah," *Ḥerut*, Oct. 16, 1952.

9. Ehud Ben Ezer, *Yamim shel laʿanah u-devash* (Tel Aviv: Am oved, 1988), 467; Shoshana Arbeli-Almozlino, *Me-hamaḥteret be-Bavel le-memshelet Yisraʾel* (Tel Aviv: Hakibutz hameukhad, 1988), 95.

10. Israel Averbach, *Yam rogesh, gevah-gali* (Tel Aviv: Hakibutz hameukhad, 1992), 168.

11. David Giladi, "Tishʿah milyonim mistaʿarim al ha-taḥburah," *Maʿariv*, Oct. 6, 1952; David Giladi, "Meẓukat ha-giyur ḥarifah gam be-London," *Maʿariv*, Oct. 7, 1952.

12. David Giladi, "Yehudim toʿim be-darkei Eyropah," *Maʿariv*, Oct. 14, 1952.

13. David Giladi, "Parẓufim ba-oniyah," *Maʿariv*, Oct. 16, 1952; idem, "Ha-nesiʿah be-Arẓah—arẓah," *Maʿariv*, Oct. 20, 1952.

14. Michelle Tir, *Ralph Klein: ha-meʾamen* (Tel Aviv: Alpha, 2000), 39. D. Segal, "Oyf der iddisher shif 'Artsa,'" *Forverts*, Oct. 10, 1955.

15. Giladi, "Ha-nesiʿah be-arẓah."

16. For a collection of oral testimonies about Chouchani's time in France, see Salomon Malka, *Monsieur Chouchani: l'énigme d'un maître du XXe siècle: entretiens avec Elie Wiesel, suivis d'une enquête* (Paris: J. C. Lattès, 1994). Levinas himself acknowledged his tremendous debt to Chouchani, while also saying remarkably little about him: Emmanuel Levinas and Richard Kerney, "Dialogue with Emmanuel Levinas," in *Face to Face with Levinas*, ed. Richard A. Cohen (Albany: State University of New York Press, 1986), 13–34. An attempt to discern the exact philosophical influence by Chouchani on Levinas is Shmuel Wygoda, "Le maître et son disciple: Chouchani et Levinas," *Cahiers d'études lévinasiennes* 1 (2002): 148–83. Historians of modern French intellectual history seem to have given up on reconstructing Chouchani's life based on archival evidence. Two examples are Samuel Moyn, *Origins of the Other: Emmanuel Levinas between Revelation and Ethics* (Ithaca, NY: Cornell University Press, 2005), 201, and Sarah Hammerschlag, *The Figural Jew: Politics and Identity in Postwar French Thought* (Chicago: University of Chicago Press, 2010), 156, n. 124. An interesting (though not peer-reviewed) attempt to reconstruct Chouchani's internal life, based on newly discovered materials, is Hodaya Har-Shefi, "Sodo shel ha-moreh ha-shotek," *Makor Rishon*, August 28, 2021.

17. Marie-Anne Lescourret, *Emmanuel Levinas* (Paris: Flammarion, 1994), 142–45; Salomon Malka, *Emmanuel Lévinas: la vie et la trace* (Paris: Albin Michel, 2005), 164–69.

18. Elie Wiesel, "Meshuga o ga'on," *Yediʿot aḥronot*, Sept. 8, 1950.

19. Elie Wiesel, "Meshuga o ga'on."

20. Elie Wiesel, "Meshuga o ga'on."

21. Elie Wiesel, "Meshuga o ga'on."

22. Wiesel mentions Chouchani often in his writing, but much of it is redundant. This is the case, for instance, in three newspaper articles he authored about him: Elie Wiesel, "Ha-rabbi aggadah modernit," *Yediʿot aḥronot*, May 15, 1964; Elie Wiesel, "Ha-moreh ha-mistori halakh le-ʿolamo," *Yediʿot aḥronot*, March 1, 1968; and Elie Wiesel, "Shoshani ha-mistori," *Ha-ẓofeh*, Dec. 6, 1968. The three most significant treatments of Chouchani in Wiesel's books are: Elie Wiesel, *Against Silence: The Voice and Vision of Elie Wiesel* (New York: Holocaust Library, 1984), 66; Elie Wiesel, *Legends of Our Time* (New York: Holt, Rinehart and Winston, 1968), 87–109; and Elie Wiesel, *One Generation After* (New York: Random House, 1970), 120–25.

23. Wiesel, *Against Silence*, 66.

24. Wiesel, *Legends of Our Time*, 87–109.

25. Wiesel, 92.

26. Wiesel, 93.

27. Wiesel, 94; Wiesel, 103.

28. Wiesel, *Legends of Our Time*, 94.

29. Johann Wolfgang von Goethe, *Faust, Part One*, trans. David Luke (Oxford: Oxford University Press, 1987), 42.

30. Wiesel, *Legends of Our Time*, 95–96.

31. Giladi, "Parẓufim ba-oniyah."

32. Giladi, "Parẓufim ba-oniyah."

33. Giladi, "Parẓufim ba-oniyah."

34. Giladi, "Parẓufim ba-oniyah."

35. Tir, *Ralph Klein: ha-meʾamen*, 40.

36. Tir, 40.

37. "Reshimat ʿolim," July 31–Dec. 30, 1952, ISA-moia-moia-0009zdl, ISA.

38. Malka, *Monsieur Chouchani*, 112.

39. So, most famously, in Natan Alterman, "El rosh ha-tor," *Davar*, Sept. 7, 1954.

40. "Reshimat ʿolim," July 31–Dec. 30, 1952, ISA-moia-moia-0009zdl, ISA.

41. Avi Picard, *ʿOlim bi-mesurah* (Beer Sheva: Ben Gurion University Press, 2013).

42. "Reshimat ʿolim," July 31–Dec. 30, 1952, ISA-moia-moia-0009zdl, ISA.

43. Rhona Seidelman, *Under Quarantine: Immigrants and Disease at Israel's Gate* (New Brunswick, NJ: Rutgers University Press, 2020).

44. "Be-hitlaked 'am," NLI K-08185-01-B.

45. "Mi-bagdad la-ma'abarah," *Davar*, March 29, 1951, 14.

46. "Sha'ar ha-'aliyah me-aḥorei gader tayil," *Ḥerut*, June 26, 1950; "Ktatah be-Sha'ar ha-'aliyah," *Ḥerut*, Sept. 26, 1954.

47. Some forty of Chouchani's notebooks have been donated recently to Israel's National Library: Monsieur Chouchani Archive, ca. 1945–68, ARC. 4* 2076, NLI. One preliminary attempt to decipher these notebooks is Hodaya Samet Har-Shefi, "Black Fire upon White Fire: The Teachings of Mr. Shoshani" (Ramat Gan, Israel: Bar-Ilan University, 2016).

48. Moyn writes about Chouchani that he is a "character who in some ways defeats the project of contextualizing intellectual history." Moyn, *Origins of the Other*, 201.

49. See forthcoming essay by Yoel Rappel in *Ha'aretz*.

50. Natan Alterman, "Magash ha-kesef," *Davar*, Nov. 21, 1947.

51. I discuss Zionists' deployments of the figure of the Wandering Jew in Yair Mintzker, "Keyẕad hafakh ha-yehudi ha-noded le-gibor yehudi," *Ḥidushim beḥeker toldot yehudey germanya u-mizraḥ eyropa* 26, no. 2 (2024): 99–122.

52. S. Yizhar, *Yeme Tsiklag*, vol. 1 (Tel Aviv: Am oved, 2009), 379.

53. Yizhar, 1:382. An interesting discussion of the figure of the Wandering Jew in 1950s Zionist ideology is Orit Rozin, *A Home for All Jews: Citizenship, Rights, and National Identity in the New Israeli State*, trans. Haim Watzman (Waltham, MA: Brandeis University Press, 2016), 93–94. On the same topic, see also Ori Yehudai, *Leaving Zion: Jewish Emigration from Palestine and Israel after World War II* (Cambridge: Cambridge University Press, 2020), 22–30.

54. Mintzker, "Keyẕad hafaḥ ha-yehudi ha-noded le-gibor yehudi," 109–14.

55. On Ben Shoushan's general whereabouts in Israel, see also what some former students wrote about him after his passing: "Ha-moreh," '*Amudim: Bit'on ha-kibbuẕ ha-dati* (Sept. 1968), 421.

56. Nahum Barukhi, *Be'erot Yiẕhak be-hityashvut u-milḥamah* (Jerusalem: Ariel, 2009).

57. Yair Sheleg, "Ḥidah yehudit shel ha-me'ah ha-'esrim," *Ha'aretz*, Sept. 26, 2003.

58. Yair Sheleg, "Ḥidah yehudit shel ha-me'ah ha-'esrim."

59. Zvi Bachrach, *Min ha-ḥavayah el ha-meḥkar* (Jerusalem: Yad Vashem, 2008).

60. Good critical engagements with Wiesel's theology include Michael Berenbaum, *Elie Wiesel: God, the Holocaust, and the Children of Israel* (West Orange, NJ: Behrman House, 1994), and Byron Sherwin, "Elie Wiesel and Jewish Theology," *Judaism* 18, no. 1 (1969): 39–52. On Bachrach, see Zvi Bachrach, "Ha-adam, ha-hashgaḥah, ve-oshwitz," *Zmanim* 6 (1981): 94. My deepest thanks to the Bachrach family for sharing materials with me.

61. Bachrach, *Min ha-havayah el ha-mehkar*, 22.

62. Zvi Bachrach, letter of July 1985 to his children, 1.

63. Bachrach family papers; Zvi Bachrach, "Ha-zikaron ha-ishi," 1–2. Bachrach family papers (emphasis in the original).

64. Bachrach, "Ha-adam, ha-hashgahah, ve-oshwitz," 96.

65. Bachrach, 96.

66. Quoted in Hava Eshkoli, *Beyn hazalah li-ge'ulah* (Jerusalem: Yad Vashem, 2004), 193.

67. Bachrach, "Ha-adam, ha-hashgahah, ve-oshwitz," 95.

68. Eshkoli, *Beyn hazalah li-ge'ulah*, 215–16.

69. Bachrach, "Ha-zikaron ha-ishi," 2.

70. Zvi Bachrach, "Professor Zvi Bachrach—re'ayon," interview by Michael Grynszpan, Aug. 2, 2014, video, 14:49, https://youtu.be/2-6os7ShoRM.

71. *Yedi'ot ha-shavu'a (Sa'ad)*, Nov. 21, 1952.

72. Avraham Hen, in *Enziklopediah shel ha-ziyonut ha-datit*, 6 vols. (Jerusalem, 1970), 2: 359–63. Information on the Center for Jewish Culture: "Hamerkaz le-tarbut toranit," ISA-ReligiousAffairs-ReligiousAffairs-0010zvp, ISA.

73. *Yedi'ot ha-shavu'a (Sa'ad)*, Nov. 21, 1952.

74. Moses Maimonides, *Ethical Writings of Maimonides*, ed. Raymond L. Weiss, trans. Charles E. Butterworth (New York: Dover Publications, 1983), 60.

75. *Yedi'ot ha-shavu'a (Sa'ad)*, Nov. 21, 1952.

76. *Yedi'ot ha-shavu'a (Sa'ad)*, Nov. 21, 1952.

77. *Yedi'ot ha-shavu'a (Sa'ad)*, Dec. 5, 1952; *Yedi'ot ha-shavua (Sa'ad)*, Jan. 25, 1953.

78. *Yedi'ot ha-shavu'a (Sa'ad)*, Jan. 9, 1953.

79. *Yedi'ot ha-shavu'a (Sa'ad)*, Feb. 20, 1953.

80. *Be'erot Yitzhak—daf yedi'ot*, Jul. 27, 1954.

81. *Be'erot Yitzhak—daf yedi'ot*, Feb. 29, 1954.

82. *Be'erot Yitzhak—daf yedi'ot*, Feb. 29, 1954.

83. *Be'erot Yitzhak—daf yedi'ot*, Feb. 29, 1954.

84. *Ha-zofeh*, Apr. 23, 1954.

85. "Hamerkaz le-tarbut toranit," p. 3.

86. *Ha-zofeh*, Sep. 4, 1953; "Hamerkaz le-tarbut toranit," p. 2.

87. *Ha-zofeh*, Nov. 23, 1954; *Ha-zofeh*, Dec. 10, 1954; *Ha-zofeh*, Dec. 12, 1954.

88. *Ha-zofeh*, Feb. 24, 1954; *Ha-zofeh*, Dec. 10, 1954; *Ha-zofeh*, Dec. 12, 1954.

89. See, for instance, Moshe Nahmani, "Mi kan Hillel?" *Makor rishon*, Feb. 2, 2011. This claim appears frequently in newspaper articles and on the internet (including Wikipedia). Though not the product of peer reviewed academic work, the claim found its way into the official description of Chouchani's materials in the catalogue of the National Library of Israel: Monsieur Chouchani Archive, NLI.

90. Basic information about Rosenbaum-Shoshani's life is A. Sh. Shtain, "Ha-Rav Yeḥezkel Rosenbaum-Shoshani," in *Radom* (Tel Aviv: Irgun Yoẓ'ey Radom be-Yisra'el, 1961), 142–43. Relevant archival materials include "Rosenbaum, Shoshani," Search Bureau for Missing Relatives, 1945, S104P\22292, CZA; Centraldossier: "Shmuel Rosenbaum-Shoshani," Statens Utlänningskommission, Swedish National Archives (hereafter SNA), Stockholm; Konseljakt, July 15, 1955, no. M 28, Justitiede-partementet, SNA. I am grateful to Marcus Hultmark for his assistance with this material.

91. Theodor Herzl, *The Complete Diaries of Theodor Herzl*, ed. Raphael Patai, trans. Harry Zohn, vol. 2 (New York: Herzl Press, 1960), 582. The emphasis is mine.

92. Saul Friedländer, *When Memory Comes*, trans. Helen R. Lane (New York: Farrar, Straus, Giroux, 1979), 9.

93. Wiesel, "Meshuga o ga'on," 5. The emphasis is mine.

94. Masha Turner and Benjamin Ish Shalom, "Erev eḥad 'im mar Shoshani: ma'aseh she-hayah," in *Be-darkhey shalom* (Jerusalem: Beit Morasha, 2007), 467–68.

95. Natan Alterman, "Mi-kol ha-'amim," *Ha'aretz*, Nov. 27, 1942.

96. I borrow this adjective from Hayim Nahman Bialik's iconic poem, "In the City of Slaughter" (1904), stanza 7.

97. A 2010 eyewitness testimony places Ben Shoushan at Bar-Ilan University "in the late 1950s" and "while the university was still quite small." Since Bar-Ilan was founded only in 1955, the scene must have taken place in that year or perhaps 1956. Either way, it is the last documented spotting of Ben Shoushan in Israel. Dov Landau, review of *Monsieur Chouchani*, by Salomon Malka, *Musaf ha-ẓofeh* (1994), http://forum.otzar.org/viewtopic.php?p=49601#p53302.

98. And see Imanuel Etkes, *Meshiḥiyut, politikah ve-halakhah: ha-ẓiyonut ha-datit ve-"hashetaḥim" 1967–1982* (Jerusalem: Karmel, 2023).

99. Y. Aviv, "Ga'on nidaḥ be-Montevideo," *Ha-ẓofeh*, Nov. 27, 1967.

100. Y. Aviv, "Ga'on nidaḥ be-Montevideo."

101. Y. Aviv, "Ga'on nidaḥ be-Montevideo."

102. One of them was Shalom Rosenberg, the late professor of Jewish Studies at the Hebrew University in Jerusalem. Another eyewitness was Tzila Arad, wife of an Israeli official in Montevideo. The latter wrote to Wiesel about Chouchani's passing in 1968: Letter from Tzila Arad to Elie Wiesel, box 244, folder 33 ("Mordechai Chouchani"), Elie Wiesel Archive, Boston, MA.

Chapter 2. When Ahasverus Turned Jewish (1873)

1. Joseph Klausner, *Historiyah shel ha-sifrut ha-'ivrit ha-ḥadashah*, vol. 6 (Jerusalem: Akhiasaf, 1952), 357–58.

2. Mendele Mokher Sefarim, *The Nag*, 30.

3. Klausner, *Historiyah shel ha-sifrut ha-'ivrit ha-ḥadashah*, 1952, 6:358.

4. Zalman Shneur, "Reshimot 'al I. Bershadsky li-mlot ḥamishim shana li-ptirato," *Davar*, March 28, 1958, 6.

5. Zalman Shneur, "Vilna," in *Shirat ha-teḥiyah ha-'ivrit*, ed. Binyamin Harshav (Tel Aviv: Ha-universita ha-petukha, 2000), 194.

6. "Le-soḥarey 'ivrit be-ḥuẓ li-medinat rusya," *Ha-levanon*, March 11, 1881, 8.

7. On this type of book trade, see Mordekhai Ehrenpraiz, *Ben mizraḥ le-ma'arav* (Tel Aviv: Am oved, 1993), 21.

8. On Devorah Romm, see Mordekhai Zalkin, "Ha-ru'aḥ ha-ḥaya be-ofney ha-hadpasa: Devorah Romm ke-sokhenet tarbut," in *Derekh sefer: shay li-Ze'ev Gris*, ed. Oded Yisre'eli, Jonatan Meir, and Avraham Reiner (Jerusalem: Karmel, 2021).

9. Two examples for setters-authors in the Romm Press are Tsvi-Nissan Golomb and Mordecai Plungian (Plunkiansky). Hirsch Nissan Golomb, "Vilna," *Ha-ẓfira*, December 11, 1883, 7; Isidore Singer et al., eds., "Golomb, Hirsch Nissan," in *The Jewish Encyclopedia: A Descriptive Record of the History, Religion, Literature, and Customs of the Jewish People from the Earliest Times to the Present Day* (New York: Funk & Wagnalls, 1901), 40. The importance of class consciousness to Jewish life in Vilnius is reflected in the biography of the important socialist leader Aaron Libermann, often called "the father of Jewish socialism." Cecil Bloom, "Aaron Libermann: The Father of Jewish Socialism," *Jewish Historical Studies* 42 (2009): 139–46.

10. Shmuel Shraga Feigenzen, "Le-toldot defus Romm," in *Yahadut Lita*, ed. Ḥayim Bar-Dayan, vol. 1 (Tel Aviv: Am hasefer, 1959), 279–80. On the expansion of the catalogue, see: Shmuel Shraga Feigenzen, "Hoda'ot: aval ashemim anaḥnu," *Ha-magid*, May 26, 1868, 167.

11. On the invention and development of rotary (stereotype) printing, see Rob Banham, "The Industrialization of the Book, 1800–1970," in *A Companion to the History of the Book*, ed. Simon Eliot and Jonathan Rose, vol. II, Blackwell Companions to Literature and Culture (Hoboken, NJ: Wiley-Blackwell, 2020), 453–569. On the rise of Russian antisemitism in the late nineteenth century, see, for instance, Israel Bartal, *Me-umah le-le'om, yehudey mizraḥ eyropa 1772–1881* (Tel Aviv: Ministry of Defense, 2002), 172–83. I take the expression "print-antisemitism" from William W. Hagen, *Anti-Jewish Violence in Poland, 1914–1920* (Cambridge: Cambridge University Press, 2018), 64.

12. Joseph Klausner, *Historiyah shel ha-sifrut ha-'ivrit ha-ḥadashah*, vol. 3 (Jerusalem: Akhiasaf, 1952), 362–75.

13. This can be glimpsed from their printed works. Some examples include Mordecai Aaron Günzburg, *Devir: kolel kevuẓat mikhtavim shonim, melizot, mishle musar ve-toldot anshe shem* (Vilna: Romm, 1844); Abraham Dov Lebensohn, *Be'urim ḥadashim: 'al Yirmeyah, Yeḥezkel ve-khol sifre tere 'asar sifre Emet, Ekhah ve-Kohelet*

(Vilna: Bi-defus Yosef Reuven b.R. Menakhem Man Romm, 1858); Vergil, *Harisot troyah be-yad ha-yevanim*, trans. Micah Joseph Lebensohn (Vilna: Defus Romm, 1869).

14. Joseph Klausner once visited Schulman in his home. "His life was as simple as can be. When I visited him in Vilnius in 1895, he inhabited two simple rooms with wooden floors, covered in sand." Klausner, *Historiyah shel ha-sifrut ha-ʿivrit ha-ḥadashah*, 1952, 3:369–70. Another description of the house is Eliʿezer Eliyahu Fridman, *Sefer ha-zikhronot: 618–686* (Tel Aviv: Defus Ahdut, 1926), 181–82.

15. Klausner, *Historiyah shel ha-sifrut ha-ʿivrit ha-ḥadashah*, 1952, 3:370.

16. For the list of Schulman's publications, see Klausner, 3:375–79.

17. Eugène Sue, *Misterey Pariz: hi ha-maḥberet ha-mikhlalah asher ḥubrah bi-leshon ẓarfat*, trans. Kalman Schulman (Vilna: Defus Romm, 1857).

18. Avraham Shalom Fridberg, *Sefer ha-zikhronot*, vol. 1 (Varsha: Defus Shuldberg, 1899), 106.

19. Klausner, *Historiyah shel ha-sifrut ha-ʿivrit ha-ḥadashah*, 1952, 3:372.

20. Lebensohn, *Be'urim ḥadashim*, xvi.

21. On Russian censorship and the Jews, see Ilia Lurie, "Ha-ẓenzurah ha-memshaltit ʿal ha-pirsumim ha-yehudiyim ba-keysarut ha-rusit," in *Toldot yehudey Rusyah*, vol. 2 (Jerusalem: Merkaz Zalman Shazar, 2010), 63–74. Shafan wrote about the censorship and the Romm press in Feigenzen, "Le-toldot defus Romm," 275. My understanding of Alexander II's reign is based on Alfred J. Rieber's pioneering work from a few decades ago. Thus, for instance, Alfred J. Rieber, "Alexander II: A Revisionist History," *Journal of Modern History* 43, no. 1 (1971): 42–58.

22. Mendele Mokher Sefarim, *The Nag*, trans. Moshe Spiegel (New York: Beechhurst Press, 1955), 170–71.

23. Mendele Mokher Sefarim, "Reshimot le-toldotay," in *Kol kitvey Mendele Mokher Sefarim*, ed. Jacob Fichman and Ludwig Schwerin (Tel Aviv: Devir, 1949), א.

24. Shlomo Srebrek, *Zikhronot* (Tel Aviv: Sh. Srebrek, n.d.), 54.

25. Srebrek, 54.

26. Srebrek, 54–55.

27. Srebrek, 55.

28. Srebrek, 55.

29. Srebrek, 56.

30. Sholem Aleichem, "Li-khvod sabi, ahuv libi, rebbe Mendele Mokher Sefarim," in *Stempenyu*, trans. Isaac Dov Berkowitz (Tel Aviv: Devir, 1950), 9–12.

31. Sholem Yankev Abramovitch, *ʿEyn mishpat* (Zhitomir: Shadova, 1866), 26.

32. Yirmeyahu Frenkel, *Perush le-susati shel Mendele Mokher Sefarim* (Tel Aviv: Yavneh, 1946), 5. For a similar evaluation, see Yosef Haim Brenner, "Ha-ʿarakhat ʿaẓmenu bi-shloshet ha-krakhim," in *Kol kitvey Y.H. Brenner*, vol. 7 (Tel Aviv: Akhdut, 1928), 222.

33. Israel Bartal, *The Jews of Eastern Europe, 1772–1881* (Philadelphia: University of Pennsylvania Press, 2005), 91.

34. Mendele Mokher Sefarim, *Mishpat shalom: osefet ma'amarim shonim* (Vilna: Defus Romm, 1860).

35. Mendele Mokher Sefarim, *Shriften*, vol. 1 (Kiev: Kultur-lige, 1928), 237.

36. Sholem Yankev Abramovitch, *Sefer toldot ha-teva* (Vilna: Defus Romm, 1863).

37. A fuller discussion of the following section is Mintzker, "Keyẓad hafaḥ ha-yehudi ha-noded le-gibor yehudi."

38. On this, see Jonathan Skolnik's important work on the topic: Jonathan Skolnik, *Jewish Pasts, German Fictions: History, Memory, and Minority Culture in Germany, 1824–1955*, Stanford Studies in Jewish History and Culture (Stanford, California: Stanford University Press, 2014), especially chapter 2: "Jewish History Under the Sign of Secularization: Berthold Auerbach's Spinoza (1837)," 23–44. Skolnik's approach to Ahasverus's reception in Jewish literature is different from mine.

39. Berthold Auerbach, *Spinoza*, trans. E. Nicholson, vol. 2 (New York: Holt, 1882), 265–66.

40. Auerbach, 2:268.

41. Auerbach, 2:272.

42. On this debate, see: Hans Otto Horch, *Auf der Suche nach der jüdischen Erzählliteratur: die Literaturkritik der "Allgemeinen Zeitung des Judentums," 1837–1922* (Frankfurt am Main: Peter Lang, 1985), 46–48.

43. Karl Gutzkow, "Mosens Ahasver," *Telegraph für Deutschland* 124 (August 1838): 985–91; Karl Gutzkow, "Mosens Ahasver," *Telegraph für Deutschland* 128 (August 1838): 1017–22.

44. Gutzkow, "Mosens Ahasver," August 1838, 987.

45. Gutzkow, "Mosens Ahasver," August 1838, 988.

46. Gutzkow, "Mosens Ahasver," August 1838, 1019.

47. Ludwig Philippson, "Ahasver, Gutzkow und Juden," *Allgemeine Zeitung des Judenthums* 2, no. 114 (1838): 460–61; Ludwig Philippson, "Ahasver, Gutzkow und Juden," *Allgemeine Zeitung des Judenthums* 2, no. 117 (1838): 472–73; and Ludwig Philippson, "Ahasver, Gutzkow und Juden," *Allgemeine Zeitung des Judenthums* 2, no. 120 (1838): 484–85.

48. Philippson, "Ahasver, Gutzkow und Juden," 1838, 460.

49. Philippson, "Ahasver, Gutzkow und Juden," 1838, 485.

50. Philippson, "Ahasver, Gutzkow und Juden," 1838, 485.

51. Mendele Mokher Sefarim, *Ha-barnash ha-katan*, trans. Shalom Luria (Jerusalem: Karmel, 2003), 141; Mendele Mokher Sefarim, *Mishpat shalom*, 99–107.

52. Mendele Mokher Sefarim, "Ha-avot ve-habanim," in *Kol kitvey Mendele Mokher Sefarim*, ed. Jacob Fichman and Ludwig Schwerin (Tel Aviv: Devir, 1949), 16.

53. Mendele Mokher Sefarim, "Ha-avot ve-habanim," 14.

54. Mendele Mokher Sefarim, "Ha-avot ve-habanim," 14.

55. Fundamental to my discussion here is Dan Miron, *A Traveller Disguised* (New York: Schocken Books, 1973), 130–68.

56. Most famously in Joseph Perl's satire *Revealer of Secrets*. Joseph Perl, *Sefer megaleh temirin* (Vienna: Gedruckt bei Anton Strauss, 1819).

57. Quoted in Miron, *A Traveller Disguised*, 141.

58. Mendele Mokher Sefarim, *The Nag*, 9.

59. Mendele Mokher Sefarim, *Shriften*, 1:237.

60. Mendele Mokher Sefarim, *Dos kleyne menshele, oder, a lebensbeshraybung fun Yitshak Avraham Takif* (New York: Hebrew Publishing Company, 1901), 5.

61. Mendele Mokher Sefarim, *Dos kleyne menshele*, 6.

62. Mendele Mokher Sefarim, *Dos kleyne menshele*, 124.

63. Miron, *A Traveller Disguised*.

64. According to one testimony, Abramovitch wrote the novel very quickly, "a sign of great internal shock." Jacob Fichman, "Shalom Yaacob Abramovitch," in *Kol kitvey Mendele Mokher Sefarim*, ed. Jacob Fichman and Ludwig Schwerin (Tel Aviv: Devir, 1949), xix.

65. Mendele Mokher Sefarim, *The Nag*, 11–12.

66. Mendele Mokher Sefarim, *The Nag*, 17.

67. Mendele Mokher Sefarim, *The Nag*, 17–18.

68. Mendele Mokher Sefarim, *The Nag*, 18.

69. This passage might also reference the fact that there were places in the Russian empire where Jewish children were literally required to learn Russian fairy tales by rote. Steven J. Zipperstein, *The Jews of Odessa: A Cultural History, 1794–1881* (Stanford, CA: Stanford University Press, 1985), 51.

70. Mendele Mokher Sefarim, *The Nag*, 19.

71. Mendele Mokher Sefarim, *The Nag*, 59.

72. Mendele Mokher Sefarim, *The Nag*, 223.

73. A classic work on the Bildungsroman in its European context is Franco Moretti, *The Way of the World: The Bildungsroman in European Culture* (London: Verso, 1987). A recent volume on the Bildungsroman in different national literatures is Sarah Graham, ed., *A History of the Bildungsroman* (Cambridge: Cambridge University Press, 2019).

74. So in the Hebrew edition of the novel: "ze ma'ase ha-haskalah ve-zeh pirya." Mendele Mokher Sefarim, "Susati," in *Kol kitvey Mendele Mokher Sefarim*, ed. Jacob Fichman and Ludwig Schwerin (Tel Aviv: Devir, 1949), 339.

75. Mendele Mokher Sefarim, *The Nag*, 21.

76. Mendele Mokher Sefarim, *The Nag*, 23–24.

77. Mendele Mokher Sefarim, *The Nag*, 28.

78. Mendele Mokher Sefarim, *The Nag*, 30.

79. Mendele Mokher Sefarim, *The Nag*, 30–31.

80. Mendele Mokher Sefarim, *The Nag*, 33–35.

81. Mendele Mokher Sefarim, *The Nag*, 35.

82. Two readers who have commented on this in the past are Frenkel, *Perush le-susati shel Mendele Mokher Sefarim*, 47; Dan Miron, "Aḥarit davar," in *Ha-susah*, by Sholem Yankev Abramovitch, ed. Menachem Peri, trans. Dan Miron (Bnei Brak: Hakibutz hameukhad, 2018), 218.

83. Mendele Mokher Sefarim, *The Nag*, 34.

84. Mendele Mokher Sefarim, *The Nag*, 31.

85. In Walter Benjamin's famous formulation: "Allegory declares itself to be beyond beauty. Allegories are, in the realm of thoughts, what ruins are in the realm of things." Walter Benjamin, *The Origin of German Tragic Drama*, trans. John Osborne (London: Lowe & Brydone Printers, 1977), 178.

86. Frenkel, *Perush le-susati shel Mendele Mokher Sefarim*, 47; Miron, "Aḥarit davar," 228–29.

87. Mendele Mokher Sefarim, *The Nag*, 59.

88. Brenner, "Ha'arakhat 'aẓmenu bi-shloshet ha-krakhim."

89. Mendele Mokher Sefarim, *The Nag*, 46–47.

90. Mendele Mokher Sefarim, *The Nag*, 201–2.

91. Mendele Mokher Sefarim, *The Nag*, 180.

92. Mendele Mokher Sefarim, *The Nag*, 47.

93. Mendele Mokher Sefarim, *The Nag*, 12.

94. Mendele Mokher Sefarim, *The Nag*, 13.

95. Sander L. Gilman, "Jews and Mental Illness: Medical Metaphors, Anti-Semitism, and the Jewish Response," *Journal of the History of the Behavioral Sciences* 20, no. 2 (1984): 150.

96. Miron, "Aḥarit davar," 222.

97. So, for instance, in controversial anticolonial activist and psychiatrist Franz Fanon's work. Frantz Fanon, *The Wretched of the Earth*, trans. Richard Philcox (New York: Grove Press, 2021), 9–16.

98. Compare also the image of the Eastern European (wandering) Jew in Joseph Roth's 1927 book, *Wandering Jews* (*Juden auf Wanderschaft*): "One doesn't want to be reminded of one's grandfather, who was from Posen or Kattowitz, by some stranger who has just arrived from Lodz. That is the ignoble, but understandable, attitude of an endangered petit-bourgeois [Jew] who is just about to climb the rather steep ladder to the terrace of the haute bourgeoisie with its free air and magnificent view. Looking at a cousin from Lodz, one can easily lose one's balance, and fall." Joseph

Roth, *The Wandering Jews*, trans. Michael Hofmann (New York: W. W. Norton, 2001), 122.

99. Some critics of Abramovitch claimed that he himself internalized anti-Jewish stereotypes, as manifested, for instance, in his novel *Fishke the Lame*. Dan Miron, "Ha-ḥinukh ha-sentimentali shel Mendele Mokher Sefarim," in *Sefer Ha-kabẓanim*, by Mendele Mokher Sefarim (Tel Aviv: Devir, 1988), 214.

100. The metaphor is Ludwig Boerne's. Ludwig Börne, *Sämtliche Schriften*, ed. Inge Rippmann and Peter Rippmann, vol. 3 (Düsseldorf: J. Melzer, 1964), 511. The influential Israeli historian Shulamit Volkov chose it for the title of one of her most important books: Shulamit Volkov, *Ba-maʿagal ha-mekhushaf: yehudim, antishemim ve-Germanim aḥerim* (Tel Aviv: Am oved, 2002).

101. George Croly, *Salathiel: A Story of the Past, the Present, and the Future* (London: Henry Colburn, 1828).

102. Mark Meir Dvorzhetski, *Yerushalayim de-Lita ba-meri u-va-shoah* (Tel Aviv: Hoẓaʾat mifleget poʿaley ereẓ yisrael, 1951), 235.

103. Abraham Sutzkever, "The Leaden Plates of Romm's Printing Works," in *Burnt Pearls: Ghetto Poems of Abraham Sutzkever*, trans. Seymour Mayne (Oakville, Ont.: Mosaic Press/Valley Editions, 1981), 41.

Chapter 3. A True Story That Never Happened (1711)

1. On the fire, see Johann Jacob Schudt, *Jüdische Merckwürdigkeiten*, Bayerische Staatsbibliothek Sig. 4 Jud. 19-1-4, vol. 2 (Frankfurt am Main und Leipzig, 1714), 70–131; Isidor Kracauer, *Die Geschichte der Judengasse in Frankfurt am Main* (Frankfurt am Main: J. Kauffmann, 1906), 334–40; and David Kaufmann, *Urkundliches aus dem Leben Samson Wertheimers* (Wien: C. Konegen, 1892), 67–71.

2. *Vorstellung der gäntzlich abgebrandten Judengaß zu Frankfurt am Main*, 1711, Kupferstich, 43 × 27.7 cm, 1711, JMF Historische Sammlung, Jüdisches Museum Frankfurt, https://sammlung.juedischesmuseum.de/objekt/vorstellung-der-gantzlich-ab-gebranden-judenga-zu-frankfurt-am-main; Friedrich Friedmann, *Das Münzkabinett*, hrsg. anläßlich der Ausstellung *Münzen und Medaillen aus dem Münzkabinett des Historischen Museum Frankfurt am Main, Oktober—Dezember 1964*, Heft 5 der Kleinen Schriften des Historischen Museum Frankfurt am Main (Frankfurt am Main: Historisches Museum, 1964), Abb. 39–40.

3. This is written on the back page of Ḥizqiya ben David da Silva, *Sefer pri ḥadash* (Amsterdam: David Tartas, 1672). JMF, Sig. JMF2014–0007.

4. Silva, *Sefer pri ḥadash*, back page.

5. Basic biographical information is from Sabine Hock, "Schudt, Johann Jacob," in *Frankfurter Biographie: Personengeschichtliches Lexikon*, ed. Wolfgang Klötzer

(Frankfurt am Main: Waldemar Kramer, 1996). On different aspects of the *Jewish Notabilia*, see Christoph Cluse and Rebekka Voß, eds., *Frankfurt's "Jewish Notabilia" ('Jüdische Merckwürdigkeiten'): Ethnographic Views of Urban Jewry in Central Europe around 1700*, vol. 40, Frankfurt Judaistische Beiträge, 2015.

6. Stephen Burnett, "Schudt and German Christian Hebraism," *Frankfurter Judaistische Beiträge* 40 (2015): 47–48.

7. "Ohn Häufte und ohne Schutz, ohne wahre freud der Seelen." Quoted in Philipp Jakob Spener, *Gläubiger Christen versicherte Beilage, aus II. Timt. I, 12., bey volkreicher Leich-begräbnus . . . Conrad Schudts* (Frankfurt am Main: Johann Dietrich Fridgen, 1680), 58.

8. Spener, *Gläubiger Christen versicherte Beilage*, 45.

9. On Spener's view on Jews within the context of contemporary Lutheran theology, See Johannes Wallmann, "Der alte und der neue Bund. Zur Haltung des Pietismus gegenüber den Juden," in *Glaubenswelt und Lebenswelten. Geschichte des Pietismus*, ed. Hartmut Lehmann, vol. 4, 4 vols. (Göttingen: Vandenhoeck & Ruprecht, 2004), 143–65.

10. Some ancient examples are to be found in Heinz Schreckenberg, *Die christlichen Adversus-Judaeos-Texte und ihr literarisches und historisches Umfeld (13.-20. Jh.)*, Europäische Hochschulschriften (Frankfurt am Main: Lang, 1994), 378, 389; Heinz Schreckenberg, *Die christlichen Adversus-Judaeos-Texte und ihr literarisches und historisches Umfeld (1.-11. Jh.)*, Europäische Hochschulschriften (Frankfurt am Main: Peter Lang, 1982), 80, 138.

11. Schudt, *Jüdische Merckwürdigkeiten*, 1714, 2:171.

12. Wallmann, "Der alte und der neue Bund. Zur Haltung des Pietismus gegenüber den Juden," 149–50. Indeed, Schudt cites Spener very often in his work, including his call to protect synagogues. Schudt, *Jüdische Merckwürdigkeiten*, 1714, 2:214.

13. The issue is still debated in the secondary literature. A recent discussion, which includes a survey of relevant literature, is Carsten L. Wilke, "From Deicide to Diaspora: The Construction of Jewish World History in Johann Jacob Schudt's Latin Writing," ed. Rebekka Voß and Christoph Cluse, *Frankfurt's "Jewish Notabilia" ("Jüdische Merckwürdigkeiten"): Ethnographic Views of Urban Jewry in Central Europe around 1700*, Frankfurter Judaistische Beiträge, 40 (2015): 153–56.

14. Schudt, *Jüdische Merckwürdigkeiten*, 1714, 2:156.

15. On Luther in Worms, including the question of what he said in his speech to the emperor, see Thomas Kaufmann, *"Hier stehe ich!": Luther in Worms: Ereignis, mediale Inszenierung, Mythos* (Stuttgart: Anton Hiersemann Verlag, 2021).

16. "June 4, 1680," Wittenberger Matrikel, 7 (1675–1709), *Album academiae vitenbergensis*, UA Halle-Wittenberg, Yo (7), 2°.

17. Burnett, "Schudt and German Christian Hebraism," 48–49.

18. A sample list of their publications can be found in Heiner Lück, *Alma Leucorea: eine Geschichte der Universität Wittenberg, 1502 bis 1817* (Halle an der Saale: Universitätsverlag Halle-Wittenberg, 2020), 176. *Catalogus disputationum philologicarum publice in Academ. Witteb. maxime, circiter ab anno MDC habitarum tomisque comprehensarum VII* (Wittenberg: Johannes Wilcke, 1686).

19. Lück, *Alma Leucorea*, 176, n. 795.

20. Andreas Sennert, *Bibliothecae Academiae Wittebergensis Publicae, Librorum qua (1.) Theologicorum (2.) Juridicorum (3.) Medicorum (4.) Philosophicorum ... & qui noviter huic de Anno LXXII. accesserunt* (Wittenberg: Johannes Wilcke, 1678).

21. Walter Friedensburg, *Geschichte der Universität Wittenberg* (Halle a.S.: Max Niemeyer, 1917), 422.

22. "Doctor, der in Streitschriften (welches bei diesen Zeiten sonderlich hochnötig ist) und anderen THEOLOGISCHEN Exercitiis wohl erfahren." Cited in Friedensburg, 419.

23. Three examples for his contentious writings against Calvinists, Catholics, and Socians, respectively, are: Abraham Calov, *Scripta anti-sociniana: quibus haeresis illa pestilentissima non tantum ex ipsis socinistarum scriptis bona fide detegitur, sed etiam e scripturis sacris, haud neglectis antiquitatis ecclesiasticae testimoniis, solide profligatur* (Ulm: Kühnen, 1684); Abraham Calov, *Discussio controversiarum hodierno tempore inter ecclesias orthodoxas et reformatos* (Wittenberg: Hake, 1656); Abraham Calov, *Mataeologia papistica e concilio potissimum Tridentino et praecipuis scriptoribus Pontificiis proposita, et testimoniis cum e scriptura sacra, tum e Romana Ecclesia confutata* (Wittenberg: Hake, 1656). About Calov as a new Torquemada: August Tholuck, *Der Geist der lutherischen Theologen Wittenbergs im Verlaufe des 17. Jahrhunderts: theilweise nach handschriftlichen Quellen* (Hamburg und Gotha: Perthes, 1852), 209. A more favorable evaluation is Timothy R. Schmerling, "Strenuus Christi Athleta Abraham Calov (1612–1686)," *Lutheran Synod Quarterly* 44, no. 4 (December 2004): 357–99.

24. Friedensburg, *Geschichte der Universität Wittenberg*, 152; Volker Jung, *Das Ganze der Heiligen Schrift: Hermeneutik und Schriftauslegung bei Abraham Calov*, Calwer theologische Monographien (Stuttgart: Calwer Verlag, 1999).

25. Friedensburg, *Geschichte der Universität Wittenberg*, 428.

26. Abraham Calov, *Die deutsche Bibel*, 3 vols. (Wittenberg, 1681).

27. Michael Marissen, "On the Jews and Their So-Called Lies in the Fourth Gospel and Bach's St. John Passion," in *Bach against Modernity*, ed. Michael Marissen (New York: Oxford University Press, 2023), 137–45.

28. The point is not to overdraw the contradictions between an allegedly philosemite Spener and an anti-Jewish Calov nor especially to deny Schudt's agency. Rather, it is to describe some common reactions to Jews in late seventeenth-century

German Lutheranism and consequently also the theology that would come to inform Johann Jacob Schudt's views on the Jews.

29. On the history of the doctrine of biblical inerrancy, see John D. Hannah, *Inerrancy and the Church* (Chicago: Moody Press, 1984).

30. Spener once wrote about Edzard that *"celeberrimum Ezardi tanti facio: ac paucos alios qui nunc vivunt, & ab eo plurima adhuc causa Dei permitto."* ("I hold the famous Edzard in particular high regard, like few contemporaries, and expect from him still many things in God's cause.") Philipp Jakob Spener, *D. Philippi Jacobi Speneri ... Consilia et judicia theologica latina,* vol. 3 (Francofurti ad Moenum: Impensis haeredum J. Davidis Aunneri & J. A. Jungii, Typis A. Heinscheitii, 1709), 3:600.

31. On Edzard's work in its Hamburg context, see Carl Wilhelm Gleiss, *Esdras Edzardus, ein alter Hamburger Judenfreund* (Hamburg: Gustav Eduward Nolte, 1871), and Joachim Whaley, *Religious Toleration and Social Change in Hamburg, 1529–1819,* Cambridge Studies in Early Modern History (Cambridge: Cambridge University Press, 1985), 86–87.

32. Johann Heinrich Höck, *Bilder aus der Geschichte der Hamburgischen Kirche seit der Reformation* (Hamburg: Verlag der Evangelischen Buchhandlung, 1900), 73.

33. Johann Jacob Schudt, *Jüdische Merckwürdigkeiten,* Bayerische Staatsbibliothek Sig. 4 Jud. 19-1-4, vol. 1 (Frankfurt am Main und Leipzig, 1714), 382.

34. Schudt, 1:379; Gleiss, *Esdras Edzardus,* 31.

35. Schudt, *Jüdische Merckwürdigkeiten,* 1714, 1:382.

36. Schudt, 1:383.

37. Hock, "Schudt, Johann Jacob," 343.

38. Schudt, *Jüdische Merckwürdigkeiten,* 1714, 1:"Vorrede."

39. Gleiss, *Esdras Edzardus,* 23.

40. The full statement is in Martin Luther, "The Freedom of a Christian," in *Three Treatises,* trans. Charles M. Jacobs, A.T.W. Steinhäuser, and W. A. Lambert (Philadelphia: Fortress Press, 1970), 261–316.

41. Gleiss, *Esdras Edzardus,* 25.

42. On Eisenmenger see, among others, Anton Theodor Hartmann, *Johann Andreas Eisenmenger und seine jüdischen Gegner* (Parchim: D. C. Historff, 1834), and Jacob Katz, *From Prejudice to Destruction: Anti-Semitism, 1700–1933* (Cambridge, MA: Harvard University Press, 1980), 13–22.

43. Katz, *From Prejudice to Destruction,* 14.

44. Johann Andreas Eisenmenger, *Entdecktes Judenthum, oder Gründlicher und Wahrhaffter Bericht, Welchergestalt die verstockte Juden die hochheilige Drey-Einigkleit, Gott Vatter, Sohn und Heil. Geist, erschrecklicher Weise lästern und verunehren* (Königsberg, 1711).

45. Benz, *Der ewige Jude,* 89.

46. "Herr Eisenmenger, mein im Leben . . . vertrauter Freund." Schudt, *Jüdische Merckwürdigkeiten*, 1714, 1:2.

47. Burnett, "Schudt and German Christian Hebraism," 51.

48. Johann Jacob Schudt, *Deliciae hebraeo-philologicae sive Tractatus de studio linguae et philologiae Hebraicae* (Francofurti ad Moenum: Friedrich Knoch, 1700), 4.

49. Johann Jacob Schudt, *Compendium historiae judaicae; de origine, incrementis & rebus gestis Judaeorum . . .* (Francofurti ad Moenum: Friedrich Knoch, 1700).

50. "[Q]uae vero de Judaeo quodam Ahasvero traduntur, dubia valde, si non prorsus sunt fabulosa, cum nec Historia S. Evangelistarum, nec Lucas in Actis Apost. nec Josephus, nec quisquam ex antiquis Ecclesiae Patribus ejus mentionem injecerit." Schudt, *Compendium historiae judaicae*, 460.

51. Johann Jacob Schudt, *Judæus Christicida gravissime peccans et vapulans, sive, perspicua & solida demonstratio, cædem & rejectionem Jesu Nazareni veram esse causam præsentis tam diuturni Judæorum exilii* (Frankfurt am Main: Published by the author, 1703).

52. Schudt, *Judæus Christicida gravissime*, 11.

53. "Quae major corporalis fingi potest miseria, quam Judaeorum praesens est fors atque conditio? Per totum fere terrarum orbem Judaei inter omnes pene nationes longe lateque dispersi misere degunt, sordido vitae genere precarium spiritum pavidi trahunt, omnibus abominabiles, totius orbis ludibrium sunt & quisquiliae, faex gentium & caeda, qui gloria quondam & omnium populorum primitiae Deique peculium fuerunt." Schudt, *Judæus Christicida gravissime*, 11.

54. Schudt, *Judæus Christicida gravissime*, 11.

55. "Qui cum Judæis conversantur & de fidei principiis ac dogmatibus cum ipsis disserunt, non sine stupore experiuntur." Schudt, *Judæus Christicida gravissime*, 16.

56. "Non vero corporalem tantum, sed spiritualem etiam & animae miseriam praesens illorum exilium tam diuturnum arguit, nam terrae Chenaan possessio signum erat evidentissimum, quod Israel in Dei sui gratia perseverabat." Schudt, *Judæus Christicida gravissime*, 15.

57. This is the claim in the book's very title.

58. Schudt, *Jüdische Merckwürdigkeiten*, 1714, 2:84.

59. Schudt, *Jüdische Merckwürdigkeiten*, 1714, 2:84.

60. Schudt, *Jüdische Merckwürdigkeiten*, 1714, 2:84.

61. Schudt, *Jüdische Merckwürdigkeiten*, 1714, 2:85.

62. Schudt, *Jüdische Merckwürdigkeiten*, 1714, 2:85.

63. Schudt, *Jüdische Merckwürdigkeiten*, 1714, 2:85.

64. Silva, *Sefer pri ḥadash*, back page.

65. Schudt, *Jüdische Merckwürdigkeiten*, 1714, 2:87.

66. Schudt, *Jüdische Merckwürdigkeiten*, 1714, 2:87.

67. Burnett, "Schudt and German Christian Hebraism," 55, n.42.

68. Schudt, *Jüdische Merckwürdigkeiten*, 1714, 1: "Vorrede."

69. Burnett, "Schudt and German Christian Hebraism," 44, n.42.

70. Schudt, *Jüdische Merckwürdigkeiten*, 1714, 1: "Vorrede."

71. All descriptions are taken from the titles of subsections in Schudt, *Jüdische Merckwürdigkeiten*, 1714.

72. Schudt, *Jüdische Merckwürdigkeiten*, 1714, 1:488.

73. Schudt, *Jüdische Merckwürdigkeiten*, 1714, 1:490.

74. Schudt, *Jüdische Merckwürdigkeiten*, 1714, 1:490.

75. Schudt, *Jüdische Merckwürdigkeiten*, 1714, 1:490.

76. Schudt, *Jüdische Merckwürdigkeiten*, 1714, 1:490–91. Compare Anderson, *The Legend of the Wandering Jew*, 123.

77. Schudt, *Compendium historiae judaicae*, 460.

78. Contained in the very title of Schudt, *Judæus Christicida*.

79. Schudt, *Jüdische Merckwürdigkeiten*, 1714, 1:491.

80. Schudt, *Jüdische Merckwürdigkeiten*, 1714, 1:490.

81. Schudt, *Jüdische Merckwürdigkeiten*, 1714, 1:492.

82. Schudt, *Jüdische Merckwürdigkeiten*, 1714, 1:492.

83. As Stephen Burnett reminds us, Schudt repeatedly calls his book "a history." Burnett, "Schudt and German Christian Hebraism," 58.

84. Schudt, *Jüdische Merckwürdigkeiten*, 1714, 1:492.

85. Schudt, *Jüdische Merckwürdigkeiten*, 1714, 1:492.

86. Schudt, *Jüdische Merckwürdigkeiten*, 1714, 1:492.

87. Schudt, *Jüdische Merckwürdigkeiten*, 1714, 1:492–93.

88. Schudt, *Jüdische Merckwürdigkeiten*, 1714, 1:496.

89. Schudt, *Jüdische Merckwürdigkeiten*, 1714, 1:513.

90. Schudt, *Jüdische Merckwürdigkeiten*, 1714, 1:513.

91. Schudt, *Jüdische Merckwürdigkeiten*, 1714, 1:494.

92. Schudt, *Jüdische Merckwürdigkeiten*, 1714, 1:495.

93. Schudt, *Jüdische Merckwürdigkeiten*, 1714, 1:503.

94. The original quote is from Erasmus Francisci, *Die lustige Schaubühne von allerhand Curiositäten* (Nürnberg: Endter, 1679), 408.

95. Three examples: Schudt, *Judæus Christicida*, 201; Schudt, *Jüdische Merckwürdigkeiten*, 1714, 2:20; Schudt, *Compendium historiae judaicae*, 474–75.

96. Schudt, *Compendium historiae judaicae*, 219.

97. Schudt, *Jüdische Merckwürdigkeiten*, 1714, 2:308.

98. Schudt, *Compendium historiae judaicae*, 219.

99. Schudt, *Compendium historiae judaicae*, 219.

100. Schudt, *Jüdische Merckwürdigkeiten*, 1714, 2:316.

101. Schudt, *Jüdische Merckwürdigkeiten*, 1714, 2:316.

102. Schudt, *Jüdische Merckwürdigkeiten*, 1714, 2:316.

Chapter 4. The Case of Ahasverus in Hamburg (1602)

1. *Kurtze Beschreibung und Erzehlung von einem Juden, mit Namen Ahasverus, welcher bey der Creutzigung Christi selbst persönlich gewesen ... und seit hero im Leben geblieben, und vor etlich Jahren gen Hamburg kommen* ... (Leyden: Creutzer, 1602), 3. BSB, Rar. 825 [VD17 12:651635F].

2. On Rabelais's use of "ces livres populaires qu'on achetait aux foires et que les colporteurs répandaient partout," see the description in Jacques Boulanger, "Introduction," in *Rabelais: oeuvres complètes*, ed. Jacques Boulanger, Bibliothèque de la Pléiade (Paris: Gallimard, 1955), 11. The original Faust Volksbuch is *Historia Von D. Johañ Fausten/dem weitbeschreyten Zauberer vnnd Schwartzkünstler* (Frankfurt am Main: Johann Spies, 1587).

3. The fullest list currently is still Neubaur, *Die Sage vom ewigen Juden*, 66–102. Many old copies Neubaur examined were lost during the Second World War and a few that he did not list have surfaced since. The author is in the process of preparing an up-to-date publication about all extant copies.

4. For a general introduction to the printing of books in the Renaissance, see, for instance: Andrew Pettegree, *The Book in the Renaissance* (New Haven, CT: Yale University Press, 2010).

5. An example of over-inking is at the BSB, Munich: VD17 12:651635F. An instance of under-inking is a copy at Stabi Bamberg, .5 B 24#11. The printer's fingerprint is clear on page 5 of the copy at UB Tübingen, Gh 732.4-OR.

6. Compare two examples from two very different parts of Germany—Dresden and Strasbourg: *Straßburgische Kriegs Sachen: Kurtze vn[d] doch warhaffte Erzehlung, Was sich von dem Ersten Tag Junij an, biß auff den 26 Julij ... jn[n]er und ausser der Statt verlauffen und zugetragen habe* (Strasbourg: Schütz, 1600); and Paul Odontius, *Kurtze vnd warhafftige Historische erzehlung, Wie vnnd welcher gestalt Paulus Odontius gewesener Euangelischer Prediger zu Walstein in Steyermarck, wegen der Lehr vnd Predigt deß Heyligen Euangelij, von der Grätzerischen Inquisition ... zum Tod vervrtheilt ... worden* (Dresden: Schütz, 1603).

7. I take the biographical information from Theodor Lockemann, "Leonhard Neubaur," *Mitteilungen des Westpreussischen Geschichtsvereins*, July 1, 1919, 25–29.

8. Philippson, "Ahasver, Gutzkow und Juden," 1838, 460–61; Philippson, "Ahasver, Gutzkow und Juden," 1838, 472–73; and Philippson, "Ahasver, Gutzkow und Juden," 1838, 484–85.

9. Neubaur, *Die Sage vom ewigen Juden*; Leonhard Neubaur, *Neue Mitteilungen über die Sage vom ewigen Juden* (Leipzig: J.C. Hinrichs, 1893); Leonhard Neubaur, "Bibliographie der Sage vom ewigen Juden," *Centralblatt für Bibliothekswesen* 10 (1893): 249–66; Leonhard Neubaur, "Zur bibliographie der Sage vom ewigen Juden," *Centralblatt für Bibliothekswesen* 28 (1911): 495–509; Leonhard Neubaur, "Zur

Geschichte der Sage vom ewigen Juden," *Zeitschrift des Vereins für Volkskunde* 22 (1912): 33–54; Leonhard Neubaur, "Zur Geschichte und Bibliographie des Volkbuchs von Ahasverus," *Zeitschrift für Bücherfreunde* 5, no. 2 (1914): 211–23.

10. Neubaur, *Neue Mitteilungen über die Sage vom ewigen Juden*, 16.

11. Anderson, *The Legend of the Wandering Jew*, 44.

12. Among the close to one hundred editions of the Bible examined for this research are all 18 pre-Luther translations into German (for example, Mentelin's in Strasbourg), Luther's own translation, and the important Catholic translations by Dietenberger and Eck, among others. I am grateful to Paul Needham of Princeton's Scheide Library for his help in this research and above all to William Theiss, who did most of it.

13. Stabi Bamberg, .5 B 24#11, page 2.

14. Based on a comparison between BSB, Rar. 825, and WLB, Kirch.G.qt.595.

15. Neubaur, *Die Sage vom ewigen Juden*, 67.

16. Neubaur, *Die Sage vom ewigen Juden*, 16; Anderson, *The Legend of the Wandering Jew*, 42–51.

17. One twentieth-century reader called the name Suchnach "a teaser" ("Vexiername"). Heinrich Dübi, "Drei spätmittelalterliche Legenden in ihrer Wanderung aus Italien durch die Schweiz nach Deutschland," *Zeitschrift des Vereins für Volkskunde* 17 (1907): 150.

18. Johann Fischart, *Die Wunderlichst Unerhörtest Legend und Beschreibung des Abgeführten, Quartirten, Gevierten und Viereckechten Vierhörnigen Hütleins Samt Ursprungs derselbigen Heyligen Quadricornischen Suiterhauben und Cornutschlappen . . .* (Strasbourg: Gangwolf Suchnach [Bernhard Jobin], 1580).

19. Arnoldus Greve, *Memoria Pauli ab Eitzen doctoris theologi et superintendentis Hamburgensis instaurata* (Hamburg: Ioannes Carolus Bohnius, 1744); Johannes Moller, *J. Molleri Cimbria litterata, sive Scriptarum Ducatus utriusque Sclesvicensis et Halsatici quibus et alii vicini quidam accensentur historia Litteraria Tripartita cum praefatione J. Grammii*, vol. 3 (Hanniae: Typis regiis, 1744), 227–36.

20. "Fabulae istius putidissimae vanitatem . . . iampridem abunde detexerunt, ac nos proinde ejusem refutatione merito supersedemus." Johannes Moller, *J. Molleri Cimbria litterata*, 3:231.

21. Thus Greve can cite the relevant page numbers in Moller's book even though the latter has not appeared in print just yet: "Ille fecit id in Cimbria Litterata, Tom III. p. 227 ad pag. 336 quam propediem typis expressam expectamus." "Praefetio," Greve, *Memoria Pauli ab Eitzen*.

22. In addition to Greve and Moller, I have also consulted the items mentioned in Heinz Scheible, ed., *Melanchthons Briefwechsel: Personen A-E* (Heidelberg: Heidelberger Akademie der Wissenschaften, 1977), 397–98, as well as Eitzen's extent letters at the StA Hamburg, 111–1 CL VII Lit Hb Nr. 1, 2; LA Schleswig-Holstein, Abt. 3,

Nrs. 300, 303; Amt 7, Nrs. 2054, 2057; and Rigsarkivet Kopenhagen (RA Copenhagen), Slesvig Bisp, 1589 L 18–208.

23. Lothar Mundt, *Lemnius und Luther: Studien und Texte zur Geschichte und Nachwirkung ihres Konflikts (1538/39)*, vol. 2 (Bern: P. Lang, 1983), 143. I am grateful to Lyndal Roper for drawing my attention to this wonderful book.

24. WB VI:21.

25. *Kurtze Beschreibung*, 3. [VD17 12:651635F].

26. Georg Gottfried Küster, *Georgii Gothofredi Kusteri, gymnasii petrini, qvod coloniae ad suevum est, conrectoris, memorabilia coloniensia* (Leipzig: Blochberger, 1731), 21–31.

27. The best description is Greve, *Memoria Pauli ab Eitzen*.

28. *Kurtze Beschreibung*, 2. [VD17 12:651635F].

29. Some relevant archival materials for the later period in Eitzen's life are to be found in RA Copenhagen and the StA Schleswig-Holstein. The most important of the Copenhagen materials is the so-called cartulary of the bishops of Schleswig, copied around 1589 and named the Schwabstedt Book (Svavstedbogen). RA Copenhagen, Slesvig Bisp, 1589 L 18–208. The only useful file in Schleswig-Holstein I was able to locate concerns the oath of office by local pastors. LA Schleswig-Holstein, Amt 16.1, Nr. 81.

30. "Evangelium an S. Johans Tage / Johan 21.," in Paul von Eitzen, *Evangelia der Fest- und Sontage durchs gantze Jar, mit kurtzen Postillen einfeltiger Auslegung* (Schleswig: Nicolaus Wegener, 1590), n.p.

31. Lee Palmer Wandel, *The Eucharist in the Reformation: Incarnation and Liturgy* (Cambridge: Cambridge University Press, 2006), 2.

32. As Neubaur already remarked. Neubaur, *Die Sage vom ewigen Juden*, 48.

33. Some examples in Luise Schorn-Schütte, ed., *Das Interim 1548/50: Herrschaftskrise und Glaubenskonflikt* (Gütersloh: Gütersloher Verlagshaus, 2005), 269–70.

34. In a letter to Georg Fabricius, August 1549. CR VII: 449. See also Thomas Kaufmann, " 'Our Lord God's Chancery' in Magdeburg and Its Fight against the Interim," *Church History* 73, no. 3 (2004): 577.

35. See, for instance, their deferential letter to him of April 16, 1549. CR VII: 366–82.

36. This is how Joachim Mörlin reports the incident to Flacius back in Magdeburg: "Hodie coepimus cum illo [Melanchthon] negotium nostrum tractare. Et quia primus motus est vehementior, oportet nos tantisper agere donec mitescat." "Morlinus ad Flacium, January 21, 1557," CR IX:32.

37. Cited in Jürgen Diestelmann, *Joachim Mörlin: Luthers Kaplan—"Papst der Lutheraner": ein Zeit- und Lebensbild aus dem 16. Jahrhundert* (Neuendettelsau: Freimund-Verlag, 2003), 225–27.

38. Johann Major, *Synodus avium: depingens miseram faciem ecclesiae propter certamina quorundam qui de primatu contendunt*, 1557.

39. StA Hamburg, 511–1 Geistlihces Ministerium III A 1 b: Akten und Briefe 1532–1601.

40. Greve, *Memoria Pauli ab Eitzen*, 139–40.

41. Greve, *Memoria Pauli ab Eitzen*, 140.

42. Greve, *Memoria Pauli ab Eitzen*, 140.

43. Diarmaid MacCulloch, *The Reformation* (New York: Penguin Books, 2005), 353.

44. Quoted in James William Richard, *The Confessional History of the Lutheran Church* (Philadelphia: Lutheran Publication Society, 1909), 500–501.

45. Greve, *Memoria Pauli ab Eitzen*, 15.

46. Greve, *Memoria Pauli ab Eitzen*, 15.

47. Quoted in Bernhard Cottret, *Calvin: A Biography*, trans. M. Wallace McDonald (Grand Rapids, MI: W. B. Eerdmans, 2000), 239.

48. Quoted in Philip Schaff, *History of the Christian Church*, vol. 7 (New York: Charles Scribner's Sons, 1898), 662.

49. "Unius tantum rei admonitum te volo: de Lutheri simiis me pridem desperasse, nec in Iacobo Andrea et similibus esse multum spei. Sed fratres nobis coniunctos opprimi barbara tyrannide nec aliquo subsidio levar vehementer mihi dolet." Calvin to Bullinger, May 1560. CR XLVI: 83–84.

50. "In Westphalo et reliquis difficile erat mihi temperare." "Calvin to Guillaume Farel, August 1557," CR XLIV: 552.

51. This understanding is misguided. Calvin wrote against the idea that the body of Christ was ubiquitous from a theological, not logical, position. See Calvin, *Institutes*, IV:17.

52. Luther, "The Heidelberg Disputation," thesis 3. LW, XXXI:39.

53. Greve, *Memoria Pauli ab Eitzen*, 40.

54. The entire discussion is in Greve, *Memoria Pauli ab Eitzen*, 38–40.

55. Greve, *Memoria Pauli ab Eitzen*, 38–40. Beza's most vehement attack on Westphal is Théodore de Bèze, *De coena Domini, plana & perspicua tractatio. In qua Ioachimi Westphali calumniae postremum editae refelluntur* (Genevae: Oliva Roberti Stephani, 1559).

56. Quoted in Lyndal Roper, *Martin Luther: Renegade and Prophet* (London: The Bodley Head, 2016), 39.

57. Greve, *Memoria Pauli ab Eitzen*, 140.

58. Greve, *Memoria Pauli ab Eitzen*, 140.

59. Susan C. Karant-Nunn, *The Reformation of Feeling: Shaping the Religious Emotions in Early Modern Germany* (Oxford: Oxford University Press, 2010), 145.

60. Tilemann Heshusius, *Verzeychnuß Und kurtzer außzug auß etlicher Hochgelehrter (auch vieler anderer Gottseliger Menner und erfarner der Hebreyschen sprach) beschreibungen von den erschrecklichen Gottslesterungen wider unsern Herrn Christum, die Jungkfraw Maria, wider alle Christen und weltliche Oberkeyt, So von den Juden teglich geübt wirdt*, 1560. [VD16 V 893]

61. Paul Frédéric Geisendorf, *Théodore de Bèze* (Genève: Labor et fides, 1949), 114–15.

62. Quoted in David C. Steinmetz, *Calvin in Context* (Oxford: Oxford University Press, 1995), 184, n.13.

63. R(EVERENDISSIMVS) ET CLA(RISSIMVS) VIR TILEMANVS HESHVSIVS S(ANCTAE) THE/OL(OGIAE) D(OCTOR) CVM AN(NOS) 35 IN 8 ECCLE(SIIS) ET SCHOLIS SIN[C]ERA DOCTRINA SEPTIESQ(VE) DVRIS EXILIIS CH(RISTV)M GLORIFICASSET IN / HAC VERO ACAD(EMIA) AN(NOS) XI PROF(ESSOREM) PRIMARIVM EG[I/SS]ET CONSTANTI FIDE SEXAGENARI(VS) ET OCTIMESTRIS PLACIDE OBIIT 25 SEPT(EMBRIS) AN(NO) D(OMI)NI 1·589.

64. Karl von Helmolt, *Tilemann Hesshus zuletzt Doktor und erster Professor der Theologie zu Helmstedt und seine sieben Exilia: ein Stück Leben aus den kirchlichen Bewegungen der zweiten Hälfte des sechzehnten Jahrhunderts* (Leipzig: Dörffling und Franke, 1859).

65. Théodore de Bèze, *Correspondance de Théodore de Bèze*, ed. Hippolyte Aubert et al., 43 vols., Travaux d'humanisme et Renaissance (Genève: Droz, 1960).

66. On "Jewishness" as rhetorical device in the Christian confessional wars of the Reformation, see David Nirenberg, *Anti-Judaism: The Western Tradition* (New York: W. W. Norton, 2013), 263–64.

Chapter 5. I, Ahasverus (2025)

1. Elena Ferrante, *In the Margins: On the Pleasures of Reading and Writing*, trans. Ann Goldstein (New York: Europa Editions, 2022), 80.

2. See Aharon Kampinsky, *Zevulun Hammer: biyografyah politit* (Ramat Gan: Bar-Ilan University Press, 2021).

3. A copy of the booklet is kept in the National Library of Israel: "Dina Bari, 8.7.75–5.10.85." NLI S 2014 A 7715. No page numbers.

4. Stefan Heym, *The Wandering Jew* (New York: Holt, Rinehart and Winston, 1984), 64.

5. Heym, 121.

6. J. D. Salinger, *Franny and Zooey* (New York: Little, Brown and Company, 2023), 49.

7. Steven J. Gold, *The Israeli Diaspora* (London: Routledge, 2002), 3.

8. So Rabin in a notorious TV interview in 1976; Yehuda Gothelf, "Ha-ḥot'im (ha-nemoshot) ve-hamaḥti'im," *Davar*, May 14, 1954, p. 12; Yehoshua Bar Yosef, *Moznaim* 42, no. 2 (January 1976): 84.

9. Preliminary data from Israel's Central Bureau of Statistics is quite striking. Dror Marmor, "Keẓev ha-yerida mi-ha'areẓ mitgaber," *Globes*, February 23, 2024, sec. Ba-areẓ, https://www.globes.co.il/news/article.aspx?did=1001471862.

10. Israeli expatriates who work on topics related to exile and wandering include Ruby Namdar, *The Ruined House*, trans. Hillel Halkin (New York: Harper, 2017); Maya Arad, *Shevaʿ midot raʿot* (Tel Aviv: Khargol, 2006); Maya Arad, *Ha-Morah le-ʿIvrit* (Tel Aviv: Khargol, 2018); and Dori Manor, ed., *Ho!* 25 (Tel Aviv: Hakibutz hameukhad, 2023). The latter is an edited collection of writings by ex-Israeli writers who continue to write in Hebrew.

11. Johann Wolfgang von Goethe, *Faust: A Tragedy*, ed. Cyrus Hamlin, trans. Walter Arndt, Norton Critical Edition (New York: W.W. Norton, 2001), 12.

12. Goethe, *Faust*, 93.

13. Toni Morrison, *Beloved* (New York: Vintage Books, 2004), 43–44.

14. Ezer Weizman, "Eineni yakhol li-sloʾaḥ be-shem ha-korbanot," *Yediot Ahronot*, January 16, 1996, sec. 24 Shaʾot, 9.

15. Ralph Waldo Emerson, "Self-Reliance," in *Self-Reliance and Other Essays* (New York: Dover Publications, 1993), 19.

16. "The first statement of an important idea which comes to full flower in the later nineteenth century—that Ahasverus is symbolic of the Jewish people as a whole—comes from Johann Jacob Schudt." Anderson, *The Legend of the Wandering Jew*, 123.

BIBLIOGRAPHY

Abramovitch, Sholem Yankev. *'Ein mishpat*. Zhitomir: Shadova, 1866.

———. *Mishpaṭ shalom: ve-hu asefat ma'amarim shonim*. Vilna: Defus Romm, 1860.

———. *Sefer toldot ha-teva*. Vilna: Defus Romm, 1863.

Aleichem, Sholem. "Li-khvod sabi, ahuv libi, rebbe Mendele Mokher Sefarim." In *Stempenyu*, translated by Isaac Dov Berkowitz. Tel Aviv: Devir, 1950.

Anderson, George K. *The Legend of the Wandering Jew*. Providence, RI: Brown University Press, 1965.

Arad, Maya. *ha-Morah le-'Ivrit*. Tel Aviv: Hargol, 2018.

———. *Shev'a midot ra'ot*. Tel Aviv: Hargol, 2006.

Arbeli-Almozlino, Shoshana. *Me-hamahteret be-Bavel le-memshelet Yisra'el*. Tel Aviv: Hakibutz hameukhad, 1988.

Arendt, Hannah. *Eichmann in Jerusalem: A Report on the Banality of Evil*. Revised and enlarged edition. New York: Penguin Books, 1994.

Auerbach, Berthold. *Spinoza*. Translated by E. Nicholson. Vol. 2. New York: Holt, 1882.

Averbach, Israel. *Yam rogesh, gevah-gali*. Tel Aviv: Hakibutz hameukhad, 1992.

Bachrach, Zvi. "Ha-adam, ha-hashgaḥah, ve-oshwitz." *Zmanim* 6 (1981): 93–97.

———. *Min ha-ḥavayah el ha-meḥkar*. Jerusalem: Yad Vashem, 2008.

Banham, Rob. "The Industrialization of the Book, 1800–1970." In *A Companion to the History of the Book*, edited by Simon Eliot and Jonathan Rose, II: 453–569. Blackwell Companions to Literature and Culture. Hoboken, NJ: Wiley-Blackwell, 2020.

Bar Yosef, Yehoshua. *Moznaim* 42, no. 2 (January 1976): 83–86.

Bartal, Israel. *The Jews of Eastern Europe, 1772–1881*. Philadelphia: University of Pennsylvania Press, 2005.

———. *Me-umah le-le'om, yehudey mizraḥ eyropa 1772–1881*. Tel Aviv: Ministry of Defense, 2002.

Barukhi, Nahum. *Be'erot Yiẓḥak be-hityashvut u-milḥamah*. Jerusalem: Ariel, 2009.

Baum, Johann Wilhelm. *Theodor Beza: nach handschriftlichen Quellen dargestellt.* Vol. 2. Leipzig: Weidmann, 1851.

Ben Ezer, Ehud. *Yamim shel la'anah u-devash.* Tel Aviv: Am oved, 1988.

Benjamin, Walter. *The Origin of German Tragic Drama.* Translated by John Osborne. London: Lowe & Brydone Printers, 1977.

Benz, Wolfgang. *"Der ewige Jude": Metaphern und Methoden nationalsozialistischer Propaganda.* Berlin: Metropol, 2010.

Berenbaum, Michael. *Elie Wiesel: God, the Holocaust, and the Children of Israel.* West Orange, NJ: Behrman House, 1994.

Beyer, Jürgen. "Jürgen und der Ewige Jude: ein lebender Heiliger wird unsterblich." *Arv. Nordic Yearbook of Folklore* 64 (2008): 125–40.

Bèze, Théodore de. *Correspondance de Théodore de Bèze.* Edited by Hippolyte Aubert, Fernand Aubert, Henri Meylan, et al. 43 vols. Travaux d'humanisme et Renaissance. Genève: Droz, 1960.

——. *De coena Domini, plana & perspicua tractatio. In qua Ioachimi Westphali calumniae postremum editae refelluntur.* Genevae: Oliva Roberti Stephani, 1559.

Birlinger, Anton, ed. *Volksthümliches aus Schwaben.* Vol. 1. Freiburg im Breisgau: Herder, 1861.

Bloom, Cecil. "Aaron Libermann: The Father of Jewish Socialism." *Jewish Historical Studies* 42 (2009): 139–46.

Börne, Ludwig. *Sämtliche Schriften.* Edited by Inge Rippmann and Peter Rippmann. Vol. 3. Düsseldorf: J. Melzer, 1964.

Boulanger, Jacques. "Introduction." In *Rabelais: oeuvres complètes,* edited by Jacques Boulanger, 7–21. Bibliothèque de la Pléiade. Paris: Gallimard, 1955.

Brenner, Yosef Haim. "Ha-arakhat 'azmenu bi-shloshet ha-krakhim." In *Kol kitvey Y.H. Brenner,* 7:219–67. Tel Aviv: Akhdut, 1928.

Burnett, Stephen. "Schudt and German Christian Hebraism." *Frankfurter Judaistische Beiträge* 40 (2015): 47–62.

Calov, Abraham. *Biblia illustrata Alten und Neuen Testaments.* 4 vols. Frankfurt am Main and Leipzig, 1672.

——. *Die deutsche Bibel.* 3 vols. Wittenberg, 1681.

——. *Discussio controversiarum hodierno tempore inter ecclesias orthodoxas et reformatos.* Wittenberg: Hake, 1656.

——. *Mataeologia papistica e concilio potissimum Tridentino et praecipuis scriptoribus Pontificiis proposita, et testimoniis cum e scriptura sacra, tum e Romana Ecclesia confutata.* Wittenberg: Hake, 1656.

——. *Scripta anti-sociniana: quibus haeresis illa pestilentissima non tantum ex ipsis socinistarum scriptis bona fide detegitur, sed etiam e scripturis sacris, haud neglectis antiquitatis ecclesiasticae testimoniis, solide profligatur.* Ulm: Kühnen, 1684.

Calvin, Jean. *Ioannis Calvini opera quae supersunt omnia.* Edited by Alfred Erichson. 58 vols. Brunsvigae: C. A. Schwetschke, 1863.

Catalogus disputationum philologicarum publice in Academ. Witteb. maxime, circiter ab anno MDC habitarum tomisque comprehensarum VII. Wittenberg: Johannes Wilcke, 1686.

Cluse, Christoph, and Rebekka Voß, eds. *Frankfurt's "Jewish Notabilia" ('Jüdische Merckwürdigkeiten'): Ethnographic Views of Urban Jewry in Central Europe around 1700.* Vol. 40. Frankfurt Judaistische Beiträge, 2015.

Cohen, Richard I., and Mirjam Rajner. "The Return of the Wandering Jew(s) in Samuel Hirszenberg's Art." *Ars Judaica* 7 (2011): 33–56.

Cottret, Bernhard. *Calvin: A Biography.* Translated by M. Wallace McDonald. Grand Rapids, MI: W. B. Eerdmans, 2000.

Croly, George. *Salathiel: A Story of the Past, the Present, and the Future.* London: Henry Colburn, 1828.

Darnton, Robert. *The Great Cat Massacre and Other Episodes in French Cultural History.* New York: Basic Books, 2009.

Daube, David. "Ahasver." *Jewish Quarterly Review* 45 (1955): 243–44.

Diestelmann, Jürgen. *Joachim Mörlin: Luthers Kaplan—"Papst der Lutheraner": ein Zeit- und Lebensbild aus dem 16. Jahrhundert.* Neuendettelsau: Freimund-Verlag, 2003.

Dübi, Heinrich. "Drei spätmittelalterliche Legenden in ihrer Wanderung aus Italien durch die Schweiz nach Deutschland." *Zeitschrift des Vereins für Volkskunde* 17 (1907): 42–65, 143–60.

Duda, Wendelin. *Sagen des Odenwaldes und westlichen Baulandes von Buchen und Walldürn nach Adelsheim und Neudenau.* Freiburg in Breisgau: Echo Verlag, 2007.

Dumas, Alexandre. *Isaac Laquedem.* Bruxelles: Meline, Cans et Cie, 1853.

Dvorzhetski, Mark Meir. *Yerushalayim de-Lita ba-meri uva-shoah.* Tel Aviv: Hotzaat mifleget poaley erets yisrael, 1951.

Ehrenpraiz, Mordekhai. *Ben mizraḥ le-ma'arav.* Tel Aviv: Am oved, 1993.

Eisenmenger, Johann Andreas. *Entdecktes Judenthum, oder Gründlicher und Wahrhaffter Bericht, Welchergestalt die verstockte Juden die hochheilige Drey-Einigkeit, Gott Vatter, Sohn und Heil. Geist, erschrecklicher Weise lästern und verunehren.* Königsberg, 1711.

Eitzen, Paul von. *Evangelia der Fest- und Sontage durchs gantze Jar, mit kurtzen Postillen einfeltiger Auslegung.* Schleswig: Nicolaus Wegener, 1590.

Emerson, Ralph Waldo. "Self-Reliance." In *Self-Reliance and Other Essays.* New York: Dover Publications, 1993.

Eötvös, József. *Die Emancipation der Juden.* Translated by Zeev Zwi Klein. 2. verm. Aufl. Pest: Gustav Heckenast, 1841.

Eshkoli, Ḥava. *Beyn haẓalah li-ge'ulah.* Jerusalem: Yad Vashem, 2004.

Etkes, Imanuel. *Meshiḥiyut, politikah ve-halakhah: ha- ẓiyonut ha-datit ye-"hashetaḥim" 1967–1982.* Jerusalem: Karmel, 2023.

Fanon, Frantz. *The Wretched of the Earth.* Translated by Richard Philcox. New York: Grove Press, 2021.

Feigenzen, Shmuel Shraga. "Hoda'ot: aval ashemim anaḥnu." *Hamagid,* May 26, 1868.

———. "Le-toldot defus Romm." In *Yahadut Lita,* edited by Ḥayim Bar-Dayan, 1: 268–96. Tel Aviv: Am hasefer, 1959.

Ferrante, Elena. *In the Margins: On the Pleasures of Reading and Writing.* Translated by Ann Goldstein. New York: Europa Editions, 2022.

Fichman, Jacob. "Shalom Yaacob Abramovitch." In *Kol kitvey Mendele Mokher Sefarim,* edited by Jacob Fichman and Ludwig Schwerin. Tel Aviv: Devir, 1949.

Fischart, Johann. *Die Wunderlichst Unerhörtest Legend und Beschreibung des Abgeführten, Quartirten, Gevierten und Viereckechten Vierhörnigen Hütleins Saṁt Ursprungs derselbigen Heyligen Quadricornischen Suiterhauben und Cornutschlappen . . .* Strasbourg: Gangwolf Suchnach [Bernhard Jobin], 1580.

Francisci, Erasmus. *Die lustige Schaubühne von allerhand Curiositäten.* Nürnberg: Endter, 1679.

Frenkel, Yirmeyahu. *Perush le-susati shel Mendele Mokher Sefarim.* Tel Aviv: Yavneh, 1946.

Fridberg, Avraham Shalom. *Sefer ha-zikhronot.* Vol. 1. Varsha: Defus Shuldberg, 1899.

Fridman, Eli'ezer Eliyahu. *Sefer ha-zikhronot: 618–686.* Tel Aviv: Defus Akhdut, 1926.

Friedensburg, Walter. *Geschichte der Universität Wittenberg.* Halle a.S.: Max Niemeyer, 1917.

Friedländer, Saul. *When Memory Comes.* Translated by Helen R. Lane. New York: Farrar, Straus, Giroux, 1979.

Friedmann, Friedrich. *Das Münzkabinett, hrsg. anläßlich der Ausstellung Münzen und Medaillen aus dem Münzkabinett des Historischen Museum Frankfurt am Main, Oktober—Dezember 1964.* Heft 5 der Kleinen Schriften des Historischen Museum Frankfurt am Main. Frankfurt am Main: Historisches Museum, 1964.

Geisendorf, Paul Frédéric. *Théodore de Bèze.* Genève: Labor et fides, 1949.

Gilbert, Martin. *The Routledge Atlas of Jewish History.* 8th ed. New York: Routledge, 2010.

Gilman, Sander L. "Jews and Mental Illness: Medical Metaphors, Anti-Semitism, and the Jewish Response." *Journal of the History of the Behavioral Sciences* 20, no. 2 (1984): 150–59.

Glanz, Rudolf. *The Jew in the Old American Folklore*. New York: Waldon Press, 1961.

Gleiss, Carl Wilhelm. *Esdras Edzardus, ein alter Hamburger Judenfreund*. Hamburg: Gustav Eduward Nolte, 1871.

Goethe, Johann Wolfgang von. *Faust: A Tragedy*. Edited by Cyrus Hamlin. Translated by Walter Arndt. Norton Critical Edition. New York: W.W. Norton, 2001.

———. *Faust, Part One*. Translated by David Luke. Oxford: Oxford University Press, 1987.

Gold, Steven J. *The Israeli Diaspora*. London: Routledge, 2002.

Goldstein, Jan. "The Wandering Jew and the Problem of Psychiatric Anti-Semitism in Fin-de-Siècle France." *Journal of Contemporary History* 20, no. 4 (October 1985): 521–52.

Golomb, Hirsch Nissan. "Vilna." *Hatsfira*, December 11, 1883.

Graham, Sarah, ed. *A History of the Bildungsroman*. Cambridge: Cambridge University Press, 2019.

Greve, Arnoldus. *Memoria Pauli ab Eitzen doctoris theologi et superintendentis Hamburgensis instaurata*. Hamburg: Ioannes Carolus Bohnius, 1744.

Gröner, Erich. *Die deutschen Kriegsschiffe, 1815–1945*. Vol. 4. München: Bernard & Graefe, 1982.

Günzburg, Mordecai Aaron. *Devir: kolel kevuẓat mikhtavim shonim, meliẓot, mishle musar ve-toldot anshe shem*. Vilna: Romm, 1844.

Gutzkow, Karl. "Mosens Ahasver." *Telegraph für Deutschland* 124 (August 1838): 985–91.

———. "Mosens Ahasver." *Telegraph für Deutschland* 128 (August 1838): 1017–22.

Haase, Hans, and Günter Schöne. *Die Universität Helmstedt: 1576–1810: Bilder aus ihrer Geschichte*. Bremen: Jacobi, 1976.

Hagen, William W. *Anti-Jewish Violence in Poland, 1914–1920*. Cambridge: Cambridge University Press, 2018.

Hammerschlag, Sarah. *The Figural Jew: Politics and Identity in Postwar French Thought*. Chicago: University of Chicago Press, 2010.

Hannah, John D. *Inerrancy and the Church*. Chicago: Moody Press, 1984.

Hartmann, Anton Theodor. *Johann Andreas Eisenmenger und seine jüdischen Gegner*. Parchim: D. C. Historff, 1834.

Hasan-Rokem, Galit. "Ahasver—The Enigma of a Name." *Jewish Quarterly Review* 100, no. 4 (Fall 2010): 544–50.

———. "Der Ewige Jude in Europa—Eine Jüdische-Christliche Koproduktion." In *Jüdischer Almanach: Grenzen*, edited by Gisela Dachs, 75–83. Berlin: Jüdischer Verlag, 2015.

Hasan-Rokem, Galit, and Alan Dundes, eds. *The Wandering Jew: Essays in the Interpretation of a Christian Legend*. Bloomington: Indiana University Press, 1986.

Helmolt, Karl von. *Tilemann Hesshus zuletzt Doktor und erster Professor der Theologie zu Helmstedt und seine sieben Exilia: ein Stück Leben aus den kirchlichen Bewegungen der zweiten Hälfte des sechzehnten Jahrhunderts*. Leipzig: Dörffling und Franke, 1859.

Herzl, Theodor. *The Complete Diaries of Theodor Herzl*. Edited by Raphael Patai. Translated by Harry Zohn. Vol. 2. 5 vols. New York: Herzl Press, 1960.

Heshusius, Tilemann. *Verzeychnuß Und kurtzer außzug auß etlicher Hochgelehrter (auch vieler anderer Gottseliger Menner und erfarner der Hebreyschen sprach) beschreibungen von den erschrecklichen Gottslesterungen wider unsern Herrn Christum, die Jungkfraw Maria, wider alle Christen und weltliche Oberkeyt, So von den Juden teglich geübt wirdt*, 1560.

Heym, Stefan. *Ahasver: Roman*. München: C. Bertelsmann, 1981.

———. *The Wandering Jew*. New York: Holt, Rinehart and Winston, 1984.

Historia Von D. Johañ Fausten/dem weitbeschreyten Zauberer vnnd Schwartzkünstler. Frankfurt am Main: Johann Spies, 1587.

Höck, Johann Heinrich. *Bilder aus der Geschichte der Hamburgischen Kirche seit der Reformation*. Hamburg: Verlag der Evangelischen Buchhandlung, 1900.

Hock, Sabine. "Schudt, Johann Jacob." In *Frankfurter Biographie: Personengeschichtliches Lexikon*, edited by Wolfgang Klötzer, 2: 343. Frankfurt am Main: Waldemar Kramer, 1996.

Horch, Hans Otto. *Auf der Suche nach der jüdischen Erzählliteratur: die Literaturkritik der "Allgemeinen Zeitung des Judentums," 1837–1922*. Frankfurt am Main: Peter Lang, 1985.

Horowitz, Tamar. *Between Neighborhood Community and Ideological Community*. Jerusalem: Makhon Henrietta Szold, 1990.

Hurwitz, S. "Ahasver, the Eternal Wanderer: Psychological Aspects." In *The Wandering Jew: Essays in the Interpretation of a Christian Legend*, edited by Galit Hasan-Rokem and Alan Dundes, 211–26. Bloomington: Indiana University Press, 1986.

Isaac-Edersheim, E. "Ahasver: A Mythic Image of the Jew." In *The Wandering Jew: Essays in the Interpretation of a Christian Legend*, edited by Galit Hasan-Rokem and Alan Dundes, 511–28. Bloomington: Indiana University Press, 1986.

Jung, Volker. *Das Ganze der Heiligen Schrift: Hermeneutik und Schriftauslegung bei Abraham Calov*. Calwer theologische Monographien. Stuttgart: Calwer Verlag, 1999.

Kampinsky, Aharon. *Zevulun Hammer: biyografyah politit*. Ramat Gan: Bar-Ilan University Press, 2021.

Kaplansky, Dan, ed. *Bet ha-sefer be-ruaḥ 'erkey tenu'at ha-'avoda: dapey rek'a le-hekerut rishonit*. Jerusalem: Haaguda lekhinukh tenuati al shem Golda Meir, 1984.

Karant-Nunn, Susan C. *The Reformation of Feeling: Shaping the Religious Emotions in Early Modern Germany*. Oxford: Oxford University Press, 2010.

Katz, Jacob. *From Prejudice to Destruction: Anti-Semitism, 1700–1933*. Cambridge, MA: Harvard University Press, 1980.

Kaufmann, David. *Urkundliches aus dem Leben Samson Wertheimers*. Wien: C. Konegen, 1892.

Kaufmann, Thomas. *"Hier stehe ich!": Luther in Worms: Ereignis, mediale Inszenierung, Mythos*. Stuttgart: Anton Hiersemann Verlag, 2021.

———. " 'Our Lord God's Chancery' in Magdeburg and Its Fight against the Interim." *Church History* 73, no. 3 (2004): 566–82.

Klausner, Joseph. *Historiyah shel ha-sifrut ha-ʿivrit ha-ḥadashah*. 6 vols. Jerusalem: Akhiasaf, 1952.

Kracauer, Isidor. *Die Geschichte der Judengasse in Frankfurt am Main*. Frankfurt am Main: J. Kauffmann, 1906.

Kühnau, Richard. *Schlesische Sagen*. Vol. 4. Leipzig: B.G. Teubner, 1910.

Kurtze Beschreibung und Erzehlung von einem Juden, mit Namen Ahasverus, welcher bey der Creutzigung Christi selbst persönlich gewesen . . . und seit hero im Leben geblieben, und vor etlich Jahren gen Hamburg kommen . . . Leyden: Creutzer, 1602.

Küster, Georg Gottfried. *Georgii Gothofredi Kusteri, gymnasii petrini, qvod coloniae ad suevum est, correctoris, memorabilia coloniensia*. Leipzig: Blochberger, 1731.

Lampert-Weissig, Lisa. *Instrument of Memory: Encounters with the Wandering Jew*. Ann Arbor: University of Michigan Press, 2024.

Las Cases, Emmanuel de. *Mémorial de Sainte-Hélène*. Edited by André Fugier. Vol. 1. Paris: Garnier, 1961.

Lebensohn, Abraham Dov. *Beʾurim ḥadashim: ʿal Yirmeyah, Yeḥezkel ve-khol sifre tere ʿasar sifre Emet, Ekhah ve-Kohelet*. Vilna: Bi-defus Yosef Reuven b.R. Menakhem Man Romm, 1858.

Lescourret, Marie-Anne. *Emmanuel Levinas*. Paris: Flammarion, 1994.

Levinas, Emmanuel, and Richard Kerney. "Dialogue with Emmanuel Levinas." In *Face to Face with Levinas*, edited by Richard A. Cohen, 13–34. Albany: State University of New York Press, 1986.

Lockemann, Theodor. "Leonhard Neubaur." *Mitteilungen des Westpreussischen Geschichtsvereins*, July 1, 1919.

Loseff, Lev. *On the Beneficence of Censorship: Aesopian Language in Modern Russian Literature*. Munich: Otto Sagner, 1984.

Lück, Heiner. *Alma Leucorea: eine Geschichte der Universität Wittenberg, 1502 bis 1817*. Halle an der Saale: Universitätsverlag Halle-Wittenberg, 2020.

Lurie, Ilia. "Ha-ẓenzurah ha-memshaltit ʿal ha-pirsumim ha-yehudiyim ba-keysarut ha-rusit." In *Toldot yehudey Rusyah*, 2: 63–74. Jerusalem: Merkaz Zalman Shazar, 2010.

Luther, Martin. *D. Martin Luthers Werke: Kritische Gesamtausgabe, Schriften.* 72 vols. Weimar: Böhlaus, 1903.

———. "The Freedom of a Christian." In *Three Treatises*, translated by Charles M. Jacobs, A.T.W. Steinhäuser, and W. A. Lambert, 261–316. Philadelphia: Fortress Press, 1970.

MacCulloch, Diarmaid. *The Reformation.* New York: Penguin Books, 2005.

Maimonides, Moses. *Ethical Writings of Maimonides.* Edited by Raymond L. Weiss. Translated by Charles E. Butterworth. New York: Dover Publications, 1983.

Major, Johann. *Synodus avium: depingens miseram faciem ecclesiae propter certamina quorundam qui de primatu contendunt*, 1557.

Malka, Salomon. *Emmanuel Lévinas: la vie et la trace.* Paris: Albin Michel, 2005.

———. *Monsieur Chouchani: l'énigme d'un maître du XXe siècle: entretiens avec Elie Wiesel, suivis d'une enquête.* Paris: J. C. Lattès, 1994.

Manor, Alexander. *Dyokano shel rav-ḥovel 'ivri.* Tel Aviv: Alef, 1963.

Manor, Dori, ed. *Ho! 25.* Tel Aviv: Hakibutz hameukhad, 2023.

Marissen, Michael. "On the Jews and Their So-Called Lies in the Fourth Gospel and Bach's St. John Passion." In *Bach against Modernity*, edited by Michael Marissen. New York: Oxford University Press, 2023.

Mendele Mokher Sefarim. *Dos kleyne menshele, oder, a lebensbeshraybung fun Yitshak Avraham Takif.* New York: Hebrew Publishing Company, 1901.

———. "Ha-avot ve-ha'banim." In *Kol kitvey Mendele Mokher Sefarim*, edited by Jacob Fichman and Ludwig Schwerin. Tel Aviv: Devir, 1949.

———. *Ha-barnash ha-katan.* Translated by Shalom Luria. Jerusalem: Karmel, 2003.

———. *Mishpat shalom: 'osefet ma'amarim shonim.* Vilna: Defus Romm, 1860.

———. *The Nag.* Translated by Moshe Spiegel. New York: Beechhurst Press, 1955.

———. "Reshimot le-toldotay." In *Kol kitvey Mendele Mokher Sefarim*, edited by Jacob Fichman and Ludwig Schwerin. Tel Aviv: Devir, 1949.

———. *Shriften.* Vol. 1. Kiev: Kultur-lige, 1928.

———. "Susati." In *Kol kitvey Mendele Mokher Sefarim*, edited by Jacob Fichman and Ludwig Schwerin, 307–49. Tel Aviv: Devir, 1949.

Mentelin, Johann, trans. *Bible.* Strasbourg: Johann Mentelin, 1466.

Mintzker, Yair. "I, Ahasuerus: Monsieur Chouchani in Israel, 1952–56." *Jewish Social Studies* 28, no. 1 (2023): 49–78.

———. "Keyẓad hafakh ha-yehudi ha-noded le-gibor yehudi." *Ḥidushim beḥeker toldot yehudey germanya u-mizraḥ eyropa* 26, no. 2 (2024): 99–122.

Miron, Dan. "Aḥarit davar." In *Ha-susah*, by Sholem Yankev Abramovitch, edited by Menachem Peri, translated by Dan Miron. Bnei Brak: Hakibutz hameukhad, 2018.

———. "Ha-ḥinukh ha-sentimentali shel Mendele Mokher Sefarim." In *Sefer Ha-kabẓanim*, by Mendele Mokher Sefarim, 201–68. Tel Aviv: Devir, 1988.

———. *A Traveller Disguised*. New York: Schocken Books, 1973.

Moller, Johannes. *J. Molleri Cimbria litterata, sive Scriptarum Ducatus utriusque Sclesvicensis et Halsatici quibus et alii vicini quidam accensentur historia Litteraria Tripartita cum praefatione J. Grammii*. Vol. 3. Hanniae: Typis regiis, 1744.

Moretti, Franco. *The Way of the World: The Bildungsroman in European Culture*. London: Verso, 1987.

Morrison, Toni. *Beloved*. New York: Vintage Books, 2004.

Moyn, Samuel. *Origins of the Other: Emmanuel Levinas between Revelation and Ethics*. Ithaca, NY: Cornell University Press, 2005.

Mundt, Lothar. *Lemnius und Luther: Studien und Texte zur Geschichte und Nachwirkung ihres Konflikts (1538/39)*. Vol. 2. Bern: P. Lang, 1983.

Namdar, Ruby. *The Ruined House*. Translated by Hillel Halkin. New York: Harper, 2017.

Neubaur, Leonhard. "Bibliographie der Sage vom ewigen Juden." *Centralblatt für Bibliothekswesen* 10 (1893): 249–66.

———. *Die Sage vom ewigen Juden*. Leipzig: J. C. Hinrichs, 1884.

———. *Neue Mitteilungen über die Sage vom ewigen Juden*. Leipzig: J. C. Hinrichs, 1893.

———. "Zur bibliographie der Sage vom ewigen Juden." *Centralblatt für Bibliothekswesen* 28 (1911): 495–509.

———. "Zur Geschichte der Sage vom ewigen Juden." *Zeitschrift des Vereins für Volkskunde* 22 (1912): 33–54.

———. "Zur Geschichte und Bibliographie des Volkbuchs von Ahasverus." *Zeitschrift für Bücherfreunde* 5, no. 2 (1914): 211–23.

Nirenberg, David. *Anti-Judaism: The Western Tradition*. New York: W. W. Norton & Company, 2013.

Odontius, Paul. *Kurtze vnd warhafftige Historische erzehlung, Wie vnnd welcher gestalt Paulus Odontius gewesener Euangelischer Prediger zu Walstein in Steyermarck, wegen der Lehr vnd Predigt deß Heyligen Euangelij, von der Grätzerischen Inquisition... zum Tod vervrtheilt... worden*. Dresden: Schütz, 1603.

Perl, Joseph. *Sefer megaleh temirin*. Vienna: Gedruckt bei Anton Strauss, 1819.

Pettegree, Andrew. *The Book in the Renaissance*. New Haven, CT: Yale University Press, 2010.

Philippson, Ludwig. "Ahasver, Gutzkow und Juden." *Allgemeine Zeitung des Judenthums* 2, no. 114 (1838): 460–61.

———. "Ahasver, Gutzkow und Juden." *Allgemeine Zeitung des Judenthums* 2, no. 117 (1838): 472–73.

————. "Ahasver, Gutzkow und Juden." *Allgemeine Zeitung des Judenthums* 2, no. 120 (1838): 484–85.

Picard, Avi. '*Olim bi-mesurah.* Beer Sheva: Ben Gurion University Press, 2013.

Richard, James William. *The Confessional History of the Lutheran Church.* Philadelphia: Lutheran Publication Society, 1909.

Rieber, Alfred J. "Alexander II: A Revisionist History." *Journal of Modern History* 43, no. 1 (1971): 42–58.

Roper, Lyndal. *Martin Luther: Renegade and Prophet.* London: Bodley Head, 2016.

Roth, Joseph. *The Wandering Jews.* Translated by Michael Hofmann. New York: W. W. Norton, 2001.

Rouart, Marie-France. *Le mythe du juif errant dans l'Europe du XIXe siècle.* Paris: J. Corti, 1988.

Rozin, Orit. *A Home for All Jews: Citizenship, Rights, and National Identity in the New Israeli State.* Translated by Haim Watzman. Waltham, MA: Brandeis University Press, 2016.

Salinger, J. D. *Franny and Zooey.* New York: Little, Brown and Company, 2023.

Samet Har-Shefi, Hodaya. "Black Fire upon White Fire: The Teachings of Mr. Shoshani." Dissertation, Bar-Ilan University, 2016.

Schaff, Philip. *History of the Christian Church.* Vol. 7. 8 vols. New York: Charles Scribner's Sons, 1898.

Scheible, Heinz, ed. *Melanchthons Briefwechsel: Personen A-E.* Heidelberg: Heidelberger Akademie der Wissenschaften, 1977.

Schmerling, Timothy R. "Strenuus Christi Athleta Abraham Calov (1612-1686)." *Lutheran Synod Quarterly* 44, no. 4 (December 2004): 357–99.

Schmidt, Arno. *Das Volksbuch vom Ewigen Juden: ein Beitrag zur Entstehungsgeschichte des Buches.* Danzig: Druck von A.W. Kafemann, 1927.

Schorn-Schütte, Luise, ed. *Das Interim 1548/50: Herrschaftskrise und Glaubenskonflikt.* Gütersloh: Gütersloher Verlagshaus, 2005.

Schreckenberg, Heinz. *Die christlichen Adversus-Judaeos-Texte und ihr literarisches und historisches Umfeld (1.-11. Jh.).* Europäische Hochschulschriften. Frankfurt am Main: Peter Lang, 1982.

————. *Die christlichen Adversus-Judaeos-Texte und ihr literarisches und historisches Umfeld (13.-20. Jh.).* Europäische Hochschulschriften. Frankfurt am Main: Lang, 1994.

Schudt, Johann Jacob. *Compendium historiae judaicae; de origine, incrementis & rebus gestis Judaeorum . . .* Francofurti ad Moenum: Friedrich Knoch, 1700.

————. *Deliciae hebraeo-philologicae sive Tractatus de studio linguae et philologiae Hebraicae.* Francofurti ad Moenum: Friedrich Knoch, 1700.

———. *Judæus Christicida gravissime peccans et vapulans, sive, perspicua & solida demonstratio, cædem & rejectionem Jesu Nazareni veram esse causam præsentis tam diuturni Judæorum exilii.* Frankfurt am Main: Self published, 1703.

———. *Jüdische Merckwürdigkeiten.* 6 vols. Frankfurt am Main und Leipzig, 1714–1717.

Seidelman, Rhona. *Under Quarantine: Immigrants and Disease at Israel's Gate.* New Brunswick, NJ: Rutgers University Press, 2020.

Sennert, Andreas. *Bibliothecae Academiae Wittebergensis Publicae, Librorum qua (1.) Theologicorum (2.) Juridicorum (3.) Medicorum (4.) Philosophicorum... & qui noviter huic de Anno LXXII. accesserunt.* Wittenberg: Johannes Wilcke, 1678.

Sherwin, Byron. "Elie Wiesel and Jewish Theology." *Judaism* 18, no. 1 (1969): 39–52.

Shneur, Zalman. "Reshimot 'al I. Bershadsky li-mlot ḥamishim shana li-ptirato." *Davar*, March 28, 1958.

———. "Vilna." In *Shirat ha-teḥiyah ha-'ivrit*, edited by Binyamin Harshav, 194. Tel Aviv: Hauniversita hapetukha, 2000.

Shtain, A. Sh. "Ha-Rav Yeḥezkel Rosenbaum-Shoshani." In *Radom*, 142–43. Tel Aviv: Irgun yotsey Radom be-Yisrael, 1961.

Silva, Hizqiya ben David da. *Sefer pri ḥadash.* Amsterdam: David Tartas, 1672.

Skolnik, Jonathan. *Jewish Pasts, German Fictions: History, Memory, and Minority Culture in Germany, 1824–1955.* Stanford Studies in Jewish History and Culture. Stanford, CA: Stanford University Press, 2014.

———. "Writing Jewish History between Gutzkow and Goethe: Auerbach's *Spinoza* and the Birth of Modern Jewish Historical Fiction." *Prooftexts* 19, no. 2 (1999): 101–25.

Smolenskin, Perez. *Ha-to'eh be-darkhey ha-ḥayim.* Vol. 4. Vilna: Defus ha-almanah ve-ha'aḥim Romm, 1901.

Sokolov, Nahum. "Sholem Yankev Abramovitch." In *Ishim*. Ktavim nivḥarim. Jerusalem: Hasifriyah hatsiyonit, 1958.

Spener, Philipp Jakob. *D. Philippi Jacobi Speneri... Consilia et judicia theologica latina.* Vol. 3. Francofurti ad Moenum: Impensis haeredum J. Davidis Aunneri & J. A. Jungii, Typis A. Heinscheitii, 1709.

———. *Gläubiger Christen versicherte Beilage, aus II. Timt. I, 12., bey volkreicher Leichbegräbnus... Conrad Schudts.* Frankfurt am Main: Johann Dietrich Fridgen, 1680.

———. *Pia desideria.* Translated by Theodore G. Tappert. Philadelphia: Fortress Press, 1964.

Srebrek, Shlomo. *Zikhronot.* Tel Aviv: Sh. Srebrek, n.d.

Steinmetz, David C. *Calvin in Context.* Oxford: Oxford University Press, 1995.

Stenographische Berichte über die Verhandlungen des Deutschen Reichstags. 2. Legislatur-Periode, II Session 1874/75. Vol. 2. Berlin: Verlag der Buchdruckerei der Norddeutschen Allgemeinen Zeitung, 1875.

Straßburgische Kriegs Sachen: Kurtze vn[d] doch warhaffte Erzehlung, Was sich von dem Ersten Tag Junij an, biß auff den 26 Julij ... jn[n]er und ausser der Statt verlauffen und zugetragen habe. Strasbourg: Schütz, 1600.

Sue, Eugène. *Misterey Pariz: hi ha-maḥberet ha-mikhlalah asher ḥubrah bi-leshon ẓarfat.* Translated by Kalman Schulman. Vilna: Defus Romm, 1857.

Sutzkever, Abraham. "The Leaden Plates of Romm's Printing Works." In *Burnt Pearls: Ghetto Poems of Abraham Sutzkever,* translated by Seymour Mayne, 41. Oakville, Ontario: Mosaic Press/Valley Editions, 1981.

Szymborska, Wisława. *View with a Grain of Sand: Selected Poems.* Translated by Stanisław Barańczak and Clare Cavanagh. New York: Harcourt, 1995.

Tholuck, August. *Der Geist der lutherischen Theologen Wittenbergs im Verlaufe des 17. Jahrhunderts: theilweise nach handschriftlichen Quellen.* Hamburg and Gotha: Perthes, 1852.

Tir, Michelle. *Ralph Klein: ha-me'amen.* Tel Aviv: Alpha, 2000.

Turner, Masha, and Benjamin Ish Shalom. "Erev eḥad 'im mar Shoshani: ma'aseh she-hayah." In *Be-darkhey shalom,* 467–68. Jerusalem: Beit Morasha, 2007.

Vergil. *Harisot troyah be-yad ha-yevanim.* Translated by Micah Joseph Lebensohn. Vilna: Defus Romm, 1869.

Verhandlungen des Reichstages 35. 1874/75. Berlin: Verlag der Buchdruckerei der Norddeutschen Allgemeinen Zeitung, 1875.

Volkov, Shulamit. *Ba-ma'agal ha-mekhushaf: yehudim, antishemim ve-germanim aḥerim.* Sifriyat ofakim. Tel Aviv: Am oved, 2002.

Vorstellung der gäntzlich abgebrandten Judengaß zu Frankfurt am Main. 1711. Kupferstich, 43 × 27.7 cm. JMF Historische Sammlung. Jüdisches Museum Frankfurt. https://sammlung.juedischesmuseum.de/objekt/vorstellung-der-gantzlich-ab-gebranden-judenga-zu-frankfurt-am-main.

Wallmann, Johannes. "Der alte und der neue Bund. Zur Haltung des Pietismus gegenüber den Juden." In *Glaubenswelt und Lebenswelten. Geschichte des Pietismus,* edited by Hartmut Lehmann, 4: 143–65. Göttingen: Vandenhoeck & Ruprecht, 2004.

Wandel, Lee Palmer. *The Eucharist in the Reformation: Incarnation and Liturgy.* Cambridge: Cambridge University Press, 2006.

Weizman, Ezer. "Eineni yakhol li-slo'aḥ be-shem ha-korbanot." *Yediot Ahronot,* January 16, 1996, sec. 24 Sha'ot.

Whaley, Joachim. *Religious Toleration and Social Change in Hamburg, 1529–1819.* Cambridge Studies in Early Modern History. Cambridge: Cambridge University Press, 1985.

Wiesel, Elie. *Against Silence: The Voice and Vision of Elie Wiesel*. New York: Holocaust Library, 1984.

———. *Legends of Our Time*. New York: Holt, Rinehart and Winston, 1968.

———. *One Generation After*. New York: Random House, 1970.

Wilke, Carsten L. "From Deicide to Diaspora: The Construction of Jewish World History in Johann Jacob Schudt's Latin Writing." In *Frankfurt's "Jewish Notabilia" ("Jüdische Merckwürdigkeiten"): Ethnographic Views of Urban Jewry in Central Europe around 1700*. Edited by Rebekka Voß and Christoph Cluse. Frankfurter Judaistische Beiträge, 40 (2015): 141–65.

Wygoda, Shmuel. "Le maître et son disciple: Chouchani et Levinas." *Cahiers d'études lévinasiennes* 1 (2002): 148–83.

Yehudai, Ori. *Leaving Zion: Jewish Emigration from Palestine and Israel after World War II*. Cambridge: Cambridge University Press, 2020.

Yizhar, S. *Yeme Tsiklag*. Vol. 1. Tel Aviv: Am oved, 2009.

Zalkin, Mordekhai. "Ha-ruaḥ ha-ḥaya be-ofney ha-hadpasa: Devorah Romm ke-sokhenet tarbut." In *Derekh sefer: shai li-Ze'ev Gris*, edited by Oded Yisreeli, Jonatan Meir, and Avraham Reiner. Jerusalem: Karmel, 2021.

Zipperstein, Steven J. *The Jews of Odessa: A Cultural History, 1794–1881*. Stanford, CA: Stanford University Press, 1985.

INDEX

Yizhar, S. (Yizhar Smilansky), 37
Yom Kippur War, 177, 185, 192

Zhitomir, 66

Zionism, 39, 41–42, 183, 185, 190, 193, 196, 199; and Ahasverus, 200; and Benjamin Netanyahu, 203; and Hapo'el Hamizrahi, 22, 38, 177; and *The Nag*, 91; and Natan Alterman, 33–34; and Rabbi Abraham Isaac Kook, 49, 53; Religious, 35, 38, 41–43, 45, 48–49, 53, 177; socialist, 177, 192; and Theodore Herzl, 37, 51, 178, 205; and Zvi (Walther) Bachrach, 41–42

Zurich, 163

A NOTE ON THE TYPE

This book has been composed in Arno, an Old-style serif typeface in the classic Venetian tradition, designed by Robert Slimbach at Adobe.